# PHILIPPIANS
### JOY IN JESUS

The Proclaim Commentary Series

THE PROCLAIM COMMENTARY SERIES

# PHILIPPIANS
## JOY IN JESUS

NEW TESTAMENT
VOLUME 11

**MATTHEW STEVEN BLACK**

WENATCHEE, WASHINGTON

Philippians: Joy in Jesus (The Proclaim Commentary Series)
Copyright © 2021 by Matthew Black
ISBN:   978-1-954858-17-6 (Print)
        978-1-954858-18-3 (eBook)

Proclaim Publishers
PO Box 2082, Wenatchee, WA 98807
proclaimpublishers.com

Cover art: *The Ruins of Philippi*

Unless otherwise quoted, Scripture quotations are from the ESV® Bible (The Holy Bible, English Standard Version®), copyright © 2001, 2016 by Crossway, a publishing ministry of Good News Publishers. Used by permission. All rights reserved.

Scripture quotations marked NASB are taken from the New American Standard Bible®, Copyright © 1960, 1962, 1963, 1968, 1971, 1972, 1973, 1975, 1977, 1995 by The Lockman Foundation. Used by permission.

Scripture quotations marked NKJV are taken from the New King James Version®. Copyright © 1982 by Thomas Nelson. Used by permission. All rights reserved.

Scripture quotations marked NIV are taken from The Holy Bible New International Version®, NIV® Copyright © 1973, 1978, 1984, 2011 by Biblica, Inc.® Used by permission. All rights reserved worldwide.

Scripture quotations marked CSB are taken from the Christian Standard Bible®, Used by permission. All rights reserved. CSB ©2017 Holman Bible Publishers.

Scripture quotations marked NLT are taken from the Holy Bible, New Living Translation, Copyright ©1996, 2004, 2007 by Tyndale House Foundation. Used by permission of Tyndale House Publishers, Inc., Carol Stream, Illinois 60188. All rights reserved.

Scripture quotations marked KJV are taken from the King James Version of the Bible.

All rights reserved. No part of this publication may be reproduced, stored in a retrieval system or transmitted in any form by any means, electronic, mechanical, photocopy, recording or otherwise, without the prior permission of the publisher, except as provided by USA copyright law.

Notes: (1) Ancient quotations have been at times changed to the ESV as well as some archaic language updated, and additional phrases added for clarification. At times verse references (non-existent until recent times) have been interspersed as well to guide the modern reader. (2) We have done our best to be careful in footnoting. Due to the nature of the sermonic material, various items are quoted freely, and may not have proper footnoting. If any great error is noticed, please contact the publisher, and it will be remedied in whatever way is available to us.

First Printing, October 2021
Manufactured in the United States of America

Dedicated to my precious daughter Katie. You shine the joy of Jesus into a dark world.

# CONTENTS

**INTRODUCTION** ............................................................................................. 19
   Author, Date, Place of Writing ................................................................. 19
   Message ..................................................................................................... 20

**1 | PHILIPPIANS 1:1-2 JOY IN JESUS** ............................................................. 21
   Background of Philippians ....................................................................... 21
      Philippi ................................................................................................... 22
      Paul's "Lonely" Imprisonment ............................................................. 23
      The Macedonian Call ............................................................................ 24
   Thankful for Our Family Tree! (1:1-2) ...................................................... 25
      People in God's Family ......................................................................... 25
         *Slaves* ................................................................................................ 27
         *Saints* ................................................................................................ 27
         *Elders and Deacons* ......................................................................... 27
      Purpose of God's Family ...................................................................... 28
   Thankful for our Family Story (1:3-8; Acts 16) ........................................ 28
      A Dear Family ....................................................................................... 29
      A Divine Family .................................................................................... 29
      A Diverse Family .................................................................................. 30
         *Lydia the Fashionista* ...................................................................... 31
         *The Slave Girl* .................................................................................. 32
         *The Ex-Military, Blue Collar GI* ....................................................... 33
   Applications .............................................................................................. 34
      1 – Attitude is everything .................................................................... 34
      2 – Loneliness is a mindset ................................................................. 34
      3 – Christian community is rich ......................................................... 35
      4 – Focus on Christ, not on circumstances ....................................... 35

**2 | PHILIPPIANS 1:3-8 THE JOY OF CHRISTIAN MATURITY** .......................... 37
   Gratitude Marks the Mature Christian (1:3) ........................................... 39
      Gratitude for People ............................................................................ 39
      Gratitude in Remembering ................................................................. 41
         *Remembering Grace* ........................................................................ 41
         *Remembering Forgiveness* .............................................................. 42
         *Remembering Love* ......................................................................... 44
   Fellowship Marks the Mature Christian (1:4-5) ...................................... 45
      Fellowship Promotes Prayer .............................................................. 45
      Fellowship Promotes Joy .................................................................... 46
      Fellowship Promotes Partnership ..................................................... 47

  *Obstacles to Corporate Fellowship* .................................................. 47
  *The Mission of Christian Fellowship* ................................................ 48
Confidence Marks the Mature Christian (1:6) ............................................ 49
 Confidence in God's Character ................................................................ 49
 Confidence in God's Commencement ..................................................... 49
 Confidence in God's Completion .............................................................. 50
Love Marks the Mature Christian (1:7-8) ................................................... 52
 Love is Deep for the Mature Christian .................................................... 52
 Love is Sacrificial for the Mature Christian ............................................ 53
 Love is Supernatural for the Mature Christian ....................................... 54

## 3 | PHILIPPIANS 1:9-11 ROOTED IN LOVING ONE ANOTHER ................ 55

Our Love Should Be Plentiful (1:9a) ........................................................... 57
 An Abundant Love ..................................................................................... 57
 An Affectionate Love .................................................................................. 58
 An Assorted Love ........................................................................................ 58
Our Love Should Be Perceptive (1:9-10a) .................................................. 60
 Love's Knowledge ...................................................................................... 60
 Love's Discernment .................................................................................... 61
 Love's Excellence ........................................................................................ 62
Our Love Should be Productive (1:10-11a) ................................................ 63
 A Growing Readiness ................................................................................. 63
 A Growing Purity ........................................................................................ 64
 A Growing Righteousness .......................................................................... 64
Our Love Should be Purposeful (1:11) ........................................................ 65
 Through Jesus Christ ................................................................................. 65
 For God's Glory ........................................................................................... 66

## 4 | PHILIPPIANS 1:12-18 JOY IN SETBACKS AND SUFFERING ............... 67

The Gospel Advances with Past Setbacks (1:12-14) .................................. 69
 Setbacks are Planned by God .................................................................... 69
  *Paul's Salvation Planned by God* ........................................................ 70
  *Paul's Suffering Planned by God* ........................................................ 70
 Setbacks Can Advance the Gospel ........................................................... 71
  *Advancing the Gospel with Roman Soldiers* ..................................... 72
 Setbacks Can Make Us Stronger ............................................................... 73
  *Stronger in Evangelism* ........................................................................ 73
  *Stronger in Faith* ................................................................................... 74
The Gospel Advances with Present Setbacks (1:15-18a) .......................... 75
 In Setbacks, we Look to God's Sovereignty ............................................. 75
 In Setbacks, We Look Past Man's Selfishness ......................................... 77
The Gospel Advances with Future Setbacks (1:18b-21) ........................... 77
 In Life or Death Christ is Glorified ........................................................... 77

## 5 | PHILIPPIANS 1:18-26 TO LIVE IS CHRIST ............................................. 81

The Christ Life is the Joyful Life (1:18-19) ....................................... 83
   A Choice to Rejoice .............................................................. 83
   Tw0 Reasons to Rejoice ........................................................ 83
      *Rejoice in the Prayers of the Saints* .................................... *84*
      *Rejoice in the Help of the Holy Spirit* ................................. *85*
      *Rejoice in Your Final Deliverance* ...................................... *85*
The Christ life is the Purposeful Life (1:20-21) ................................ 86
   A Clarifying Purpose ............................................................ 86
   A Magnifying Purpose .......................................................... 87
   An All-Consuming Purpose ................................................... 87
The Christ Life is the Longing Life (1:22-24) ................................... 88
   We Long for Spiritual Fruit ................................................... 88
   We Long to be Present with Christ ........................................ 89
      *Death Will Be an Encounter* ............................................. *89*
      *Death Will Be Much Better* ............................................... *90*
   We Long to Camp Out .......................................................... 90
The Christ Life is the Growing Life (1:25-26) .................................. 91
   Growth in Joy ...................................................................... 91
   Growth in Glory ................................................................... 92

## 6 | PHILIPPIANS 1:27 WALK WORTHY OF THE GOSPEL ............................. 93

The Exhortation to Walk Worthy (1:27a) .......................................... 94
   An Important Exhortation .................................................... 94
   A New Mindset .................................................................... 95
   A Divine Imperative ............................................................. 96
      *The Unrepentant Sinner* .................................................. *96*
      *The Self-Righteous Sinner* ............................................... *97*
      *The Humble Saint* ........................................................... *98*
   A Glorious Gospel ................................................................ 98
Ways to Walk Worthy (1:27b) ......................................................... 99
   Walk in Consistent Obedience ............................................... 99
      *A Cosmic Consistency* .................................................... *100*
      *A Growing Consistency* .................................................. *100*
      *A Militant Consistency* ................................................... *102*
      *A Persevering Consistency* .............................................. *102*
   Walk in the Fear of God ...................................................... 103
      *Adam in the Garden* ...................................................... *104*
      *Joseph in the Old Testament* .......................................... *104*
   Walk in Unity ..................................................................... 105
      *Unity Flows from the Holy Spirit's Work* ......................... *105*
      *Unity Flows from Hard Work* ......................................... *105*
      *Unity Flows from Our High Calling* ................................ *106*

## 7 | PHILIPPIANS 1:27-30 THE COURAGE TO SUFFER ... 109

### Have Courage to Suffer with Faithfulness (1:27) ... 111
- Faithfulness is Manifested by Spirit ... 111
- Faithfulness Marks the New Birth ... 112
- Faithfulness Moves Us to Victory ... 112
  - *Scriptural Examples* ... *113*
  - *Applications* ... *113*

### Have Courage to Suffer with Forcefulness (1:27) ... 114
- Pictures of Forcefulness: Soldiers & Athletes ... 114
- The Power of Forcefulness ... 116

### Have Courage to Suffer with Fearlessness (1:28) ... 116
- Courage is a Sign for the Saved ... 116
- Courage is a Sign for the Lost ... 117

### Have Courage to Suffer with Favor (1:29-30) ... 118
- We are Favored with the Ability to Believe ... 118
- We are Favored with the Ability to Suffer ... 119

## 8 | PHILIPPIANS 2:1-11 EVERY KNEE SHALL BOW ... 123

### The Power for Humility (2:1-4) ... 125
- Look to the Truine God ... 125
  - *We are Encouraged by the Son's Sacrifice* ... *126*
  - *We are Comforted by the Father's Love* ... *126*
  - *We are Enriched by the Spirit's Fellowship* ... *126*
  - *We are Supported by the Church's Sympathy* ... *127*
- Love the Body of Christ ... 127
  - *Be Harmonious Together* ... *128*
  - *Be Humble Together* ... *128*
  - *Be Helpful Together* ... *129*

### The Pathway to Humility (2:5-8) ... 129
- Have the Mind of Christ (2:5) ... 130
- Consider the Humility of Christ (2:6-8) ... 131
  - *He Relinquished His Place (2:6a)* ... *131*
  - *He Refused His Privileges (2:6-7a)* ... *133*
  - *He Restricted His Presence (2:7b)* ... *134*
  - *He Realized His Purpose (2:8)* ... *135*

### The Practice of Humility (2:9-11) ... 135
- The Father Exalts Christ ... 135
- All People & Angels Exalt Christ ... 136
- All Confess Christ as Yahweh ... 136

## 9 | 1 PETER 2:12-13 HOW CAN I CHANGE? ... 139

### Spiritual Growth is Personal (2:12) ... 141
- A Transcendent Labor ... 141
- A Strenuous Labor ... 142

| | |
|---|---|
| A Personal Labor | 144 |
| A Practical Labor | 145 |
| Spiritual Growth is Progressive (2:12) | 146 |
|     Justification: An Event | 147 |
|     Sanctification: A Journey | 147 |
|     Glorification: Our Final Destination | 148 |
| Spiritual Growth is Praise-Driven (2:12) | 149 |
|     The Focus of Our Praise | 149 |
|     The Fear of Our Praise | 151 |
| Spiritual Growth is Predestined (2:13) | 151 |
|     God's Plan Reaches Beyond Time | 151 |
|     God's Plan Requires Your Cooperation | 152 |
|     God's Plan Guarantees Your Growth | 152 |
|     God's Plan Rejects Laziness | 153 |
|         *Tension in Evangelism* | *153* |
|         *Tension in Sanctification* | *153* |

## 10 | PHILIPPIANS 2:14-18 BE AN INFLUENCER! .......... 155

| | |
|---|---|
| We Live the Life (2:14-15) | 157 |
|     An Appreciative Life | 157 |
|     A Hopeful Life | 159 |
|     A Happy Life | 160 |
|     A Blameless Life | 161 |
| We Shine the Light (2:15b) | 161 |
|     Shine Amidst Sinners | 162 |
|     Shine as Stars | 163 |
|     Stay Bright! | 163 |
| We Speak the Word (2:16) | 164 |
|     The Power of the Word | 165 |
|         *The Word's Supremacy* | *165* |
|         *The Word Spoken* | *166* |
|     The Purpose of the Word | 166 |
|     The Practice of the Word | 168 |
| We Sacrifice for the Kingdom (2:17-18) | 169 |
|     Resolve to Sacrifice | 169 |
|     Rejoice in Sacrifice | 170 |

## 11 | PHILIPPIANS 2:19-30 MODELS OF MINISTRY .......... 171

| | |
|---|---|
| Paul: A Model of Selflessness (2:19-21) | 172 |
|     The Joy of Selfless Ministry | 173 |
|         *Radical Selflessness is Seen in Paul* | *174* |
|         *Joy is the Mark of True Discipleship* | *174* |
|     The Hard Work of Selfless Ministry | 175 |
|         *Metaphors for Discipleship Imply Work* | *175* |
|         *Models for Discipleship Require Work* | *176* |

The Reward of Selfless Ministry ........................................................... 177
   *The Reward of Reproducing a Pastor*............................................. *177*
   *The Reward of Reproducing a Church*............................................ *178*
Timothy: A Model of Service (2:19-24)................................................178
  Big Vision Service ................................................................................ 179
   *Excuses for Small Vision*................................................................. *180*
  Big Hearted Service (2:20-21) ........................................................... 181
   *Timothy's Imprisonment*.................................................................. *182*
   *How to Maintain a Big Heart (And Avoid Burnout)* .................... *182*
  Big Dividend Service........................................................................... 183
Epaphroditus: A Model of Sacrifice (2:25-30)....................................183
  The Example of Sacrifice ................................................................... 183
  The Honor of Sacrifice ....................................................................... 186

## 12 | PHILIPPIANS 3:1-3 INCREASE YOUR JOY .......................................189

Increase Your Wellspring of Joy (3:1) ..................................................191
  The Reason to Rejoice ........................................................................ 191
  The Command to Rejoice .................................................................. 192
  The Choice to Rejoice......................................................................... 193
  The Safety of Rejoicing ...................................................................... 193
Increase Your Watchfulness of Joy (3:2)..............................................195
  A Description of Joy Stealers ............................................................ 195
   *Dogs* ................................................................................................... *195*
   *Evil Doers*.......................................................................................... *196*
   *False Teachers* .................................................................................. *196*
  Watch Out for Joy Stealers ................................................................ 196
Increase Your Worship through Joy (3:3) ...........................................197
  A Sensitive Heart ................................................................................ 198
  A Spirit-Filled Heart ........................................................................... 199
  A Crucified Heart................................................................................ 200

## 13 | PHILIPPIANS 3:4-11 THE GREAT CHANGE.......................................201

Life Before Christ (3:4-6) ....................................................................... 202
  Impressive Beginning ........................................................................ 202
  Impressive Nationality ...................................................................... 203
  Impressive Lineage ............................................................................. 203
  Impressive Upbringing ...................................................................... 204
  Impressive Standard........................................................................... 205
  Impressive Sincerity .......................................................................... 205
  Impressive Morality ........................................................................... 206
   *Paul Had Everything But Jesus*...................................................... *206*
   *Everything Minus Jesus Equals Nothing*....................................... *207*
Coming to Know Christ (3:7-9; Acts 9:1-5) ........................................ 207
  We Know the Reach of Christ .......................................................... 207
   *A Surprising Love*............................................................................ *209*

    *A Saving Love* .................................................................................. *210*
    *A Love Embraced through Faith* ....................................................... *210*
   We Know the Riches of Christ ............................................................ 211
   We Know the Righteousness of Christ ................................................ 212
Growing in Christ (3:10-11) ....................................................................... 213

## 14 | PHILIPPIANS 3:10-16 PRESSING ON TO THE PRIZE ................... 217

Run with Ambition (3:10-11) ..................................................................... 219
   A Personal Ambition ............................................................................ 219
    *Knowing Christ Personally is Objective* .............................................. *219*
    *Knowing Christ Personally is Subjective* ............................................ *220*
    *Knowing Christ Personally is Progressive* ........................................... *221*
    *Knowing Christ Personally is Substantive* .......................................... *222*
   A Powerful Ambition ........................................................................... 222
   A Passionate Ambition ........................................................................ 223
   A Prayerful Ambition ........................................................................... 223
    *What is Certain* ................................................................................ *224*
    *What is Not Certain* ......................................................................... *224*
    *Christianity is a Lens, Not a List* ...................................................... *224*
Run with Endurance (3:12-14) ................................................................... 225
   Enduring with A Proper View of the Present ..................................... 225
    *Paul is Humble* ................................................................................ *225*
    *Paul is Hungry* ................................................................................. *226*
   Enduring with A Proper View of the Past .......................................... 227
   Enduring with A Proper View of the Future ...................................... 228
Run with Grace (3:15-16) ........................................................................... 229
   Grace to Engage ................................................................................... 230
   Grace to Persevere ............................................................................... 230

## 15 | PHILIPPIANS 3:17-21 CITIZENS OF HEAVEN ............................... 233

Citizens are Disciples (3:17) ........................................................................ 234
   A Disciple is Counter Cultural ............................................................ 236
   A Disciple is a Prototype ..................................................................... 236
   A Disciple is a Partner ......................................................................... 237
Citizens are Discerning (3:18-19) ............................................................... 238
   Discerning But Compassionate ........................................................... 239
   Discerning In Enemy Territory ........................................................... 239
   Discerning Idols of the Heart .............................................................. 241
    *The Destiny of Idolatry* .................................................................... *241*
    *The Demand of Idolatry* .................................................................. *241*
    *The Depravity of Idolatry* ................................................................ *242*
    *The Desire of Idolatry* ..................................................................... *242*
Citizens are Devoted (3:20-21) .................................................................. 243
   Devoted to our Homeland ................................................................... 243
   Devoted to our King ............................................................................ 244

Devoted to Our Future ............................................................... 244

## 16 | PHILIPPIANS 4:1-5 DISARMING DISHARMONY ........................... 247

A Big Heart (4:1) ............................................................................ 249
   A Big Heart Because of Our Family ............................................. 249
   A Big Heart Because of Our Future .............................................. 251
   A Big Heart Because of Our Focus ............................................... 251
A Warm Embrace (4:2-3) ............................................................... 253
   Embrace in the Lord ................................................................... 254
      *1. Go straight to Jesus.* ............................................................. *255*
      *2. Deal with your own heart: repent & forgive.* ........................... *256*
      *3. If you need to talk, have the right attitude.* ............................ *256*
      *4. If you know someone is offended, fix it.* ................................ *256*
      *5. If you need help, get it.* ....................................................... *257*
   Embrace Help ............................................................................. 257
A Lasting Joy (4:4-5) ..................................................................... 258
   Joy In Christ Enriches My Own Heart ........................................... 258
   Joy In Christ Enriches the Hearts of Others .................................. 259
   Joy In Christ Encourages Us That Time is Short ........................... 259

## 17 | PHILIPPIANS 4:4-9 WHEN PANIC ATTACKS .............................. 261

   *The Terror Defined* ................................................................... *262*
   *The Terror Described Physiologically* ......................................... *262*
   *The Terror Described Personally* ................................................ *263*
Rejoice (4:4-5) .............................................................................. 265
   Rejoice in the Lord ..................................................................... 265
   Rejoice Always ........................................................................... 266
   Rejoice Again and Again ............................................................. 267
   Rejoice Restfully ......................................................................... 267
   Rejoice Expectantly .................................................................... 268
Rest in God's Peace (4:6-7) ............................................................ 268
   God's Rest Should Be Universal .................................................. 269
      *There is a Healthy Fear* ........................................................... *269*
      *There is a Sinful Fear* .............................................................. *270*
   God's Rest is Possible ................................................................. 271
      *Focus on God's Care* ............................................................... *271*
      *Focus on God's Supply* ............................................................ *271*
      *Focus on God's Final Plan* ....................................................... *272*
   God's Rest is Delightful .............................................................. 272
Renew Your mind (4:8-9) ............................................................... 273
   The Practice of Mind Renewal ..................................................... 273
   The Power of Mind Renewal ........................................................ 274

## 18 | PHILIPPIANS 4:10-14 HAPPY IN JESUS ALONE ........................... 275

Happy in Christ with or without People (4:10-11) .......................... 276

The Principle of Happiness with People ..................................................... 277
The Practice of Happiness with People ...................................................... 278
The Person that Gives True Happiness ...................................................... 279
Happy in Christ with or without Money (4:12-13) ................................. 280
Happy in Christ with or without Trials (4:14) ........................................ 281
    God is in Control of Trials ..................................................................... 281
    Trials are a Test for the False Convert .................................................... 282
    Trials are a Gift for the Believer .............................................................. 282
    God's Plan for Your Trials ....................................................................... 283

## 19 | PHILIPPIANS 4:15-23 GROWING THROUGH GENEROSITY ............ 285

*People and Money* ............................................................................................. 287
*The Bible and Money* ........................................................................................ 288
Giving Grows us through Partnership (4:14-17) .................................. 288
    The Power of Partnership ....................................................................... 290
    *How Do I Partner with People for the Gospel?* ........................................ 290
    The Fruit of Partnership .......................................................................... 291
Giving Grows us through Worship (4:18) ............................................... 292
    A Full Payment ........................................................................................ 293
    A Fragrant Offering ................................................................................. 293
    *David's Generosity* ................................................................................... 294
    *Your Generosity* ....................................................................................... 294
Giving Grows us through Stewardship (4:19-23) ................................. 295
    God's Care for You .................................................................................. 295
    We Care about God's Glory .................................................................... 295
    We Care for God's Family ....................................................................... 296

# ABBREVIATIONS

## *Common*

cf – Latin "conferatur", compare, or see, or see also
ff – and following (pages or verses)
i.e. – Latin "id est", that is
e.g. – Latin "exempli gratia", for example

## *Books of the Bible*

OLD TESTAMENT

| | | | |
|---|---|---|---|
| Genesis | Gen | Job | Job |
| Exodus | Exo | Psalms | Psa |
| Leviticus | Lev | Proverbs | Pro |
| Numbers | Num | Ecclesiastes | Ecc |
| Deuteronomy | Deut | Song of Solomon | Song |
| Joshua | Josh | Isaiah | Isa |
| Judges | Jdg | Jeremiah | Jer |
| Ruth | Rth | Lamentations | Lam |
| 1 Samuel | 1 Sam | Ezekiel | Eze |
| 2 Samuel | 2 Sam | Daniel | Dan |
| 1 Kings | 1 Kgs | Hosea | Hos |
| 2 Kings | 2 Kgs | Joel | Joel |
| 1 Chronicles | 1 Chr | Amos | Amos |
| 2 Chronicles | 2 Chr | Obadiah | Oba |
| Ezra | Ezr | Jonah | Jonah |
| Nehemiah | Neh | Micah | Mic |
| Esther | Est | Nahum | Nah |

| | | | |
|---|---|---|---|
| Habakkuk | Hab | Zechariah | Zech |
| Zephaniah | Zeph | Malachi | Mal |
| Haggai | Hag | | |

### New Testament

| | | | |
|---|---|---|---|
| Matthew | Mt | Philemon | Phm |
| Mark | Mk | Hebrews | Heb |
| Luke | Lk | James | Jas |
| John | Jn | 1 Peter | 1 Pet |
| Acts | Acts | 2 Peter | 2 Pet |
| Romans | Rom | 1 John | 1 Jn |
| 1 Corinthians | 1 Cor | 2 John | 2 Jn |
| 2 Corinthians | 2 Cor | 3 John | 3 Jn |
| Galatians | Gal | Jude | Jud |
| Ephesians | Eph | Revelation | Rev |
| Philippians | Phil | | |
| Colossians | Col | | |
| 1 Thessalonians | 1 Thess | | |
| 2 Thessalonians | 2 Thess | | |
| 1 Timothy | 1 Tim | | |
| 2 Timothy | 2 Tim | | |
| Titus | Titus | | |

# INTRODUCTION

*Rejoice in the Lord always; again I will say, rejoice.*
PHILIPPIANS 4:4

The book of Philippians overflows with joy and thanksgiving. Paul wrote to the church in Philippi to thank them for a gift. He reported the joyful news that Epaphroditus, who had brought their gift to Paul, had recovered from his illness and was returning to Philippi. Paul said that he had learned the secret of being content in any situation, and he told them about his situation in prison. He expressed joy that more people were hearing about Christ even if some were proclaiming the gospel with bad motives. Wanting the Christians in Philippi to be unified, he challenged them to be servants just as Jesus was when he "himself emptied" and became a man rather than clinging to the rights of his divine nature (2:1–11).

## AUTHOR, DATE, PLACE OF WRITING

The early church was unanimous in its testimony that Philippians was written by the apostle Paul (*cf* 1:1). Internally the letter reveals the stamp of genuineness. The many personal references of the author fit what we know of Paul from other New Testament books.

It is evident that Paul wrote the letter from prison (*cf* 1:13-14). Some have argued that this imprisonment took place in Ephesus, perhaps c. A.D. 53-55; others put it in Caesarea c. 57-59. Best evidence, however, favors Rome as the place of origin and the date as c. 61. This fits well with the account of Paul's house arrest in Acts 28:14-31. When he wrote Philippians, he was not in the Mamertine dungeon as he was when he wrote 2 Timothy. He was in his own rented house, where for two years he was free to impart the gospel to all who came to him.

Many of the Philippians were retired military men who had been given land in the vicinity and who in turn served as a military presence in this frontier city. Their pride in Roman citizenship brings Paul to say that our citizenship is in heaven (3:20). That Philippi was a Roman colony may explain why there were not enough Jews there to permit the establishment of a synagogue and why Paul does not quote the Old Testament in the Philippian letter.

## **MESSAGE**

Philippians is one of Paul's most informal letters. With this church he did not feel the need to assert his apostolic authority. His overflowing love for them is obvious. He even allowed them to send him money (*cf* 1:5,7; 4:15), which was very unusual for him.

Joy in suffering is the overwhelming theme of this letter. Paul is imprisoned, yet he uses the term for joy (noun and verb) over sixteen times. His peace and hope were not based on circumstances, but on knowing Christ (3:10) and pursing that prize as his highest ambition. All was dung compared to this goal (3:8).

There is an element of false teaching present in the church (*cf* 3:2, 18-19). These heretics seem to be similar to those in the churches of Galatia, who were called Judaizers. They insisted that one had to become a Jew before one could be a Christian. There is also a conflict resolution needed in this letter (4:1-5).

This letter includes an example of an early Christian hymn, creed, or liturgical poem (*cf* 2:6-11). It is one of the finest Christological passages in the entire New Testament (*cf* Jn 1:1-14; Col 1:13-20; Heb 1:2-3). Paul uses it as an example of Christ's humility to be imitated by every believer (*cf* 2:1-5), not primarily in a doctrinal sense.

In a book of 104 verses, Jesus' name or title occurs 51 times. It is obvious who is central in Paul's heart, mind, and theology.

I was personally moved by Paul's desire to apprehend Christ as he himself was apprehended by Christ (3:12). This was the prize Paul was reaching for. Paul was clear that knowing Christ is a lifelong endeavor. We are called to know him more and more each day.

Matthew Steven Black
Elgin, Illinois
October 1, 2021

# 1 | PHILIPPIANS 1:1-2
## JOY IN JESUS

*Grace to you and peace from God our
Father and the Lord Jesus Christ.*
PHILIPPIANS 1:2

Paul's overarching concern in Philippians is with the gospel, a word that appears more in Philippians than in any other letter (per hundred words), as scholar Gordon Fee points outs.[1] The word "gospel" means "good news". The theme of the book of Philippians is "joy in Jesus." Joy comes through sharing in Christ's presence in a new community that God has created through the gospel.

There is almost no correction in the book of Philippians. It is a book that is written to maturing Christians. The key to Christian maturity we find in this letter is to: rejoice in the Lord. Get your focus off yourself; get your focus off your circumstances, and rejoice in Christ, in your forever family, and in all the spiritual blessings God has given you. We see this taught and lived out in this letter.

### BACKGROUND OF PHILIPPIANS

Paul is going to have a number of things to say about his forever family in Jesus. Here is a guy who should be, by all accounts, absolutely

---

[1] Gordon Fee. *Paul's Letter to the Philippians*, vol 14, The New International Commentary on the New Testament (Grand Rapids, MI: Eerdmans, 1995) 82.

depressed because of loneliness. He has nothing that you and I would seek to cure our loneliness. He's writing from prison. He has no wife. No kids. No grandkids. No home. No hometown he can return to. No home church that is nearby (he was sent from Antioch). He's in prison. He's not in proximity with people.

## Philippi

His friends are far away in a town called Philippi. Philippi was founded by the father of Alexander the Great, Phillip II of Macedonia. It had a population of about 2000 people. It became established because it was considered a port city, not too far from the Mediterranean Sea. It also was supplied with gold mines nearby.

Paul is writing the Philippians a letter from Rome where he is imprisoned. There in the cell he is shackled next to a Roman soldier under house arrest. It's normally a lot worse, but Paul is a Roman citizen. There he can receive guests and write letters. He's wrote four letters called the "prison epistles": Galatians, Ephesians, Philippians, and Colossians.[2] He doesn't have a lot in common with these people. Most are married. He's single. Many of them have children. He doesn't. They are going to work. He's going to jail, right? They're really at different phases of their life. And he writes them a letter, as a friend, and he talks about how much joy he has because of their Gospel partnership with him. Here is a striking fact in our text: *Paul is not lonely*. He rejoices in the fellowship he has with God's people everywhere. He rejoices that God is building his community, his forever family, even though he's in prison. As Jesus said, "I will build my church, and the gates of hell shall not prevail against it" (Mt 16:18). He rejoices in Christ who said, "I will never leave you nor forsake you" (Heb 13:5).

Paul was never totally alone, because Christ was always with him. Paul reminds us that joy isn't derived from comfortable circumstances, but from a living, encouraging encounter and communion with Christ.

**Philippians 1:1-11** | Paul and Timothy, servants of Christ Jesus, To all the saints in Christ Jesus who are at Philippi, with the overseers and deacons: [2] Grace to you and peace from God our Father

---

[2] You can remember the prison epistles with the mnemonic device: General Electric Power Company, the initials for the prison epistles – Galatians, Ephesians, Philippians, and Colossians.

and the Lord Jesus Christ. ³ I thank my God in all my remembrance of you, ⁴ always in every prayer of mine for you all making my prayer with joy, ⁵ because of your partnership in the gospel from the first day until now. ⁶ And I am sure of this, that he who began a good work in you will bring it to completion at the day of Jesus Christ. ⁷ It is right for me to feel this way about you all, because I hold you in my heart, for you are all partakers with me of grace, both in my imprisonment and in the defense and confirmation of the gospel. ⁸ For God is my witness, how I yearn for you all with the affection of Christ Jesus. ⁹ And it is my prayer that your love may abound more and more, with knowledge and all discernment, ¹⁰ so that you may approve what is excellent, and so be pure and blameless for the day of Christ, ¹¹ filled with the fruit of righteousness that comes through Jesus Christ, to the glory and praise of God.

Why are we people so lonely? Theologically, to get you to understand why we're in this state, I'll briefly summarize for you the Bible's teaching of why isolation, loneliness, is our state. And that is, to begin the character of God. God, by definition, according to Scripture, is Trinitarian in nature. One God, three persons. Father, Son, Spirit. Mysterious? Indeed. But the Bible says that within the very character of God, there is love, community, respect, relationship. God never gets lonely. God did not make mankind because he was lonely. That would be impossible since God is completely fulfilled within himself. God made man for his glory.

Loneliness is ultimately caused by sin which separates us from God. That's why even if you are in a crowd of people, you can feel lonely. You can be a mother in the home with a husband and many children and be lonely. The cure for loneliness is salvation in Jesus. When you come to know Jesus, he takes away your sins. He takes away the separation. He unites you with himself and you are adopted and chosen into God's family. You are never alone again. And at that moment God brings you into fellowship with all Christians. *Fellowship* is sharing in the presence of God.

### Paul's "Lonely" Imprisonment

Paul is sitting in prison, facing death, lonely, hurting. He is hungry. He is broke. He is beaten. He is probably sick, and he writes a letter to his friends. And he opens with this word to explain to the depth of the relationship that they have in their Gospel partnership. He opens with this. "Grace to you."

Paul knew about the grace of God. He spoke of it at every opportunity. He was under house arrest in Rome, and he shared his testimony of Jesus "throughout the whole imperial guard" (1:13). The imperial guard, known as the Praetorians, were the elite of the Roman army and were paid double a normal soldier's wage for their service. There were 10,000 specifically to guard the emperor of Rome. Paul's testimony spread throughout the Praetorian Guard, and even saints deep in "Caesar's household," i.e., those in and about the emperor's palace and among his family (4:22).

Paul was held a bit at Caesarea Maratima on the Coast of the Mediterranean Sea, the capitol of Judea at the time. He was likely held there in a broken cistern that is still there today. There is even a plaque there dedicated to Pontius Pilate. He was then transferred to Rome and was there under house arrest for two years (Acts 28:30) with some of the imperial guard, very elite. Paul was a Roman citizen and got great treatment. Non-Roman citizens, even of high status, were often harshly treated. In contrast, house arrest was typically more comfortable for the prisoner, who was usually physically chained to a guard but could still host visitors.

Upon entering the city of Rome, "Julius, a centurion of the Augustan Regiment" (Acts 27:1) handed Paul over to the Prefect of the Praetorian Guard (the commanding officer). The official duty of the Prefect was to keep in custody all accused persons who were to be tried before the Emperor. "Now when we came to Rome, the centurion delivered the prisoners to the captain of the guard; but Paul was permitted to dwell by himself with the soldier who guarded him" (Acts 28:16).

Paul had been delivered to the Praetorian Guard to await trial before the Emperor. Paul is twice referred to as having been "bound in chains" (Acts 28:20; Eph 6:20). The *chains* referred to were a short length of chain by which the wrist of a prisoner was bound to the wrist of a soldier who was guarding him, so that escape was impossible, both for Paul, *and* the guard!

## The Macedonian Call

Every congregation has a beginning. The church at Jerusalem began on Pentecost with the coming of the Holy Spirit and the preaching of the apostles (Acts 2). The church in Samaria began with Philip's preaching the word (Acts 8). The church at Philippi began with Paul hearing the Macedonian call (Acts 16:9). Paul and his team of missionaries were going to circle Asia and head back East, but the Holy Spirit forbid them to preach in Asia and Bithynia. The Spirit gave Paul a vision of a man saying, "Come over into Macedonia, and help us" (Acts 16:9).

> And they went through the region of Phrygia and Galatia, having been forbidden by the Holy Spirit to speak the word in Asia. [7] And when they had come up to Mysia, they attempted to go into Bithynia, but the Spirit of Jesus did not allow them. [8] So, passing by Mysia, they went down to Troas. [9] And a vision appeared to Paul in the night: a man of Macedonia was standing there, urging him and saying, "Come over to Macedonia and help us." [10] And when Paul had seen the vision, immediately we sought to go on into Macedonia, concluding that God had called us to preach the gospel to them. —*Acts 16:6-10*

In obedience Paul, Silas, Timothy, and Luke went straight through Asia to Macedonia (modern day Greece, Macedonia and Bulgaria). It seems the Lord wanted the gospel to impact Philippi, an important port city. For the first time the gospel was preached in Europe. Paul shared a special friendship with the Christians at Philippi. That friendship started in a strange way, which is described in the 16th chapter of Acts. Paul and his companions had been on a missionary journey. They had an itinerary—they knew where they were going. Bithynia was the next place on the list. They travelled so much and were ready to go east to Bithynia. But when they tried to enter Bithynia, Acts says, "the Spirit didn't allow them" (Acts 16:7).

Then, during the night, Paul saw a vision of a man from Macedonia begging him, "Come over into Macedonia and help us" (Acts 16:9). Paul and his companions caught the next ship to Macedonia, and proceeded to Philippi, its leading city.

## THANKFUL FOR OUR FAMILY TREE! (1:1-2)

### People in God's Family

Every family has its structure. You have mom and dad, children, sometimes Grandma and Grandpa. Everyone knows their place. Ten years ago, my oldest brother gave me the book of the genealogy of my family. How many of you have done research in your family tree? You can find interesting characters in every family tree.

Growing up, I remember listening to stories from my grandfather, Charles Cunningham Black, who everyone called "Scottie" because he was from Scotland, born in 1899. "He was 15 years old when he joined the British Army and fought in World War I. His sister Mary signed the papers for him so that he could get away from his father, who he didn't get along with. He was caught in a battle and spent 3 months in a prison camp. After the war ended he was sent to Cairo Egypt."[3] Once his service was ended he opted to go to the United States. He landed at Ellis Island on the 4th of March, 1923. Later he would put on three round exhibition fights for Al Capone, who paid him $50 a night (a very good wage back then!).

Genealogies are fascinating! On my grandmother's side, I found out that 150 years ago (in 1866), my great grandfather Henry Becker moved to 248 North Street, Elgin, Illinois, about 2 miles from where I presently live.[4] Some of my ancestors were saved in the Great Awakening under the preaching of John Wesley. People used to say they that my family [the Butt family] were born with hymnbooks in their hands – "singing instead of crying!"[5]

My mom had a great aunt (through marriage). We all think our Aunts are great! Unfortunately, this great aunt was an outlaw. So I'm also related to Belle Starr, one of the most famous female outlaw in the Wild West.[6] In 1941 a famous movie was made about her.

As I went back, I found out I'm related to James Scott, Duke of Monmouth whose father was King Charles II of England (through Lucy Walter – via the Vanstone / Butt families[7]).

---

[3] Charles Black. "We Relate" From werelate.org. http://www.werelate.org/wiki/Person:Charles_Black_%2811%29 . Accessed December 8, 2012.

[4] Henry Becker. "We Relate" http://www.werelate.org/wiki/Person:Henry_Becker_%285%29

[5] Hannah Butt Taylor Letter. "We Relate" From werelate.org. http://www.werelate.org/wiki/MySource:Srblac/Hannah_Butt_Taylor_Letter Accessed December 8, 2012.

[6] Alma Becker. "We Relate" http://www.werelate.org/wiki/Person:Alma_Becker_%282%29 . Alma Becker was married to Jack Reed. Jack's uncle was James C. Reed, whose mother was Myra Maybelle Shirley, AKA Belle Starr.

[7] Charles II of England. "We Relate" http://www.werelate.org/wiki/Person:Charles_II_of_England_%281%29

Of course, my most famous relative is James Scott, Great Grandson of King James I (King James Bible fame). Duke James Scott of Monmouth (a protestant) actually tried to usurp the throne from his uncle King James II (a catholic).

We don't choose our family, that's for sure! But we also don't choose the church. Jesus promised: "I will build my church and the gates of hell will not prevail against it" (Mt 16:18). As Paul writes to these Philippian friends, let's look at the family structure.

### Slaves

Paul and Timothy are writing, and they introduce themselves as slaves [*doulos*] of Jesus.

**Philippians 1:1a** | Paul and Timothy, servants of Christ Jesus.

Though we are sons spiritually, adopted into the family of God, when it comes to obedience and holiness, we are slaves of righteousness for Christ.

Timothy had a very special relationship with Paul. Though he was somewhat young, he radical commitment to Christ and was Paul's spiritual son in the faith. This is a beautiful picture of spiritual leadership. At other churches, they have to say, we are God's ordained apostles, but here, we have a church that is spiritually mature, and you see this in so many ways in this letter. When leaders are good and gentle and kind, you know you have a mature church. You see this tenderness in all of Paul's letters. He says, I'm a slave of Jesus. I want to wash your feet, like he washed his disciples' feet.

### Saints

**Philippians 1:1b** | Paul To all the saints in Christ Jesus who are at Philippi.

Who are these people he calls "saints"? A saint is simply a "holy one." It means "one separated unto God, set apart for God's service." If you are a Christian, then you are a saint.

### Elders and Deacons

**Philippians 1:1c** | with the overseers and deacons.

These saints at Philippi are overseen by the pastors and elders. The word overseer here is one of many words used for elders: pastor, bishop, overseer, teacher, shepherd. These are all good words used for the same office. It had been 12 years since the jailhouse conversion of the Philippian jailer, the slave girl, and Lydia and her family, and now there is an established church in Philippi. There are elders overseeing them. There are deacons caring for the needs of congregation. We don't know who these church leaders were. Perhaps one of the elders is the Philippian jailer. It's been 12 years since the night he was converted.

### Purpose of God's Family

Paul greets the Philippians with gospel words:

> **Philippians 1:2** | Grace to you and peace from God our Father and the Lord Jesus Christ.

Grace is not only God's unmerited favor but also his infinite power to help his children. Peace is that reconciliation with God. We are no longer enemies but have been brought into a sweet relationship with God through his Son Jesus. So we get an example of how God grows the church here and around the world. How does Jesus build his church? First through the grace and peace of conversion. That's how Paul starts his letter off.

Have you been converted? Have you placed your faith in Jesus? Are you a saint? This position of sainthood is not like in the Roman Catholic church where has to prove that you've done two authentic miracles before you are canonized as a saint. To be a saint, you need trust Christ with repentant faith, and your robe of sin is put on Jesus, and he robes you in his righteousness. That's sainthood, and it is possible through a total surrender to Christ. You surrender your sin to him, and you receive his righteousness. You are justified before a holy God because of the blood of Christ.

I want you to remember the words of Jesus who said, "I will build my church, and the gates of hell shall not prevail against it" (Mt 16:18). Jesus promised to build his church but let me show you how it began.

## THANKFUL FOR OUR FAMILY STORY (1:3-8; ACTS 16)

We read of Paul's deep affection for the Philippians. This was a ragtag church when it started, but don't judge the finished product by the ingredients. There is a cooking show called *Chopped*. It's a favorite of mine because they take all these diverse and strange ingredients, and the challenge is to make an inviting and edible dish. They usually are able to accomplish it, but you can't judge the finished product on the initial ingredients. You have to wait for the reveal.

## A Dear Family

> **Philippians 1:3-5** | I thank my God every time I remember you. ⁴ In all my prayers for all of you, I always pray with joy ⁵ because of your partnership in the gospel from the first day until now.

Paul has such affection when he remembers his forever Philippian family. As Paul mused in his Roman cell, his mind ranged across Italy and the Adriatic to Macedonia and over the *Via Egnatia* to "little Rome," the pretentious Roman colony of Philippi—and the beloved faces of Lydia and her clan, the jailer and his family, Euodia and Syntyche and Clement and scores of others who had been added to the church. And Paul smiled as he writes about his gratitude for this sweetheart church.[8]

Paul's little epistle to the church at Philippi is overflowing with terms of deep affection. These expressions of love begin in Paul's opening thanksgiving for God's transforming work in the Philippian believers: "I hold you in my heart" (1:7); and then "I yearn for you all with the affection of Christ Jesus" (1:8). Later he will call them "my beloved" (2:12) and "my brothers, whom I love and long for, my joy and my crown" (4:1). Not only does Paul speak tenderly to this church, he also spares them the sharp scolding that he felt compelled to speak to others. Clearly, the church at Philippi has a very special place in Paul's heart.[9]

## A Divine Family

> **Philippians 1:6** | Being confident of this, that he who began a good work in you will carry it on to completion until the day of Christ Jesus.

---

[8] R. Kent Hughes, *Philippians: The Fellowship of the Gospel*, Preaching the Word (Wheaton, IL: Crossway Books, 2007), 24.
[9] Dennis E. Johnson, *Philippians*, ed. Richard D. Phillips, Philip Graham Ryken, and Daniel M. Doriani, 1st ed., Reformed Expository Commentary (Phillipsburg, NJ: P&R Publishing, 2013), 21.

God's going to finish the work. Some of what he has to work with is lumpy or difficult. But he's the Potter, and we are the clay. The context makes it clear that the one who began this good work is God himself. The good work in view is the entire work of salvation from beginning to end, stretching from initial regeneration and justification to final glorification (*cf* Rom 8:29–30; Eph 1:3–14).[10]

Paul is *confident* as he prays, with a confidence not based on the Philippians' own abilities or past achievements, but on the power and love of God and because God can be relied upon to bring what he begins *to completion*. When we see that God has begun a good work in people's lives, we can be sure that it is his purpose to continue—that can always be our confidence in praying for our fellow-Christians.[11]

The day that the completed work of God will be admired is "the day of Christ Jesus" or what we might refer to as his Second Coming. In that moment we will bear the image of Christ's character perfectly. Sin and Satan will be no more. Believers are "predestined to become conformed to the image of God's Son" (Rom 8:29), because "in a moment, in the twinkling of an eye, at the last trumpet. For the trumpet will sound, and the dead will be raised imperishable, and we shall be changed" (1 Cor 15:52). "We know that when he appears we shall be like him, because we shall see him as he is" (1 Jn 3:2). Finally, God's work in us will be finished! No more trials. No more growing. We will be fully mature in Christ, reflecting the image of our glorious Bridegroom.

## A Diverse Family

> **Philippians 1:7-8** | It is right for me to feel this way about all of you, since I have you in my heart and, whether I am in chains or defending and confirming the gospel, all of you share in God's grace with me. ⁸ God can testify how I long for all of you with the affection of Christ Jesus.

Paul has this deep affection. He compares his love for the Philippians to Christ's love, it is so strong. Paul can remember how extraordi-

---

[10] Matthew S. Harmon, *Philippians: A Mentor Commentary*, Mentor Commentaries (Great Britain; Ross-shire: Mentor, 2015), 84.
[11] Francis Foulkes, "Philippians," in *New Bible Commentary: 21st Century Edition*, ed. D. A. Carson et al., 4th ed. (Leicester, England; Downers Grove, IL: Inter-Varsity Press, 1994), 1250.

nary this church is. I want to look at it from Acts 16. In the Jewish Mishnah (collection of Jewish history and traditions) it is said that a Jewish man would thank God daily for three things: that he was not a woman, a slave, or a Gentile. That's interesting because that was the founding group for the Philippian church.

### Lydia the Fashionista

If we look to Acts 16, Lydia we find is from Thyatira, but has a home in Philippi. She's a rich woman. She has a booming business in selling purple fabric for clothing. A "seller of purple" (Acts 16:14) meant Lydia sold purple clothes or cloth. At the time, such clothes were so expensive they were only worn by royalty and the rich. Let's read about her. They came to a city, it says in Acts 16:12, named…

> …Philippi, which is a leading city of the district of Macedonia and a Roman colony. We remained in this city some days. [13] And on the Sabbath day we went outside the gate to the riverside, where we supposed there was a place of prayer, and we sat down and spoke to the women who had come together. [14] One who heard us was a woman named Lydia, from the city of Thyatira, a seller of purple goods, who was a worshiper of God. The Lord opened her heart to pay attention to what was said by Paul. [15] And after she was baptized, and her household as well, she urged us, saying, "If you have judged me to be faithful to the Lord, come to my house and stay." And she prevailed upon us. —Acts 16:12-15

Thyatira and Philippi are cities with booming economies. Lydia then is basically a Greek fashionista, CEO, on top of some fashion empire. Today we might say she has a house in Chicago and in Paris. She's a serious mover in her world. Isn't it wonderful that God can humble someone like Lydia? She's what the Bible calls a "God-fearer." Here's what that means. She's rejected paganism and polytheism. She does not believe that there are dozens of gods: god of the wind, the rain, the purple cloth; god of the sea, god of the fashion world… She's come to believe there is only one God ruling the universe. So a God-fearer is that she is a monotheist. She's in the synagogue. She's listening to the teaching of the Jews. She's trying to live a moral life. I want you to see how God goes after her. She is an intellect. She is a seeker. She understands the law, if she knows the Torah. She knows she needs forgiveness. She knows she needs a blood sacrifice. She needs atonement. She needs to be justified before God. But she's confused.

Enter Paul. He enters into what is basically a women's Bible study and pauses the Kay Arthur or Nancy Leigh DeMoss DVD and begins to teach them. Paul basically connects the dots for them. God opens her eyes. Lydia is a thinker. She's an intellect. She's a God fearer. She is listening to the word of God, and she experiences the wisdom of God when God opens her eyes. After her conversion, she "constrained" the missionaries to use this house as a base of operations, so it must have been much larger than needed. Her home in Philippi became the place where the new church met (Acts 16:40).

### *The Slave Girl*

Back in Acts 16, we are introduced to a slave girl. She's manic. She's mental. She's possessed by a demon. She's making tons of money for her handlers. She's following Paul and Silas and Luke around, causing trouble. She's interrupting and screaming speaking of Paul and his Savior Jesus. That sounds good, but it's not. She's screaming and causing a scene for them. This is an evil spirit that has her tongue. Let's read about her.

> As we were going to the place of prayer, we were met by a slave girl who had a spirit of divination and brought her owners much gain by fortune-telling. [17] She followed Paul and us, crying out, "These men are servants of the Most High God, who proclaim to you the way of salvation." [18] And this she kept doing for many days. Paul, having become greatly annoyed, turned and said to the spirit, "I command you in the name of Jesus Christ to come out of her." And it came out that very hour. —*Acts 16:16-18.*

I love what the Scripture says. Paul was "annoyed." He had a holy annoyance. Don't misunderstand. Paul is a man filled with the Holy Spirit. He knows what this girl needs. He is annoyed that this girl is under the power of the wicked one. She needs to experience the power of the gospel not merely through wisdom, which she knew and had been spouting off about. Mere knowledge was not enough to convert this girl. She needed to experience Christ as the power of God. So Paul commands the demon to come out of her. There's convert number two. The slave girl is converted through the power of God.

This conversion eventually causes a riot, because the gospel has major economic consequences for the city of Philippi. Even though Paul is a Roman citizen, he is thrown into prison with Silas. It seems Luke and Timothy are in Philippi, but they are not arrested. But when her owners saw that their hope of gain was gone, they seized Paul and Silas and dragged them into the marketplace before the rulers. 20 And when they had brought them to the magistrates, they said, "These men are Jews, and they are disturbing our city. 21 They advocate customs that are not lawful for us as Romans to accept or practice." 22 The crowd joined in attacking them, and the magistrates tore the garments off them and gave orders to beat them with rods. 23 And when they had inflicted many blows upon them, they threw them into prison, ordering the jailer to keep them safely. 24 Having received this order, he put them into the inner prison and fastened their feet in the stocks (Acts 16:19-24).

### *The Ex-Military, Blue Collar GI*

So here we have an introduction to our Ex-Roman military Philippian jailer. He's likely a GI, a Roman soldier that is now a warden. He's a tough guy. We know that because he's supposed to keep Paul and Silas safe, but he tortures them.

Not only does he beat them, but he puts them in stocks. Now when we modern people think of stocks, we think of the 1700s when a person would have their hands and their head restrained by stocks. The Roman practice of stocks was not nearly as kind. Stocks in Roman practice was a form of torture in the prisoners would be shackled to the wall in painful positions.

This jailer is not just keeping them safe. He's torturing them. He's going above and beyond in making sure they never want to cause a problem in Philippi again. But something happens.

> About midnight Paul and Silas were praying and singing hymns to God, and the prisoners were listening to them, 26 and suddenly there was a great earthquake, so that the foundations of the prison were shaken. And immediately all the doors were opened, and everyone's bonds were unfastened. 27 When the jailer woke and saw that the prison doors were open, he drew his sword and was about to kill himself, supposing that the prisoners had escaped. 28 But Paul cried with a loud voice, "Do not harm yourself, for we are all here." 29 And the jailer called for lights and rushed in, and trembling with fear he fell down before Paul and Silas. 30 Then he brought them out and said, "Sirs, what must I do to be saved?" 31 And they said, "Believe in the Lord Jesus, and you will be saved, you and your household."32 And they spoke the word of the Lord to him and to all who were in his house.33 And he took them the same hour of the night and washed

their wounds; and he was baptized at once, he and all his family. ³⁴ Then he brought them up into his house and set food before them. And he rejoiced along with his entire household that he had believed in God. —*Acts 16:25-34*

God delivers them, and the Philippians jailer and his whole family come to know the Lord.

## APPLICATIONS

Let me leave you with some applications.

### 1 – Attitude is everything

So what is Paul's attitude when he's in jail? We can hear his heart in the book of Philippians. If they want to kill him, he says, "To die is gain." If they want to beat him, he says, "Rejoice in the Lord always, and again I say rejoice." If they set him free, he says, "For me to live is Christ." If they torture him, he breaks out in prayer and singing, and brings an earthquake to the entire jail complex. You are a Christian. God is working through you. One of the great marks of God on your life is the joy of knowing Jesus. Look at Paul: joy doesn't come from your circumstances – it comes from your walk with Christ.

### 2 – Loneliness is a mindset

As we have created technology to connect more and more people, ironically, loneliness has increased. I want to share with you a set of statistics from the book called, *Bowling Alone*. It's authored by a professor at the Harvard Business School, and he traces a decline in friendship and relationship, and an increase in loneliness and isolation over the course of the last 25 years, roughly.

He says an evening with the neighbors is down 33 percent. And many of us don't even know our neighbors. We don't know who they are. You're just, "That's the weird guy. He mows his lawn in dress socks. Over there is the loud guy: he talks loud; his music is loud. There's the angry lady. She's always yelling at people. We don't even know who they are, you know? As Christians, we need to take the time to get to know our neighbors. Lots of Christians complain about loneliness. But Proverbs tells us: "A man that has friends must show himself friendly" (Prov 18:24).

### 3 – Christian community is rich

God's family is diverse. Look at the Philippian church: it started with a woman, a slave girl and a Gentile jailer and his family. Let us enjoy the diversity of every ethnicity under heaven. Let us remember that "Grace erases race." We celebrate our ethnicity, but we also remember we are all the same blood. There is one human race. Let me challenge you, if you are struggling with loneliness, start getting to know people. Don't just stay in your comfort zone hanging out with people just like you. If you are young, love on an elderly person. Next time you have lunch out, invite someone completely different than you.

### 4 – Focus on Christ, not on circumstances

One thing we have in common with all Christians is a radical focus on Christ. Paul doesn't begin this letter bemoaning his prison sentence. He starts out rejoicing with a heart filled with grace and peace. That's how Paul greets his friends in Philippi. Paul is focused on Christ in grace and peace. Are you walking in the power of grace? God's grace is forgiving enough to cleanse you of your sins and powerful enough to give you the strength to live the Christian life. Can you testify that the grace of Jesus is sufficient for every test and trial to give you joy?

A lot of people talk about the grace of God. But you will know you are enjoying the grace of God when you experience the peace of God. Are you walking in God's peace? Do you have a clean conscience? Is there any sin that is condemning you in your conscience? Remember what Paul says:

> Do not be anxious about anything, but in everything by prayer and supplication with thanksgiving let your requests be made known to God. [7] And the peace of God, which surpasses all understanding, will guard your hearts and your minds in Christ Jesus.
> —*Philippians 4:6-7*

Or as Paul says a few verses earlier, "Rejoice in the Lord always; again I will say, rejoice" (4:4). Joy comes from Jesus. Jesus is what brought this congregation together. Jesus is what fills us with joy. Paul is in prison, and he has such joy knowing what Jesus is doing in this congregation.

### Conclusion

Where is your joy? Where is your focus? If we focus on each other, we will be discouraged, but if we focus on Christ, we will rejoice! In the local church we have so much diversity, just like the Philippians church. We have people who were raised in different parts of the world, people of many diverse contexts, family backgrounds. We are a church that looks like heaven from every tribe, tongue, language and nation. Let us act like we are from heaven, by focusing on Christ. What is your family story? How you came to know Christ may have different details, but one detail is always the say: we found our joy in the love and forgiveness of Jesus! Tell that story everywhere!

# 2 | PHILIPPIANS 1:3-8
## THE JOY OF CHRISTIAN MATURITY

*And I am sure of this, that he who began a good work in you will bring it to completion at the day of Jesus Christ.*
PHILIPPIANS 1:6

I am so glad to be saved. Where would any of us be without Jesus? The joyful life is the mature life. It's a life of constant growing and changing. The Bible not only commands Christians to grow, it promises that every Christian will grow in grace and be conformed to the image of Christ. Peter says, "Grow in grace and in the knowledge of our Lord and Savior Jesus Christ" (1 Pet 3:18). Paul says in Romans 8:29 that all Christians are predestined "to be conformed to the image of God's dear Son." That means you were meant to grow! The growing life is the joyful life.

Something that brings me joy is when I think about the maple tree that my brother David planted at our home in Oak Forest, Illinois when we were kids. David was so proud of that tree. He planted it and watered it. He watched it grow. My dad wasn't so fond of that tree. When he noticed it in the corner of the yard, he didn't want it there, and so he took the lawn mower and cut it down. But David kept watering it. Eventually the seasons changed and underneath the ground during fall and winter and spring, that root system grew. By late spring, my dad just gave up and let the tree grow. Today, that tree is so big, you can see it from the satellite photos. That maple tree refused to die. There was such life in it that it kept growing.

That's what happened when you came to know Christ. There was a principle of life in you that guarantees that you will grow in God's grace and into the image of Christ. That's the joyful life. No matter what is happening. No matter what trials or burdens, you can have joy because God is growing you. He's making you stronger. If you've gone astray, he's bringing you back. You are God's child. He'll never let go of you. That's the theme of our passage today.

> **Philippians 1:6** | And I am sure of this, that he who began a good work in you will bring it to completion at the day of Jesus Christ.

In his letter to the Philippians, Paul emphasizes joy in the life of the Christian. In fact, he spoke of gladness, joy, and rejoicing some sixteen times (1:4,18,25; 2:2,17,18,28,29; 3:1; 4:1,4,10). The word for joy simply means, "the experience of gladness."[12] Paul speaks of a Christian joy that is informed by God's love and sovereignty. Thus with Paul joy "is an understanding of existence that encompasses both elation and depression, that can accept with submission events that bring delight or dismay, because joy allows one to see beyond any particular event to the sovereign Lord who stands above all events and ultimately has control over them."[13] True biblical joy, is a "quality or attitude of delight and happiness, which is ultimately grounded in the work of God as Father, Son and Holy Spirit." Let us notice four fruits of joyful living in Christ from the letter to the Philippians. The Bible commands:

> Rejoice in the Lord always; again I will say, rejoice. —*Philippians 4:4*

Paul goes on to say in 4:6-7 to be anxious for nothing and be prayerful and joyful in everything.

> Do not be anxious about anything, but in everything by prayer and supplication with thanksgiving let your requests be made known to God. ⁷ And the peace of God, which surpasses all understanding, will guard your hearts and your minds in Christ Jesus.

---

[12] Arndt, W., Danker, F. W., & Bauer, W. *A Greek-English Lexicon of the New Testament and other early Christian Literature*, 3rd ed.(Chicago: University of Chicago Press, 2000), 1077.

[13] G. F. Hawthorne. (2004). *Philippians*, Vol. 43 (Dallas: Word, Inc., 2004), 21.

*— Philippians 4:6-7*

Paul is not talking about sweeping our problems under the rug, but having a deep, rich, abiding joy in Jesus. Because of Jesus we can be filled with joy in every circumstance.

**Philippians 1:3-8** | I thank my God in all my remembrance of you, ⁴ always in every prayer of mine for you all making my prayer with joy, ⁵ because of your partnership in the gospel from the first day until now. ⁶ And I am sure of this, that he who began a good work in you will bring it to completion at the day of Jesus Christ. ⁷ It is right for me to feel this way about you all, because I hold you in my heart, for you are all partakers with me of grace, both in my imprisonment and in the defense and confirmation of the gospel. ⁸ For God is my witness, how I yearn for you all with the affection of Christ Jesus.

Paul demonstrates Christian maturity. The mature life is the joyful life. You cannot be joyful unless you are growing and changing in Christ. Paul gives us four areas of Christian maturity. They are really marks of a God-focused life. A God-focused life will bring you joy. The first mark of a joyful, God-focused life, is gratitude.

## GRATITUDE MARKS THE MATURE CHRISTIAN (1:3)

### Gratitude for People

What was it about those folks in Philippi that brought Paul so much joy? First, he had happy memories of the people. Look at how Paul begins his gratitude:

**Philippians 1:3** | I thank my God in all my remembrance of you.

What were Paul's happy memories? He had no regrets, he nursed no ill feelings, he struggled through no unresolved conflicts. He looked back over a full decade and when he thought of the Philippians, he laughed with joy! "I'm so thankful!" Gratitude is at the very core of what it means to understand grace. However bad your day is going, your year is going, your life is going – you are not in hell! Amazing grace how sweet the sound that saved a wretch like me! Wow, God is so good. Gratitude. It's one of the main mark that you are maturing in Christ. Are you a grateful person?

Ingratitude was at the heart of the fall, and at the heart of what's fallen about us to this day. Adam and Eve thought God was holding back goodness from them. Ingratitude led to the very first sin and to all sin (Rom 1:21). Gratitude takes nothing for granted. It acknowledges each favor, each gift—both big and small. It also recognizes the giver—the relative who shows her love by giving you a gift; the friend who remembers to call you; the person who gives you a compliment or goes out of his way to invite you to go for a walk on a beautiful day; the spouse or friend who brings you a cup of coffee when you're exhausted, cooks you a fine dinner, or throws a party for you.

When we stop to think about it, we have received many gifts from many people, and especially from God. We have much to be thankful for.And Paul says: "When I pray to God, I just tell him how grateful I am for you!" Were there difficulties? Yes! That Philippian jailer beat Paul's body bloody. But now, what a joy that he worships God. You better believe he brought some difficult baggage into the Christian life, but Paul sees the end result for the whole church. He sees them growing and changing in Christ. God's going to finish the work, he says (1:6).

I wonder how many pastors can say that about former churches they have served? Could you say that about former friends you have had? Or places where you have worked? Are yours happy memories? Unfortunately, the memory of certain people makes us churn. When we call them to mind, they bring sad or disappointing mental images. Paul knew no such memories from his days in Philippi.[14]

I want you to know something. This gratitude isn't a platitude. People are hard to love. Look in the mirror. Are you easy to love? The Philippian church was not perfect. Imagine the baggage of the Philippian jailer and the slave girl. Yet Paul was sincerely grateful for them—all of them! Look at the phrase "all of you" in verses 4, 7, and 8.

Based on chapter 2, this church needed to continue to grow in humility, and in chapter 4, some individuals needed a pastoral rebuke, yet Paul was grateful. The conflict didn't crush his gratitude. That's impressive. That's instructive. That's hopeful. If you're a super-critical person, always focusing on what's wrong, then you won't be a grateful person. Don't look for perfection before you show gratitude; look for

---

[14] Charles R. Swindoll. *Laugh Again Hope Again: Two Books to Inspire a Joy-Filled Life* (Nashville: Thomas Nelson. Kindle Edition) Kindle Locations 495-497.

evidences of grace in people's lives. Be quick to thank God for Christian virtues in others and remember that sanctification is a slow process.

Do you give thanks to God in prayer for others? Paul rarely thanked God for things. Paul thanked God for people, who, despite whatever trouble they may have been to him, remained a source of joy and thanksgiving. Paul even wrote a word of thanksgiving for the crazy Corinthians (1 Cor 1:4)!

Do you allow conflict to crush your joy? Don't misunderstand. Paul doesn't overlook the conflict; he addresses it. He doesn't say he enjoys conflict. He simply is able to rejoice in the Lord despite the conflict. This again shows us that we had better have a well of joy that is much more satisfying and sustaining than a fountain filled with comfortable circumstances to stimulate joy. You must go to the gospel for this kind of joy.

## Gratitude in Remembering

Look at how Paul begins his gratitude:

**Philippians 1:3** | I thank my God in all my remembrance of you.

Remarkably, Paul is filled with joy while in prison. Do you find this challenging? I do. Do you think you need something other than Jesus to find real joy? Better-behaved kids? A better job? A different address? More vacation time? In America we often think "bigger" is the answer—bigger house, bigger muscles, bigger church, etc.—but what we really need is a bigger vision of God. Nothing else is an ultimate source of joy. You can have all of those and never know this joy. If you have everything but Jesus, you will be longing for more. If you have nothing but Jesus, you have everything you need for joy. Look at the decadence and the excess of modern culture. None of it provides what people desire.

### *Remembering Grace*

Paul had an attitude and practice of gratitude. He knew that though people are sinners, and sheep sometimes "bite", that God was not finished with the Philippian church yet. Why was Paul so filled with joy when he remembered the Philippians? Was this a perfect church with perfect people? No. Why was he grateful? He chose to notice and focus on God's gifts. These people were once pagans. Now they were growing in Christ (1:6, 9-11). They were once proud, and now they were putting on humility (2:1-11). They were now pressing on to the mark of the high call of Christian maturity (3:14-16). They were growing in their thought life and thinking on whatever was true and honorable, just and pure (4:8).

Paul must have often remembered that, after he left Macedonia, the Philippian church was the only one that helped him financially (4:15-16). Those devoted believers continued their generosity by contributing toward the collection Paul made for the needy believers in Jerusalem (2 Cor 8:1-5).[15]

### *Remembering Forgiveness*

Paul didn't just think about gratitude, he walked in it. He practiced it. He wasn't someone to hold on to bitterness or unforgiveness. Rather than be bitter or gossip, he went to the source if he had a problem. That's how you maintain joy. Do you have a problem with a church member or a leader at Living Hope? Are you nursing a hurt? You cannot be hurt and be joyful at the same time.

Focus on the good things God is doing! Make sure you are bold enough to bring your hurt to the person who hurt you. If you are talking about it with others, you are likely guilty of gossip or slander. It's not right. Don't wait for the person to come to you if you are hurt. The Bible commands us to go to the person who hurt us. The person who is hurt is required to go according to Matthew 18. Go and tell your dear brother or sister who hurt you about the hurt. Be ready to forgive. Listen to the wise words of Jonathan Edwards:

> Proud people tend to speak of others' sins, the miserable delusion of hypocrites, the deadness of some saints with bitterness, or the opposition to holiness of many believers. Pure Christian humility, however, is silent about the sins of others, or speaks of them with grief and pity. The spiritually proud person finds fault with other saints for their lack of progress in grace, while the humble Christian sees so much evil in his own heart, and is so concerned about it, that he is not apt to be very busy with other hearts. He complains most of himself and his own spiritual coldness and readily hopes that most everybody has more love and thankfulness to God than he.[16]

---

[15] John F. MacArthur Jr., *Philippians*, MacArthur New Testament Commentary (Chicago: Moody Press, 2001), 20.

[16] Jonathan Edwards. *Some Thoughts Concerning the Present Revival of Religion in New-England* (Boston: Kneeland & Green Publishing, 1742), 202.

One of the best stories of the difficulty, but joy of forgiveness is one told by Corrie Ten Boom. She had seen her sister die in the Ravensbruck concentration camp. She was telling about it at a church after the war in Munich, Germany. It was there she saw one of her tormentors during the war. She says:

> It was in a church in Munich where I was speaking in 1947 that I saw him – a balding heavyset man in a gray overcoat, a brown felt hat clutched between his hands. One moment I saw the overcoat and the brown hat, the next, (*at least in my mind, I saw*) a blue uniform and a visored cap with its skull and crossbones.
>
> Memories of the concentration camp came back with a rush: the huge room with its harsh overhead lights, the pathetic pile of dresses and shoes in the center of the floor, the shame of walking naked past this man. I could see my sister's frail form ahead of me, ribs sharp beneath the parchment of skin.
>
> *My sister* Betsie and I had been arrested for concealing Jews in our home during the Nazi occupation of Holland. This man had been a guard at Ravensbruck concentration camp where we were sent.
>
> Now he was in front of me, hand thrust out: "A fine message, fraulein! How good it is to know that, as you say, all our sins are at the bottom of the sea!"
>
> It was the first time since my release that I had been face to face with one of my captors and my blood seemed to freeze.
>
> "You mentioned Ravensbruck in your talk," he was saying. "I was a guard there. But since that time," he went on, "I have become a Christian. I know that God has forgiven me for the cruel things I did there, but I would like to hear it from your lips as well. Fraulein – again the hand came out – "will you forgive me?"
>
> And I stood there – and could not. Betsie had died in that place – could he erase her slow terrible death simply for the asking?
>
> It could not have been many seconds that he stood there, hand held out, but to me it seemed hours as I wrestled with the most difficult thing I had ever had to do.
>
> For I had to do it – I knew that. The message that God forgives has a prior condition: that we forgive those who have injured us. "If you do not forgive men their trespasses," Jesus says, "neither will your Father in Heaven forgive your trespasses."

> Still, I stood there with this coldness clutching my heart. But forgiveness is an act of the will, and the will can function regardless of the temperature of the heart. "Jesus, help me!" I prayed silently. "I can lift my hand. I can do that much. Lord, you supply the feeling."
>
> And so woodenly, mechanically, I thrust my hand into the one stretched out to me. And as I did, an incredible thing took place. The current started in my shoulder, raced down my arm, sprang into our joined hands. And then this healing warmth seemed to flood my whole being, bringing tears to my eyes.
>
> "I forgive you, brother!" I cried. "With all my heart!"
>
> For a long moment we grasped each other's hands, the former guard and former prisoner. I had never known God's love so intensely as I did then.[17]

What a joy it is to forgive. What a pure joy that now Corrie could remember that this former soldier's sins were cast into the bottom of the sea of God's forgetfulness. What a pure joy that she could remember they are together in the kingdom of God. Joy is not there because we tuck others' sins under the rug. The joy of remembering our brothers and sisters is there because we forgive them as we are forgiven.

### *Remembering Love*

Paul talks about the messiness of loving Christ's bride and preaching his gospel. Consider the pain Paul experienced in 2 Corinthians 6. He didn't hold it against anyone, but actually rejoiced that he could lay down his life for Christ.

> As servants of God we commend ourselves in every way: by great endurance, in afflictions, hardships, calamities, ⁵ beatings, imprisonments, riots, labors, sleepless nights, hunger; ⁶ by purity, knowledge, patience, kindness, the Holy Spirit, genuine love; ⁷ by truthful speech, and the power of God; with the weapons of righteousness for the right hand and for the left; ⁸ through honor and dishonor, through slander and praise. We are treated as impostors, and yet are true; ⁹ as unknown, and yet well known; as dying, and behold, we live; as punished, and yet not killed; ¹⁰ as sorrowful, yet always rejoicing; as poor, yet making many rich; as having nothing, yet possessing everything.
> —*2 Corinthians 6:4-10*

---

[17] Corrie ten Boom. "I'm Still Learning to Forgive" Guideposts Magazine. Copyright © 1972 by Guideposts Associates, Inc., Carmel, New York 10512.

Paul never let the conflict that the truth brings stop him from loving God's people. Truth brings conflict. Look at the Philippian jailer who beat Paul and Silas before he came to salvation. Look at the slave girl that harassed Paul and his team for days before she was converted. People come with baggage. If you love people, you have to be patient with their baggage. You come with baggage. But we thank God, like Paul did, for every remembrance. Because one day the war will be over. One day we will see Jesus. One day we will all be presented blameless to Jesus Christ. Paul could see that day coming. It filled his heart with gratitude for the Philippians. One way you can tell if you are growing in Christ is if you are grateful. In order to be grateful to people, you have to be forgiving and tender and kind in your heart to them (Eph 4:22-31).

## FELLOWSHIP MARKS THE MATURE CHRISTIAN (1:4-5)

### Fellowship Promotes Prayer

Paul begins to tell of his prayer life. He fellowships with God and rejoices over his fellowship with the saints in Philippi. Paul was never too busy to pray and thank God. That's the secret behind Paul's joy. He prayed without ceasing. E. M. Bounds was right when he said: "He who is too busy to pray will be too busy to live a holy life."[18]

We cannot life a joyful life without fellowship with God. We are so weak and easily overcome. Life is impossible, wouldn't you agree? We are so weak. We were never made to walk this life alone. That's why the person who is growing in Christ is a person of deep prayer. You know the importance of prayer. You feel your weakness. To pray you have to be humble. There is a humility to the person who prays. Listen to Paul.

> **Philippians 1:4-5a** | Always in every prayer of mine for you all making my prayer.

Prayer indicates our weakness. Paul attributes all the success of his life and the Philippians to God. That's what gratitude and prayer are all about. We can preach and teach and spend hours preparing. But the truth is: I did nothing. You did nothing. The word of God did everything. Jesus is absolutely correct when he says, "Without me you can

---

[18] E.M. Bounds. *Purpose in Prayer* (New York: Fleming H. Revell Co., 1920), 105.

do nothing" (Jn 15:5). How weak Paul was. He considered himself "the chief of sinners." He was often given pain in his life that left him feeling debilitated. Look over at 2 Corinthians 12. Paul says:

> To keep me from becoming conceited because of the surpassing greatness of the revelations, a thorn was given me in the flesh, a messenger of Satan to harass me, to keep me from becoming conceited. [8] Three times I pleaded with the Lord about this, that it should leave me. [9] But he said to me, "My grace is sufficient for you, for my power is made perfect in weakness." Therefore I will boast all the more gladly of my weaknesses, so that the power of Christ may rest upon me. [10] For the sake of Christ, then, I am content with weaknesses, insults, hardships, persecutions, and calamities. For when I am weak, then I am strong.  —*2 Corinthians 12:7-10*

Pain drove Paul to prayer. And even in the pain, Paul started rejoicing. "Lord thank you for this thorn in my side." Maybe that thorn was the difficult situations in the Corinthian church that tore him up. Maybe it was physical. But even the pain led him to rejoice in his weakness. His weakness helped him to know Christ better! Prayer is a place where we can rejoice and thank God that we are not alone. We have fellowship with God. We are never alone. But we also have fellowship with people.

### Fellowship Promotes Joy

Paul's great prayer focus is on his partnership with the Philippian church. He's so thankful to be united with them in Christ. His joy began the first day he met them until now. Listen to Paul.

**Philippians 1:4b** | Making my prayer with joy.

What does "gospel partnership" mean? Paul really believed he was on a mission together with all the Christians everywhere, including the Philippians. *Partnership* from the Greek *koinonia* (*cf* 1:5,7; 2:1; 3:10; 4:14,15). We often translate it as "fellowship." It means "sharing in the presence of God" and sharing in his presence with each other.

We need this fellowship. It's what makes life satisfying. When you are dying, you don't say, "Bring me my high school or college diploma." You don't say, "Bring me my trophies from third grade or my awards from work." No. You want people. We all want to have those intimate connections with people. Fellowship is knowing God is near and knowing his people are near.

## Fellowship Promotes Partnership

**Philippians 1:4** | Because of your partnership in the gospel from the first day until now.

This *koinonia* – this gospel partnership meant they supplied prayers, missionary helpers, and also financial support.

> And you Philippians yourselves know that in the beginning of the gospel, when I left Macedonia, no church entered into partnership with me in giving and receiving, except you only. —*Philippians 4:15*

It seems the fellowship they had with Paul included communication, financial support, expanding the gospel, etc. We can also imagine that Paul must have sent workers to Philippi to train the elders and the deacons. Fellowship means that we are one in Christ. There is a divine unity that we have in the Spirit of God that brings us together. Fellowship with Christ brings great and inexpressible joy! Though you have not seen him, you love him.

> Though you do not now see him, you believe in him and rejoice with joy that is inexpressible and filled with glory. —*1 Peter 1:8*

Fellowship with God is more to be desired than the greatest of earthly delights.

> That I may know him and the power of his resurrection, and the fellowship of his sufferings, becoming like him in his death.
> —*Philippians 3:10*

But fellowship always extends to the Body of Christ. We are one in Christ. We enjoy fellowship together. There is a personal partnership in God's forever family, where we share in Christ's fellowship by coming together. That's why we gather on Sunday mornings and for small groups and for times of prayer and instruction. Jesus is present with us.

### Obstacles to Corporate Fellowship

At least four obstacles will keep you from having such enjoyable and edifying relationships as a Christian: sensationalism, mysticism, idealism, and individualism.

*Sensationalists* don't find Christian community exciting enough to participate in it. However, the Christian life isn't about shock and awe, but lowly acts of service and love (Phil 2:3-4), which are extraordinarily significant. In other words, we fellowship at church for the presence of God, not a light show or a rock concert. God is here. That's more than enough!

*Mystics* make the Christian life into a series of quiet times, isolated from the rest of the church. They desire to live a "me and Jesus" kind of Christianity without the church. But Christianity is "we and Jesus," not just "me and Jesus."

*Idealists* struggle in Christian community because they have, in the words of Bonhoeffer, a "wish dream" of what the church ought to be, and it never lives up to their expectations.[19] The idealists are never satisfied with any church. Let me just say that if you come to church for Jesus, with your eyes on Jesus, Jesus and Jesus alone will satisfy you.

*Individualists* fall prey to culture that only enjoys community online. Privatization coupled with this technological video-game culture kills people's ability to relate to others. We have a culture of "busy loneliness": people do a lot of stuff, but they remain extremely lonesome.

### *The Mission of Christian Fellowship*

Ultimately, fellowship has a mission: to bring Christ to every creature. You need gospel partners, those united together in Christ by the Spirit, from every tribe and tongue, who live on the gospel. These are friends that will fall and fail but who need the same grace and mercy of Jesus that you need. You need more than friendships; you gospel partners who are on mission with you.[20] Godly fellowship does not just result in deep friendships, and a deep walk with God. If you fellowship with God and others, you will share that presence with the lost and expand the kingdom of God. Ultimately, we are partnering with God to proclaim his gospel to lost sinners. You will also partner by giving to others who are going to places you cannot go.

Now it's not just our gathering together in fellowship and preaching and teaching the word in Christian fellowship or even giving to missions that advances God's kingdom. It's God himself who has to work in us for real transformation. Mature, joyful Christians have a deep

---

[19] Bonhoeffer. *Life Together*, 27.
[20] Francis Chan and Tony Merida. *Exalting Jesus in Philippians* (Christ-Centered Exposition Commentary) (Nashville, TN: B&H Publishing Group, 2016), 25.

confidence in God. Confidence is another sign of the mature and joyful life.

## CONFIDENCE MARKS THE MATURE CHRISTIAN (1:6)

Paul's confidence in God was a settled fact. He knew that God was at work and in control. He was confident that God was bringing about whatever was happening for his glory. When we possess that kind of confidence, we have a solid platform built within us—a solid platform upon which joy can rest. This is a glorious mark of Christian maturity.

> **Philippians 1:6** | And I am sure of this, that he who began a good work in you will bring it to completion at the day of Jesus Christ.

### Confidence in God's Character

> **Philippians 1:6b** | He who began a good work.

Paul's confidence was much more than human hope; it was the absolute confidence that comes from knowing and believing God's promise that the God who began a good work in him will perfect it until the day of Christ Jesus. Salvation is wholly God's work, and for that reason its completion is as certain as if it were already accomplished.[21]

The focus is on the word *completion*. God will finish his work in you. That's what he promises. How do we know? He gave his only Son to guarantee it. Travel back in your mind to the cross where Christ was crucified. See the Savior lifted up, paying for the sins of the world. There were seven sayings that Christ uttered from the cross, commonly called the seven last words of Christ. One of them our Lord cried out was a single word, *Tetelestai*! Translated, it means, "It is finished!" Telos is the root Greek term, the same root of the word translated perfect. Paul was saying, "He who began a good work in you when you were converted ten years ago, Philippians, will bring it to completion. It will be finished! Jesus will see to it. And that gives me joy."

### Confidence in God's Commencement

> **Philippians 1:6b** | He who began a good work.

Paul had no trouble persuading himself that God had begun a good work in the Philippians. God began the work. Yes Paul planted, others

---

[21] MacArthur, *Philippians*, 26.

watered, but it was our great God who gives the increase (1 Cor 3:6). The apostle could see plenty of proof that the dear Philippian believers were soundly saved. Their outward good works were evidence of the inward good work begun in their hearts by the Holy Spirit. Their good works had not resulted in salvation (an impossibility), but their good works had resulted from salvation (an expectation). God puts a new heart in each believer. Out of that heart comes the fruit of the Spirit. God is at work.

The good work of God begins in us when the Holy Spirit takes up permanent residence in our hearts. He brings with Him the life of God: eternal, immaculate, spiritual life. We are immediately aware of this new life by a fresh consciousness of the old life (Rom 7). The world becomes aware of this new life when love breaks through: love for God, love for God's people, love for lost people, love outflowing as a result of life infilling.[22]

## Confidence in God's Completion

**Philippians 1:6c** | He will ... bring it to completion at the day of Jesus Christ.

Christ will complete his work in every child of God. We are predestined for holiness. We see God's predestination unto holiness for all genuine Christians in Romans 8:28-30. We are *predestined* to be conformed to the image of Christ. All who God *"foreknew"* and *"called"* and *"justified"* (i.e. all true Christians) are predestined to live in some measure of holiness and blamelessness, being *"conformed to the image of his Son."* Who is Paul talking about? Again, it must be emphasized that Paul is speaking of all true Christians without exception. All who are predestined are called. All who are called are justified. All whom God justified, he is conforming to the image of his Son, and he will one day glorify them with a sinlessly perfect nature and body in glory. Paul is referring to the entire glorified church of God and only those in that Body. When Jesus comes again, God will unveil his completed work in

---

[22] John Phillips, *Exploring Ephesians & Philippians: An Expository Commentary*, The John Phillips Commentary Series (Kregel Publications; WORDsearch Corp., 2009), Php 1:6a.

every believer, and the work is so amazing that if you could see a glorified saint, you might be tempted to bow down and worship him or her, they would be so amazing. C.S. Lewis imagined what it might be like.

> The dullest most uninteresting [believer] you can talk to may one day be a creature which, if you saw it now, you would be strongly tempted to worship...[23]

Every selfish part of our character, God is removing, and one day, it will be completely removed. Paul is teaching us that God's not just powerful to save you from the *penalty* of sin when we called on him for salvation as Savior and Lord. He is powerful to save you from the *power* and *place* of sin through the ongoing process of growth in the Christian's life (*cf* Phil 2:12).[24] Indeed, "Sin is no longer your master.... Instead, you live under the freedom of God's grace" (Rom 6:14, NLT). Since God began a work of Christian growth, he will complete that growth, not only removing the penalty of sin and the power of sin, but at the day of Christ Jesus, the second coming, he will remove the very *presence* of sin all together. During this life we can be free from giving in to temptation, but temptation is still all around us. Can you imagine, when we see Jesus face to face, that there will be no more temptation? No more harassment from Satan. No more spiritual warfare. The war will be completely won, and we will live forever in the fruits of Jesus' victory! Paul reminds us that we do have ultimate victory so that we will live in that victory right now.

You want a fresh burst of encouragement? You may be stuck in neutral in your growth in Christ. You were growing but now you've stopped. You've hit a wall. The Lord has not folded his arms and looked the other way. Find encouragement in this firm confidence: The One who began a good work in you will bring it to completion; he will finish the task. He's not done with you. He's not done with your family. He's not done with your church. He will bring the work he's begun to completion. Each day, he is there to guide you by his hand and even carry you to a place of complete victory over sin. We may stumble into sin here and there because of our ignorance, but no Christian should live in it. We may step in the "cow dung" of sin here and there, but we don't

---

[23] C.S. Lewis, *The Weight of Glory and Other Addresses* (New York: HarperOne, 2001), 45.

[24] Moises Silva, *Philippians*, WEC (Chicago: Moody, 1988), 51–52.

move into the pigpen and roll in the dung. We should seek to live now with the confident mindset of our final victory against sin at all times.

## LOVE MARKS THE MATURE CHRISTIAN (1:7-8)

Finally, the last mark Paul mentions in verses 7-8 is affection. Love. Isn't that the ultimate mark of Christian maturity? Name all the virtues of Christian maturity. Paul says, you can prophesy, you can have faith to remove mountains, you can have hope and full assurance of salvation, but the greatest of these is what? Love. Paul has a deep love for his church family in Philippi that he compares to the love of Christ.

> **Philippians 1:7-8** | It is right for me to feel this way about you all, because I hold you in my heart, for you are all partakers with me of grace, both in my imprisonment and in the defense and confirmation of the gospel. ⁸ For God is my witness, how I yearn for you all with the affection of Christ Jesus.

### Love is Deep for the Mature Christian

> **Philippians 1:7a** | It is right for me to feel this way about you all, because I hold you in my heart.

Paul's love was deep and consuming for the Philippians. He had mature love, based on God's everlasting love. I've heard God's people say or at least imply: "I love God. I love walking with Jesus and the Holy Spirit. I just don't like his people all the time." Mature love from a believer is never divorced from the Body of Christ. It's always intimately connected to our union with Jesus Christ. Cyprian (c. 200) said, "He cannot have God for his Father who has not the Church for his mother."[25] John said it simply:

> We know that we have passed out of death into life, because we love the brothers. —*1 John 3:16*

Paul was not like that. He always looked at people through the lens of God's work in them. It's easy to get down, depressed, bitter, and jaded in close relationships. There are toxic emotions that we all experience which threatens our love for one another. Bitterness, discouragement, and just plain *giving up* will rob us of our joy. Paul had a

---

[25] Cyprian of North Africa (c.200) in Edward White Benson. *Cyprian: His Life, His Times, His Work* (New York: The Macmillan Company, 1897), 183.

sweet love for the people at Philippi that we can learn from. Paul says, "I hold you in my heart" (1:7), and "I yearn for you all with the affection of Christ Jesus" (1:8). It was right for Paul to love the Philippians this way because he loved them with a deep, agape love.

The term Paul uses to draw attention to his affection is, literally, the Greek word for "bowels." He says, in essence, "I love you with all my bowels." That would not be a flattering statement for a modern believer, but in the first century it was believed that the intestines, the stomach, the liver, even the lungs, held the most tender parts of human emotions. That explains why this joyful man would use "bowels" in reference to "affection." He says, in effect, "As I share with you my feelings, I open my whole inner being to you and tell you that the level of my affection is deep and tender." Too many people live with the inaccurate impression that Paul was somewhat cold and uncaring. Not according to this statement; in fact, quite the contrary! When he was with those he loved, Paul went to the warmest depths in conversation and affection.

## Love is Sacrificial for the Mature Christian

**Philippians 1:7b** | For you are all partakers with me of grace, both in my imprisonment and in the defense and confirmation of the gospel.

Mature agape love is always self-sacrificing. Paul gladly sacrificed for the Philippians while he wrote them under Roman imprisonment. Paul's circumstances at the time he wrote this letter were dire. He was imprisoned in Rome, possibly facing execution. As it turned out, he was released from this imprisonment, but he was not certain that would be the case when he wrote Philippians. He was under house arrest (Acts 28:23, 30), chained at every moment to a Roman solider from Caesar's Praetorian Guard (Acts 28:16) to prevent any possibility of escape. Paul languished there, unable to do the work he loved.[26] Nevertheless, his heart overflowed with joy that both the Philippians believers and Paul could together partake of God's grace and love in two vital ways: in both *apologetics* (defense) and in *evangelism* (confirmation of the gospel). Paul affirmed that the Philippian church selflessly and sacrificially stood by him to give encouragement, to help alleviate his suffering, and

---

[26] MacArthur, *Philippians*, 17–18.

to meet his needs in every way they could. They were his spiritual partners, partakers of grace with him, in the fullest sense. They exercised mature love, gladly sacrificing for one another.

## Love is Supernatural for the Mature Christian

**Philippians 1:8** | God is my witness, how I yearn for you all with the affection of Christ Jesus.

All of the believers at Philippi, with no exceptions, were the objects of Paul's great affection, an affection so deep and pervasive as to reflect that of Christ Jesus himself. It was enhanced and enriched by their warm and compassionate care for him that touched him so deeply. It was, in fact, a supernatural affection, instilled by the Lord both in his heart and theirs. [27] It was no less than "the love of God [that had] been poured out within [their] hearts through the Holy Spirit" (Rom 5:5). Paul wrote of this God-given love to the Thessalonians:

> Now as to the love of the brethren, you have no need for anyone to write to you, for you yourselves are taught by God to love one another.
> —*1 Thessalonians 4:9*

### Conclusion

Are you growing spiritually? Are you living the joyful life? It begins with gratitude. As you grow in Christ so will your gratitude grow. So will your fellowship with God and others grow. So will your prayer life grow. So will confidence in God's work grow. So will your deep love for fellow Christians. Real maturity in Christ is seen in making much of Jesus.

---

[27] Ibid., 32.

# 3 | PHILIPPIANS 1:9-11
## ROOTED IN LOVING ONE ANOTHER

*It is my prayer that your love may abound more and more, with knowledge and all discernment, so that you may approve what is excellent, and so be pure and blameless for the day of Christ.*
PHILIPPIANS 1:9-10

Paul has a special relationship with the Philippian church. As I read this and studied this passage, I noticed the primary words in the passage have to do with Paul's emotions for the Philippian church: Feel, heart, longing, affection, love. Paul has a peculiar relationship with the churches that can be described by love. We might think that because of his important position as apostle, he was disconnected or heartless, or aloof. Perhaps his urgency was so great, maybe he didn't have much time for vulnerability and emotion. What we find in this passage is that Paul was not disconnected of aloof. He was passionate for God's people. He had a heart that was filled with love for those who were under his care.

Sometimes there are Christians that they are virtually devoid of emotion. They belong to what I heard someone refer to as the "First

Church of Christ Frigidaire." Paul is not part of the frozen chosen. He is chosen, but he is very much thawed out, filled with the living love of Jesus!

> **Philippians 1:9-11** | And it is my prayer that your love may abound more and more, with knowledge and all discernment, [10] so that you may approve what is excellent, and so be pure and blameless for the day of Christ, [11] filled with the fruit of righteousness that comes through Jesus Christ, to the glory and praise of God

Paul is moved with deep love for the Philippian believers. His affections and emotions are running over – so much so that he prays for this church. That's one of the marks of really loving one another: prayer. Most people never associate prayer with pop music, but there is an interesting country song that's been around for a few years by a guy named Jaron Lowenstein. And it's a song called "I pray for you." It's a song based upon the bitter breakup that he had with his girlfriend, and he puts an interesting twist on prayer.

He said, *"I haven't been to church since I don't remember when. Things were going great till they fell apart again. So I listened to the preacher, he told me what to do. He said, you can't go hating on others who have done wrong to you. Sometimes we get angry, but we must not condemn. Let the good Lord do his job and you just pray for them."*

So his chorus is, *"I pray your breaks go out running down a hill. I pray a flowerpot falls from a windowsill and knocks you in the head like I'd like to. I pray your birthday comes and nobody calls. I pray you're flying high when your engine stalls. I pray all your dreams never come true. Just know wherever you are, honey, I pray for you."*

I pray that none of us pray that way! That's the point, real prayer is soaked in love. We often say that we love one another, but do we really? Do we truly care about our brothers and sisters? Love is the distinguishing mark of a Christian.

Jesus said, "by this all men will know you are my disciples, by the love you have for one another" (Jn 13:35). The most important expression of our Christian faith is love. Love is the hallmark of their faith, right? He said, "now abide faith, hope, and love, and the greatest of these is love" (1 Cor 13:13). The apostle John said,

> We know that we have passed out of death into life, because we love the brothers. —*1 John 3:14*

Dwight L. Moody once said something interesting. He said,

> There is no use trying to do church work without love. A doctor or a lawyer may do good work without love, but God's work cannot be done without love.[28]

## OUR LOVE SHOULD BE PLENTIFUL (1:9A)

Christians should be growing in love more and more. I love gardening. I don't get to do it a lot. But I love planting a seed and watching it grow. In this text, we understand the power of love. Love grows us into the image of Christ.

### An Abundant Love

The first attribute of Christian love is this: our love should be plentiful. Look at verse 9 and notice the goal of Paul's prayer:

**Philippians 1:9a** | And it is my prayer that your love may abound more and more.

The word "abound" means to super abound or to exceed a fixed number or a fixed measure. Do you agree that it is hard to love? Love is not just some robotic duty. We are commanded to love, but our love must be sincere. What would you think of my love for Jill if I told her "Happy Anniversary" and gave her flowers? And she said, "Thank you." But I said, "Don't mention it. I have to do it. God commands me to love you." That's not true love.

Should we obey God? Yes! But God doesn't just want to change our actions. He wants to transform our hearts. "Let love be without hypocrisy" (Rom 12:9). God wants our love to be genuine. Paul it seems is referring to the specific demonstration of love to one another within the church. I don't think he's speaking of loving God, though that's of highest importance. I don't think he's speaking of loving the world of lost people in evangelism, but that's important as well. I think he is specifically speaking of loving God's people, the church. Why do I say this? Because he writes the same thing almost in 1 Thessalonians 3.

> May the Lord make your love increase and overflow for each other.
> — *1 Thessalonians 3:12*

---

[28] D.L. Moody in William R. Moody. *The Life of Dwight Lyman Moody* (New York: Revell, 1900), 140.

So many times in marriage or in the church or anytime you get close to someone, you are going to get hurt. Remember we are all porcupines.

## An Affectionate Love

How can Paul tell us to abound in love? How can our love be plentiful? To learn to love, let's look at Paul as an example. He's already told them: "I long for all of you with the affection of Christ Jesus" (1:8). Longing or yearning has the idea of homesickness. "I am homesick for you," he says in effect, "restless till we can be together again."[29]

The word affection is a very powerful word. Literally Paul says, "I love you with the bowels of Jesus." The love of Christ in Paul was so powerful that it was as if as though the heart of Jesus had taken over.[30] This was the way people expressed themselves in ancient times. It was like saying, "I love you with all my guts." the word *splanchna* ("bowels" or "affections") is used as a metaphor for one's deepest inner affections.[31] But this word bowels, or affection, is a very intense word. It was saying, I love you with the powerful love of Jesus. I love you so much it hurts! The power of the gospel is shown in the supernatural affection that it produces, not only for Jesus Christ himself, but also for those who belong to Jesus Christ.[32]

## An Assorted Love

So as Paul thinks of how much he loves the Philippians, he prays that their love for each other may abound through various families and cultures. We already know a slave girl is there. A business woman name Lydia is there. We also have a soldier there. And Paul prays for them all.

> **Philippians 1:9a** | And it is my prayer that your love may abound more and more.

As I said before, the word "abound" means to super abound or to exceed a fixed number or a fixed measure. Local assemblies of Chris-

---

[29] J. A. Motyer, *The Message of Philippians*, The Bible Speaks Today (Downers Grove, IL: InterVarsity Press, 1984), 54.
[30] Ibid., 55.
[31] J. Phillips, *Exploring Philippians*, Php 1:8.
[32] Harmon, *Philippians*, 95.

tians should display a loving unity not explicable along merely sociological lines. The world is separated by race, economics, and politics. Not so in the church. Our race is that we are covered with the blood of Christ. Our economics is that we have treasure laid up in heaven. Our political affiliation is that we bow our knee to King Jesus. People who have little or nothing in common on economic, social, political or ethnic bases are brought together by the Holy Spirit in unified devotion to Christ and the advance of his gospel. [33]

Interesting, one of the Church historians named Tertullian writes that the Roman government was disturbed about the early church. Christians were increasing in number by leaps and bounds. Because they wouldn't take even a pinch of incense and put it before the image of the emperor, the Romans felt they might be disloyal. Spies went into the Christian gatherings and came back with a report something like this:

> These Christians are very strange people. They meet together in an empty room to worship. They do not have an image. They speak of One by the name of Jesus, who is absent, but whom they seem to be expecting at any time. And my, how they love him and how they love one another.[34]

Interesting that an unbelieving spy in a Christian congregation made note of the fact that *they loved one another so intensely*. So take that little test in your mind right now. And ask yourself this, "Does my own love abound?" Would that be a word that describes the expression of your love? Think about your marriage. Is your love toward your spouse an abounding love? Or in your home toward your children, or toward your parents, or among your friends? Would you say that that is a good description of your own love experience in your life?

Are you the kind of person that love just keeps growing and growing in love and abounding more and more? You say, is that even possible? Well, yes, it is possible. It is possible because in Romans chapter 5 Paul said, "the love of God has been poured out in our hearts by the Holy Spirit" (Rom 5:5). The love of God has been poured out or literally it gushes out. It implies there is no limit to it at all. What that means then is that we have an unlimited capacity to love. If you're one of those

---

[33] Ibid.
[34] J. Vernon McGee. *John, Thru the Bible* (Nashville: Thomas Nelson Publishers, 1995), 69.

type of people, and I've met a few, who say I'm just fresh out of love, I've loved all the love out, I've got no more love to give. It's all gone now. I say, well, you need a better connection. Because the love of God gushes out, is poured out by the Holy Spirit. And last time I checked, he never ran out. Is your heart growing bigger and bigger? The more you love Jesus, the bigger your heart will grow.

## OUR LOVE SHOULD BE PERCEPTIVE (1:9-10A)

Love has boundaries. Now watch what the apostle does. You know, Paul could have just said, I pray that your love may abound still more and more period. He tells us exactly *how* our love should abound: in knowledge and discernment and excellence.

> **Philippians 1:9-10a** | And it is my prayer that your love may abound more and more, with knowledge and all discernment, [10] so that you may approve what is excellent.

There are two banks for the river of love: knowledge and discernment. You see, overflowing love sounds really great, but it is like a river. And if that water has free flow without any direction or discretion, it can hurt people.

A couple years ago the three rivers that surround my sister's town in Louisiana overflowed their banks. They had a hundred-year flood. It destroyed her home. My sister was huddled with her children in her car and someone came and rescued her. And it was all because of a river that overflowed its banks. Water is a blessing, but that much water that just flows wherever it wants to, can destroy people's lives. And so too with love. Real biblical love is not just pure emotion. Agape love is informed by the truth and knowledge of the Bible.

### Love's Knowledge

> **Philippians 1:9a** | And it is my prayer that your love may abound more and more, with knowledge.

What is knowledge? To be a Christian one must come to know the truth. You must know and believe the gospel that the blood of Jesus cleanses you and makes you right with God. That's knowledge. In order for love to be informed, we need to have knowledge. Discernment is to go a step further and "grasp the significance" of something. To really love as Jesus loves, we must know how to discern and apply the knowledge of God's word.

Just because you "feel" something is God's will doesn't mean it is. Love has a riverbank that guides it: knowledge. Biblical knowledge is a "lamp" unto your feet and a "light" to your path. Discernment helps you choose the way. You can say you love God and others, but you cannot actually love God and others without counseling yourself with the word of God. If you don't counsel yourself with God's word you will just do what's in your heart man, whatever you feel like doing. That is the most dangerous, irresponsible thing you could ever do. And you would be a dangerous person to live that way. So many people allow themselves to be counseled by their selfish wicked heart. They end up in a disaster.

When we add knowledge to our love, it means we are constantly counseling ourselves with the word of God and disregarding what our hearts are telling us. How do we let knowledge guide our love? You can't trust your heart. Our heart of our old nature is "deceitful and desperately wicked above all things: who can know it?" (Jer 17:9). We are called to "trust in the Lord with all our heart and lean not to our own understanding" (Prov 3:5-6).

Instead, we inform our love by constantly counseling ourselves with the word of God. You may feel that love is letting another Christian do whatever he or she wants to do. That's where you need knowledge. The knowledge of Matthew chapter 18 where Jesus said, "sometimes the most loving thing you can do is to confront another brother or sister." And that's love. So mature love is not sentimentality, nor is it emotion. It has banks and the first bank is knowledge. The second is discernment.

## Love's Discernment

> **Philippians 1:9c** | And it is my prayer that your love may abound more and more, with ... all discernment.

Love needs a direction. There needs to be discernment. Sometimes love needs to be tender. Sometimes it needs to be tough. As love grows, knowledge grows. We need to grow in our knowledge of Christ. We need to grow in "all discernment" as well. Every parent knows this, that love is expressed in different ways at different times to the same child. One day a parent will give a gift to a child. Another day a parent will spank a child. Both are legitimate expressions of love.

Another example is that of Jesus Christ. Sometimes He'd heal a person, another day he would overturn the tables in the temple and with a whip drive out the money changers. Both are expressions of love but in two different contexts. One day Jesus would say to the crowd, "You are blessed." Another day he'd look at another crowd filled with Pharisees and say, "You whitewashed sepulchers." Both are expressions of love from the one who is the Author of love himself.

## Love's Excellence

> **Philippians 1:9-10a** | And it is my prayer that your love may abound more and more, with knowledge and all discernment, ¹⁰ so that you may approve what is excellent.

As you grow in love, you will grow in knowledge and discernment. And you will be able to test what is the very best to give glory to God. As you activate a wise kind of love, you will "approve things that are excellent" (1:10). Godly love leads to a balanced life of excellence, a life engaged in the things that matter. We need to test and examine all things to see if they rise to the worthy standard of God's excellence.

In verse 10 we see a wonderful byproduct of love guided by knowledge and discernment: testing and approving that which is excellent. Excellence is referring to us mere mortals reflecting God's refulgent excellence, his glory, his beauty. Approve the things that really matter. What are you allowing in your life, your marriage or singleness, your job, your mind, your thoughts, your actions? Are you allowing things into your life that matter? Are you reflecting God's glory in everything? Do you have a life of excellence?

At Philippi, love showed itself to be of the very essence of the new nature given to the believer. No sooner had Lydia become a Christian than she pressed Paul and his company to become her houseguests. No sooner had the jailor become a Christian than, though he had earlier fastened the apostle's feet in the stocks, he began to bathe his wounds.[35]

Now most of us know that the most frequently used Greek word for love in the New Testament is what, tell me? Agape. Agape is the Greek word for love that expresses God's love for us. Generally, love for one another is to be at that supreme, superior, that's what we aspire to, agape love. Well, make sure that your agape isn't sloppy. Don't love

---

[35] Motyer, *Message of Philippians*, 55.

with sloppy agape. Sloppy agape is saying you love somebody but it's really a selfish love. I'm going to do something or say something because I don't want to be disliked by that person. That's sloppy agape.

## OUR LOVE SHOULD BE PRODUCTIVE (1:10-11A)

The excellence of love has a profound effect on our character. Love grows us. The effect of living a life of love is profound.

> **Philippians 1:9-11** | And it is my prayer that your love may abound more and more, with knowledge and all discernment, [10] so that you may approve what is excellent, and so be pure and blameless for the day of Christ, [11] filled with the fruit of righteousness that comes through Jesus Christ, to the glory and praise of God.

### A Growing Readiness

Notice there is a there is a program of growth, starting with a seed of "love abounding more and more" (vs 9) and ending with a harvest of being "filled with the fruit of righteousness" (vs 11). Paul takes this metaphor of growth very seriously. Why? Because Christian growth, says Paul, is for *the day of Christ*, that is, with a view to Christ's Second Coming.

> **Philippians 1:10b** | So that you may approve what is excellent, and so be pure and blameless for the day of Christ.

Those who are truly born again have the love of God poured into them by the Holy Spirit (Rom 5). But we have to stir up that love, getting ready for Jesus' coming. Jesus can return any moment, and we must be prepared for him. The responsibility to be ready for his coming is wholly ours. Does this in any way contradict the truth we noted at verse 6, that salvation is all of God ("He who has begun a good work will finish it"), leaving no room for effort or contribution from us? Certainly not! Paul says later: "Work out your own salvation with fear and trembling, [13] for it is God who works in you, both to will and to work for his good pleasure" (2:12-13).

Remember the grace which saves is also the grace that energizes through the Holy Spirit. The free gift of salvation is a gift of new life. The Christian, saved by grace, demonstrates the authenticity of what has happened by exercising new energies in the Spirit. Consequently—

Paul prays that love may abound more and more. It is our responsibility to stir up love and affection for fellow Christians.

The word of God calls all Christians to act—to work, run, imitate, to be a soldier, athlete and farmer. We are called to a life of good works planned out by God for those whom he has re-created in Christ (Eph 2:10). In other words, it is by *obedience*—active, costly, personal, voluntary, disciplined obedience—that we enter into conscious experience of what our salvation in Christ means. This is why the Bible can say that God gives the Holy Spirit to those who obey him. "God has given the Holy Spirit to those who obey him" (Acts 5:32). In other words, you can recognize those who have the Holy Spirit by their lives of obedience.

## A Growing Purity

**Philippians 1:10c** | Be pure and blameless for the day of Christ.

Love affects our character. When love abounds in us, we are able to test and approve and examine what is excellent, what is best. And the result is that we are pure and blameless. Pure refers to our *inward* character. Blameless refers to our *outward* character.

The word referring to our pure inward character has to do with integrity. The idea is a sincere life. The word here means literally: "without wax." Some of you speak Spanish. The word sincere comes from the Latin – *sin cera* – which means *without wax*. Back in the day deceitful merchants would fill in the flaws of a clay vessel – the plate or the cup – with wax to hide the cracks. The Christian is "sin cera" without wax. We live a life of integrity because the love of Christ has changed our inward character.

As I said before blameless refers to our *outward* character. Daily we put off old habits and put on new habits. We put off gossip and put on godly and edifying speech. We put off bitterness and put on tenderness, kindness, and forgiveness. We put off fear and put on faith. We put off worldliness and put on love for God. Every day our heart and life are more and more conformed to Jesus.

## A Growing Righteousness

Love brings a wonderful harvest of righteousness. When love abounds more and more, you become "filled with the fruit of righteousness."

**Philippians 1:11** | Filled with the fruit of righteousness that comes through Jesus Christ, to the glory and praise of God.

You say, "Pastor Matt, will I really be filled completely with the fruit of righteousness?" Sanctification is a promise that comes "through Jesus Christ." We grow in the Christlike righteousness as we take hold of Christ. John Owen says, "The Holy Spirit will not move you as a Christian until you first take hold of the means of grace. Rather, he is communicated through the means of grace." [36] Therefore, we seek to encounter Jesus through all the ways Jesus reveals himself (the means of grace). What does he mean? You will not grow in love without those things (the means) through which God gives grace. How do we encounter Jesus? Here are a few ordinary ways we encounter God: study the word, preaching of the word, fellowship, baptism, communion, prayer, evangelism. We could go on and on, but this is how you are going to be "filled with the fruit of righteousness that comes through Jesus Christ" (1:11a). God's love through the Holy Spirit is productive in the believer's life. We are always *making progress* as we come through Jesus Christ.

## OUR LOVE SHOULD BE PURPOSEFUL (1:11)

Excellence is attained through Christ alone. Paul says this purity and righteousness of life "comes through Jesus" and bring praise to God.

**Philippians 1:11** | Filled with the fruit of righteousness that comes through Jesus Christ, to the glory and praise of God.

### Through Jesus Christ

You say, "How can I have this life of love?" Turn your eyes upon Jesus. This life of excellence is not attainable through human power or manipulation. There must be a sincere surrender to the Lordship of Jesus. Jesus paid it all. So come and see what God can do for you. What has he done for you. Do you see it? What has he done that would make you love him more and more? Our God is about redeeming your wrecks. He's about making beauty from ashes. Do you know this one who is the rose of Sharon? He can make your stinking life clean and smell good, with the aroma of righteousness.

---

[36] John Owen. *Works, Volume 3*, "Mortification of Sin" (Carlisle, PA: Banner of Truth, 1966), 554. (Originally published in 1656).

## For God's Glory

The purpose of all love as a Christian is to glorify God. You know how I know that? Because that's the purpose of all life. All of life is to glorify God. I exist to glorify God. I do. In Revelation 4 the 24 elders bowed down saying "for thy pleasure all things were created." That's why I exist. Paul says: "Whether you eat or whatever you do, do all for the glory of God" (1 Cor 10:31). Whatever you do, all things, for the glory of God. Loving is under the category of all things. Whatever you do, do all for the glory of God. So now we have the ultimate test to know if this expression of our love is approved or not. And it's simple. Does it glorify Jesus Christ?

## Conclusion

What joy Paul had to write the Philippian believers. That joy came from an overwhelming love not based on us. We have so many sins and mistakes. If you want to truly love someone whether they are a brother in Christ or a lost person, a family member who is hard to love, there is a way to love them. Think of them as saved and one day fully glorified. God's still working on me. Have patience with me. Love me in spite of me. Can I tell you that Jesus was a carpenter? He is the best carpenter, isn't he? He's not done working on you. It took him just six days to make the moon and the stars, but he's still working on you and me!

# 4 | PHILIPPIANS 1:12-18
## JOY IN SETBACKS AND SUFFERING

> *Some indeed preach Christ from envy and rivalry, but others from good will. The latter do it out of love, knowing that I am put here for the defense of the gospel. The former proclaim Christ out of selfish ambition, not sincerely but thinking to afflict me in my imprisonment. What then? Only that in every way, whether in pretense or in truth, Christ is proclaimed, and in that I rejoice.*
> PHILIPPIANS 1:15-18

It's funny when we come to the day to set back clocks, and I have a sermon on setbacks! For the 100th year, we turned our clocks back an hour, banishing the gloom of dark mornings but robbing us of those beautiful daylit evenings. We gain an hour of sleep, but we lose an hour of daylight in the evening. Some people get frustrated with the falling back and the Springing forward. One thing we can do with Daylight Savings Time is blame Canada. They started it in 1908, a hundred years ago. It's Canada's fault.

For some of us, the best thing about Daylight Savings time is that the clock in your car and microwave are finally correct! There are consequences that go with having earlier sun downs. Today, sundown is at 4:43pm. That means at 5pm tonight, it'll look like midnight, but it'll only be 5 o'clock!

According to a government survey—74 percent of Americans say a lack of daylight affects their mood and their productivity. John Sharp, M.D., psychiatrist on faculty at Harvard Medical School, who helped with the study says, the darkness of winter "really affects us and can cause people to be irritable, sleepy, and want to quit the day earlier. It's easier just to shut it all down at 5pm."[37] Some of you are asking, "What do I do if I'm just grumpy all year long?!" Seriously, the darkness of winter has an adverse effect on some people. Think of it, back in June, we had 15 hours of daylight. Today we have only 10. By the end of the year we'll have only 9 hours of daylight. Because of the lack of daylight for the next three months, some people get the winter blues, and many of them do what all sane people should do in these Chicago winters: they move to Florida. All in favor? Say Amen!

As we look to the book of Philippians, we know it's not just winter that might dampen our mood. There are some serious dark and cold circumstances and setbacks in our lives that very well might steal our joy. I don't want that to happen. You don't want that to happen. And you know what? God doesn't want that to happen. In the passage before us, we are going to see how the greatest setbacks. What is a setback? The dictionary defines setback as "an obstacle to progress; a reverse or defeat."

I came across a website for the criminal justice system, called *corrections.com*, in which this statement was on it. Most prisoners are unhappy. And many of them are unhappy all the time. Many contemplate or attempt suicide or self-mutilation. The suicide rate for American prisoners is between 5 to 15 times greater than it is for the general American population. I'm sharing that with you to begin with, because I just want you to keep in mind that we are reading the letter of a prisoner. It's no joke to be in prison. Paul is in prison as he is writing the

---

[37] Manning-Schaffel, Vivian. "The Clocks 'fall Back' Sunday at 2:00 a.m. Here's How to Survive the Darker Days." NBCNews.com. November 03, 2018. Accessed November 03, 2018. https://www.nbcnews.com/better/health/clocks-fall-back-daylight-saving-time-ends-sunday-here-s-ncna930016.

book of Philippians. In fact, he writes four prison epistles: Galatians, Ephesians, Philippians and Colossians. Being in prison is very difficult. Yet Paul is filled with joy. Paul is writing this letter to the Philippians from prison, under house arrest. He's got a Roman soldier chained to him 24/7 for more than two years. This seems like a major setback for the gospel. Yet Paul says: my setbacks, past, present and future are really advances for the gospel. What?! That sounds extreme. Yet that's exactly what Paul says. Let's read about it.

> **Philippians 1:12-21** | I want you to know, brothers, that what has happened to me has really served to advance the gospel, [13] so that it has become known throughout the whole imperial guard and to all the rest that my imprisonment is for Christ. [14] And most of the brothers, having become confident in the Lord by my imprisonment, are much more bold to speak the word without fear. [15] Some indeed preach Christ from envy and rivalry, but others from good will. [16] The latter do it out of love, knowing that I am put here for the defense of the gospel. [17] The former proclaim Christ out of selfish ambition, not sincerely but thinking to afflict me in my imprisonment. [18] What then? Only that in every way, whether in pretense or in truth, Christ is proclaimed, and in that I rejoice. Yes, and I will rejoice, [19] for I know that through your prayers and the help of the Spirit of Jesus Christ this will turn out for my deliverance, [20] as it is my eager expectation and hope that I will not be at all ashamed, but that with full courage now as always Christ will be honored in my body, whether by life or by death. [21] For to me to live is Christ, and to die is gain.

## THE GOSPEL ADVANCES WITH PAST SETBACKS (1:12-14)

### Setbacks are Planned by God

You may be a Christian and in a terrible circumstance. Perhaps your circumstance is stealing your joy. Isn't it true that sometimes things happen to us in our past that set us back and steal our joy? Paul was a man who would not allow his joy to be stolen. How? He believed his setbacks were planned by God.

> **Philippians 1:12** | I want you to know, brothers, that what has happened to me has really served to advance the gospel.

### Paul's Salvation Planned by God

He says, what's happened in my life seems to be something to steal my joy, but it's not. It seems like something that would make the gospel decline, but it's not. It's actually working to advance the gospel. This was true of his former life. He says in Philippians 3:8, "I count everything as loss because of the surpassing worth of knowing Christ Jesus my Lord." It's all garbage compared to knowing Christ. Can we all agree that all our past failures as well as our past successes are equally refuse compared to knowing Christ? But Paul goes further. Here is a terrible, difficult circumstance that puts Paul in jail. It looks like the prospects for the gospel's advance are declining. It looks like the gospel is in a downturn. Paul's in jail. The chief leader for the gospel is in chains. What a set back! Paul says: no. It's not a setback. It's a steppingstone. It's an advance.

### Paul's Suffering Planned by God

Here's what happened. After Paul's third missionary journey, he goes back to Jerusalem. He's warned in advance by the Holy Spirit (Acts 20:23) that he's going to have trouble in Jerusalem and get arrested. According to Acts 21:27-36, Paul's in the temple area with another fellow going through a ceremonial ritual. Some of the leaders spot Paul there. They start a riot, and they attack him. A Roman soldier arrests Paul—not to punish him, but to protect him from the mob—he takes Paul, is about to have Paul beaten. Paul pulls his Roman citizenship card out and says, you can't beat me. I'm a Roman citizen. And everywhere Paul goes, he preaches the gospel – he tells his story. He's in the barracks in Jerusalem, and he tells his story, "As I was on my way and drew near to Damascus, about noon a great light from heaven suddenly shone around me..." (Acts 22:6).

He is then taken from Jerusalem to Caesarea by the sea, where he spends two years. And he goes through three trials in two years. He stands before Felix, and he tells his story (Acts 24:24, Felix "sent for Paul and heard him speak about faith in Christ Jesus"). He stands before Festus and King Herod Agrippa, and he tells his story (Acts 26:12ff, "I journeyed to Damascus ... 13 At midday, O king, I saw on the way a light from heaven, brighter than the sun"). And after two years, he finally says, I'm done. This judicial process is crazy. I appeal my case to Caesar in Rome. Every Roman citizen had that right. So they put him on a ship. It is not a cruise ship. It's not a Princess Cruise. It is the Prison cruise ship! And they send him to Rome. He almost doesn't make it to Rome. The ship sinks. He has to swim to shore. Paul made sure all the prisoners were accounted for. But he finally goes to Rome, where he's put in jail again – under house arrest.

## Setbacks Can Advance the Gospel

All of that is under this banner, Paul says, "the things which happened to me" (1:12). A lot had happened to Paul. Now that set of circumstances is enough to change any joyful person into a depressed person quickly. But not Paul. He's not depressed. How could he be depressed? The gospel is going forth. He's telling the gospel everywhere to kings and governors, to fellow prisoners, and eventually to Roman soldiers when he's put under house arrest. Paul says: these things are not a defeat or a setback. They are an advance.

The Greek word for "advance' means a forward movement overcoming any kind of obstacles. Obstacles are involved. God can use setbacks to put you in a position to actually advances the gospel overcoming any obstacles. The word for advance was used of pioneers cutting undergrowth away, so you could walk with ease. It was also used for soldiers advancing against an enemy. This advance of the gospel was a forward movement overcoming all obstacles.

Did you ever get into superheroes when you were a kid? Are some of you still into superheroes? My son Evan's favorite superhero is Captain America. My favorite has always been Superman. I love to tell Ava my superman jokes. *What does Superman use to eat his cereal? A Super Bowl.* Ok I'll quit while I'm ahead. I like Superman because he's the man of steel. You can throw anything at him, and he crushes it. Throw volts of electricity, and he absorbs it. There is no possible challenge. Superman has one weakness though. Remember what it is? Kryptonite.

Our God has no weakness. When we totally commit our lives to him, he can absorb any setback and turn it into a steppingstone. Daniel's lions were not a setback but a steppingstone for the faith of the King of Persia. Shadrach, Meshach, and Abednego looked done for in the fiery furnace. But God turned that setback into a great victory! Joseph had setback after setback, from the pit to slavery to the prison. But God turned that setback into a steppingstone to the palace. Moses had a setback at the Red Sea. But God through Moses said, "Stand back and see the salvation of the Lord!" Job lost everything. What a setback. But look what God did. God turned his setback into a comeback. Today Job's life encourages suffering people more than any book in the Bible. God doesn't want you to be a dropout when the setback comes. He wants you to be a billboard of his sufficient grace! And now, though Paul was in prison, he was advancing the gospel like never before. Here we have two ways the gospel is advanced through setbacks while Paul is in prison.

### *Advancing the Gospel with Roman Soldiers*

For Paul, his setbacks opened the door for an audience of Roman soldiers to hear the gospel and believe on Christ. God's plan has been furthered for the palace guard. How many Roman soldiers were coming to the Christian churches in Rome? None. How many Roman soldiers were they reaching before Paul was imprisoned? If you count the Philippian jailer, supposing he was at one time a Roman soldier, it's about one! Isn't God's grace amazing? What looks like a setback is actually an advance.

> **Philippians 1:13** | So that it has become known throughout the whole imperial guard and to all the rest that my imprisonment is for Christ.

The whole imperial guard was reached with the gospel. The Imperial Guard was the elite personal soldiers for the emperor. There was about 10,000 of them in the Roman Empire. They were the bodyguards of the emperor. Now Paul is incarcerated in Rome. He's not in the palace. He's in a rented home likely provided by another believer or a church, the Book of Acts tells us (Acts 28:30). Paul is chained to a guard 24 hours a day in a rented house. But the people chained to him are the elite soldiers of the Imperial Guard. That would be like being chained to the Secret Service or to the CIA, the elite of the elite.

Here's the issue. Roman soldiers were unlikely to go to Paul's evangelistic talks. These were men who were rough and hard hearted. They weren't philosophizing about eternal life. After their shift they were ready for a beer at the pub. They were ready for the equivalent of a game of pool. They weren't about to seek out a converted Jew and talk to him. So God says, "That's fine, but I want to evangelize the soldiers, and I have an unusual turn of events for you Paul. Since they're not coming to the Bible studies, I'm going to send the evangelist apostle to them." This isn't a prison ministry where Paul gets to walk in and walk out.

He's going to be incarcerated with one soldier after another being chained to Paul. Wow!

How does God advance the gospel with this great setback? Paul's chained to these Roman soldiers. Think of what it was like to be chained to Paul the Apostle for six hours. That's how it worked. There are 24 hours a day. Four soldiers chained six hours at a time to Paul. Paul couldn't eat without being chained. He couldn't sleep without being chained. Everything he did 24 hours was chained to a guard. Now we often think, oh, Paul was in chains. But think of it the other way. *So was the soldier.*

Can you imagine what it's like to listen to Paul? What do you think Paul brought up during those six hours? The gospel: "Jesus died for sinners. Jesus can forgive you. Let me tell you about this Jesus. I was walking on the Damascus road..." You couldn't shut him up. Paul talked a lot about his conversion. Have you ever shared with somebody in a conversation, and you bring up the gospel? They don't like what you have to say. So they walk away. Paul's audience of Roman soldiers *couldn't* walk away. Talk about a captive audience.

## Setbacks Can Make Us Stronger

We see the gospel has done it's work so that the whole palace guard knows he's imprisoned for Christ. Some of them are getting converted. The gospel is advancing. The Roman Christians as well are now beginning to speak more boldly without fear. As a result of these setbacks, with Paul in jail, they are growing in their faith and boldness.

> **Philippians 1:14** | And most of the brothers, having become confident in the Lord by my imprisonment, are much more bold to speak the word without fear.

### *Stronger in Evangelism*

Christian brothers would visit Paul in his confinement. They didn't have seminaries and Bible colleges to train people back then. Their great theologian was in prison. With a Roman soldier looking on and listening, Paul would speak to the brothers who would visit him. He would encourage them to speak boldly. He would pray for them when they departed. "O God, I thank you that you put me in here. And I thank you that my brother came to see me. And I thank you for the guy that's chained to me here Lord. And I thank you that he's got to hear everything we've said. And I thank you for the soldier earlier in the day, on the day shift, he got to hear it too. O God you are in control." The brothers left Paul, and they must have been like "Did you see that Roman soldier, how he was listening? God opened his heart. We too can witness like Paul."

Maybe that Roman soldier went to the local pub, and he says, "You know we have got one weird guy I have to guard at the moment." And here's this timid Christian. And he's sitting over in a corner and overhears all this. And there's a courage that rises in him, "But he's quite a man you know." And he finds stirring and rising within him a renewed confidence. And he speaks the word of the gospel there in that pub without fear. God is surely with Paul in his circumstance to give him boldness. God is most certainly with me in my circumstance. I need to be more bold in the faith.

We've got to get over our fear and realize that God is in control of your setbacks. We can't shut down in our trials. We've got to reach out for that grace. Share Christ. Be bold. He's got you just where he wants you. He wants you to use your setback to show the strength of God and to embolden his people.

Don't let your setback hold you back. Let it make you more bold. Paul was in a terrible circumstance. God was not so interested in changing Paul's circumstance. Sometimes God puts us in very difficult places in our lives. Our prayers during those times is "God get me out of this and then I'll be an effective witness." God's logic is very different from our own. We assume if we are going to be effective Christians, the circumstances have to be right. But God is concerned with making really effective Christians even if the circumstances are wrong. That's why we shouldn't spend so much time trying to change our circumstances. We need to get on with sharing the gospel whatever our circumstances are. That's what Paul did.

*Stronger in Faith*

God's given you a setback. He doesn't want you to change your circumstances, but he wants you to trust him with a living faith. He's growing your faith in him. Are there any circumstances or setbacks that are too hard for the Lord? Have faith. He's working all things together for your good, for the kingdom's growth, and for the glory of his name. God wanted some Roman soldiers saved, so he sovereignly placed Paul in jail through a setback. It looks like a setback, but it's really a comeback. What is your setback? Speak it in your mind. You know what it is. For Paul it was a prison. He looked at what had put him there in his past. He didn't regret how things turned out. He said it actually advanced the gospel. What's your setback in the past that you wish you could change? Maybe the Lord is turning your setback into a mission field. Do you believe God can turn your setback into a triumph for the gospel?

For me, there have been times in my life I wish I could change the time of my conversion. I wish I had Christian parents that cared for me. I have so much baggage from my childhood. It's painful. But you see the Lord took my pain and turned into his gain. Because of my own pain I feel other people's pain. I have empathy for people. That pain helps me to listen to others. I don't want anyone to live without Christ, so it emboldens me to speak the gospel with deep compassion.

You're the same way. God's in total control of your past. He wants you to turn your setback into a mission field. Maybe you had an awful childhood. Maybe you were raised in a false religion. Maybe you were on the streets at a young age. Maybe you saw your parents get a divorce. Whatever your setback, God wants you to use it to advance his cause, his gospel. Jesus died for sinners. There are plenty of people who are hurting and need someone like you to listen to them and then to give them the hope of eternal life in Jesus. God is in total control of your past, present and future if you are his child. Acknowledge that. Realize he's advancing the gospel through your pain and setbacks.

## THE GOSPEL ADVANCES WITH PRESENT SETBACKS (1:15-18A)

The advance of the gospel must shape how we evaluate our present circumstances.

### In Setbacks, we Look to God's Sovereignty

Paul is in jail, and he can do nothing about those in the church who are making the gospel about themselves. He sees that some preach Christ with wrong motives (like envy and rivalry and self-promition). But he's not out of sorts. He remembers others who love him and know as he says, "I am put here" for the gospel.

**Philippians 1:15-16** | Some indeed preach Christ from envy and rivalry, but others from good will. ¹⁶ The latter do it out of love, knowing that I am put here for the defense of the gospel.

You'd think that if God wanted Paul to defend the gospel, he'd certainly get him out of prison. From the outside it looked like Paul was being put on the shelf. And people using his imprisonment to promote themselves, even "thinking to afflict [Paul] in [his] imprisonment" (1:17).

"He's not preaching right, that's why he's in prison."

"There must be sin in his life."

"We have a more holy way of living than Paul."

"Paul's not as articulate as our pastor."

"He's got such a far-reaching ministry, he must be compromising for so many to come to Christ."

And they were causing him harm and gossiping and making stuff up about him.

One factor that controlled Paul's thinking is the sovereignty of God. Paul had planned to go on from Rome to Spain, Gaul, the frontier lands along the Rhine, and lands where Huns and Goths and Vandals sat in pagan darkness. The islands of Britannia also beckoned. His plans for evangelism had been as wide as the world.

But Paul was in chains. A lesser man would have questioned God's ways, fretted over his enforced inaction, and perhaps become embittered. Not Paul! He knew his chains were divinely planned and God made no mistakes; he knew God had not lost control.³⁸

God put Paul there in the prison. God is in control. It's not just true for Paul or special people. It is true for every believer, for in each and every case "he who began a good work in you will carry it on to completion at the day of Jesus Christ" (1:6). God rules. The pressures of life are the hands of the Potter, who is also our Father; the fires of life are those of the Refiner (Mal 3:3).³⁹

Our setbacks form us to be what God wants us to be.

A man long ago said, "I watched some stone workers hewing an odd-shaped stone as it lay on the ground.

"What are you going to do with that?" someone asked.

---

³⁸ J. Phillips, *Exploring Philippians*, Php 1:12.

³⁹ Motyer, *Message of Philippians*, 65.

"We are cutting it here, so it will fit in up there," the worker answered, pointing to an opening high on the tower of the great building."

That's what God is doing with our setbacks. He's forming us. He's shaping us. Trust God's sovereignty. He knows what he's doing for you. But he's also doing something for this lost world through you.

## In Setbacks, We Look Past Man's Selfishness

Paul is in jail, and he sees that the church is in trouble. There are factions and people promoting themselves more than Christ.

> **Philippians 1:17-18a** | The former proclaim Christ out of selfish ambition, not sincerely but thinking to afflict me in my imprisonment. [18] What then? Only that in every way, whether in pretense or in truth, Christ is proclaimed, and in that I rejoice.

There was envy, rivalry, and selfish ambition. There were those even in the early church that wanted their brand of Christianity. They were preaching the gospel, but saying perhaps that theirs was a more pure form of the gospel or of holiness. It even says they were "proclaiming Christ out of selfish ambition, not sincerely but thinking to afflict me in my imprisonment" (1:17).

There were and are those in the church that get their eyes more on their own ministry than on Christ. Isn't that strange that ministry itself can be an idol. We have to be careful. There are some that promote Christ for their own selfish ambition. They promote Christ because they want to be known as a great evangelist or a great teacher. And they were saying, "Our church is the best church. You don't want to go to that church down the street. They don't have the gospel as clear as our church." Paul exposed these false motives, as he should have. But he didn't go negative. He says, "I rejoice" that Christ is proclaimed!

# THE GOSPEL ADVANCES WITH FUTURE SETBACKS (1:18B-21)

The advance of the gospel must shape how we evaluate our future circumstances.

## In Life or Death Christ is Glorified

Paul now turns to the future. What's the worst that could happen? Well Paul prays for his deliverance, but he is content with either life or death. Because of contentment, he is able to rejoice whether he glorifies God by living or by dying. Paul can't help but rejoice.

**Philippians 1:18b-21** | Yes, and I will rejoice, [19] for I know that through your prayers and the help of the Spirit of Jesus Christ this will turn out for my deliverance,[20] as it is my eager expectation and hope that I will not be at all ashamed, but that with full courage now as always Christ will be honored in my body, whether by life or by death. [21] For to me to live is Christ, and to die is gain.

Paul says, I'm not afraid of the future because whether by life or by death, I want to honor and glorify Christ. "For me to live is Christ and to die is gain" (1:21).

As a Christian, you don't have to worry about the past, the present, or the future because whatever you are going through is there to set you up to glorify God. Honor him. He's sovereign in your setbacks. What's the absolute worst thing that could happen to Paul or to you? Death. Death is victory for the Christian. No matter what happens, in life, I will honor Christ. I will spread his gospel. In death, I will be with Christ, what could be better?! You need to have a Philippians 1:21 outlook on life. All is gain. To live is Christ and to die is gain! Romans 8:29-30 says the same. All things work together for your good and God's glory for the child of God.

What about you? Is Philippians 1:21 your motto? My friend, if you're not ready to die, you're not ready to live. If you don't know Christ, your you can advance your career, your family, your finances. But if you don't know Christ, your greatest setback will be death. If you are without Christ today, you need to come to him. Believe that he died for your sins and rose again for you. Your sins separate you from God, but Christ will cleanse you of your sins and bring you to God.

## Conclusion

When I was in high school, I was defensive end for the Ponchatoula Green wave in high school. Our goal was to sack the quarterback. One game we found a weakness in the offensive line. My friend Bobby Smith sacrifice himself and throw himself against a couple of the front linemen, and I would one of us would sack the quarterback and advance our team!

Maybe God has you in a place of sacrifice and suffering. You feel like your pain is in vain. But really, it's a way that God can advance the gospel. Any pain you have is there to advance the gospel for his glory. Remember in your setbacks there is no obstacle that can hold you back the gospel. Your setback is a mission field. Preach Christ! Remember

Jesus said, "I will build my church and the gates of hell will not prevail against it" (Mt 16:18).

# 5 | PHILIPPIANS 1:18-26
## TO LIVE IS CHRIST

*For to me to live is Christ, and to die is gain.*
PHILIPPIANS 1:21

The passage before us is all about the struggle in our hearts to want to be in heaven. Paul is under house arrest, chained to a Roman soldier. He wants to depart, but he also wants to preach Christ.

About ten days ago, I was reminded of the preciousness of this verse. I was turning left onto a side road near our church. My car was stationary, and all the sudden a big Ford F-350 careened into me at almost full speed, pushing me into oncoming traffic. That's when another truck smashed into me head on. I thought I was going to die. In that moment, I had no fear of dying. I felt the overwhelming love and grace of God. But this text has renewed meaning to me. "For me to live is Christ and to die is gain." Near death experiences help us to gain perspective as to what is important in life and in death.

Make no mistake: the only thing that matters in life and in death is Jesus Christ – not what is your stock portfolio, the size of your family, your wealth or how many vacations you've been on. The only thing that matters is your union with Christ. That's what Paul says: "For me to live is Christ and to die is gain." What does Paul mean when he says: "to live is Christ"? How do you live Christ? He's talking about his union with Christ.

According to Wayne Grudem union with Christ is "*the fact that we are in Christ, Christ is in us, we are like Christ, and we are with Christ.*"[40] In other words, union with Christ is our nearness to God through Christ. We are united to God in Christ. He is with you, before you, behind you, above you, below you, and inside you. Everything that happens in your life is God working good for you by bringing you nearer and nearer to him. No matter what is happening in your life, God is working it out for your good and his glory.

> And we know that for those who love God all things work together for good, for those who are called according to his purpose. [29] For those whom he foreknew he also predestined to be conformed to the image of his Son. —Romans 8:28-29

> Oh, fear the Lord, you his saints, for those who fear him have no lack! The young lions suffer want and hunger; but those who seek the Lord lack no good thing. —Psalm 34:9-10

I'll say it again: the only thing that matters in life and in death is Jesus Christ. Someone once said, "Only one life, 'twill soon be past, only what's done for Christ will last." True statement. The only life worth living is the Christ-centered life. This was Paul's creed. That creed was expressed to the church in ancient Philippi, located in the country of Turkey today. He said, "For me to live is Christ and to die is gain" (1:21). This should be our purpose statement. It's our doctrinal statement. It's our creed. It's our purpose. How can I live a meaningful life for Christ? Paul gives four pillars in the passage.

> **Philippians 1:18b-26** | Yes, and I will rejoice, [19] for I know that through your prayers and the help of the Spirit of Jesus Christ this will turn out for my deliverance, [20] as it is my eager expectation and hope that I will not be at all ashamed, but that with full courage now as always Christ will be honored in my body, whether by life or by death. [21] For to me to live is Christ, and to die is gain. [22] If I am to live in the flesh, that means fruitful labor for me. Yet which I shall choose I cannot tell. [23] I am hard pressed between the two. My desire is to depart and be with

---

[40] Wayne A. Grudem, *Systematic Theology: An Introduction to Biblical Doctrine* (Leicester, England; Grand Rapids, MI: Inter-Varsity Press; Zondervan Pub. House, 2004), 840.

Christ, for that is far better. ²⁴ But to remain in the flesh is more necessary on your account. ²⁵ Convinced of this, I know that I will remain and continue with you all, for your progress and joy in the faith, ²⁶ so that in me you may have ample cause to glory in Christ Jesus, because of my coming to you again.

## THE CHRIST LIFE IS THE JOYFUL LIFE (1:18-19)

### A Choice to Rejoice

**Philippians 1:18b** | Yes, and I will rejoice.

Despite what is happening in life, I have cause for rejoicing. Despite of my circumstances. Despite my failures and pride, I can rejoice. Make the choice to rejoice. Paul was under house arrest in Rome, and he could have chosen worry, anger, and a whole slew of toxic emotions. He chose to rejoice. We need to choose to rejoice in every circumstance. Paul elaborates further in Philippians 4:4, "Rejoice in the Lord always: and again I say, Rejoice." There are many reasons to rejoice, but Paul's main reason is that he is eternally connected to Christ, and so are you if you have entrusted your life to him. "For me to live is Christ." Therefore, rejoice. Everything that happens in your life is a sovereign act of God designed to draw you nearer to him. And it ends in a fully realized union with Christ: "For me to live is Christ and to die is gain."

### Two Reasons to Rejoice

Paul could choose to rejoice because God was going to work everything out for his salvation and deliverance into the arms of Jesus. There is coming a day when we will all hear, "Well done, good and faithful servant." We will hear that because of the work God began in us and promises to complete when Jesus returns in glory (1:6). There are many ways that God is doing this good work in us, so there are many ways in which we all ought to daily rejoice. Can I show you several things you should rejoice in right now?

There are two things that Paul says will "turn out" for his "deliverance" so that he will not be ashamed when Christ comes: help through *prayer* and help through the *Holy Spirit*. God is working on our behalf through both human and divine means.

### Rejoice in the Prayers of the Saints

**Philippians 1:18b-19** | Yes, and I will rejoice, ¹⁹ for I know that through your prayers and the help of the Spirit of Jesus Christ this will turn out for my deliverance.

God promises to sustain you through the prayers of the saints. That's what he promised Paul and that's what he promises you. We all have a responsibility to pray for one another. The prophet Samuel once said, "God forbid that I should sin in ceasing to pray for you" (1 Sam 12:23). There are many kinds of prayer but praying for the saints is called intercession. We are called to listen to the prompts of the Spirit to pray for one another. Pray for one another. God is working your final deliverance through the prayers of the saints. Rejoice that God's people are praying for you. So much of the prayers that take place for you are anonymous. You don't even realize all the prayers that are going up for you. Rejoice! Prayer changes things. Prayer is working on your behalf. The fountain of all prayer is the ministry of intercession going on right now by our Lord Jesus. And his prayers are moving in all of us who know the Lord. His prayers move in us to pray for one another. Listen to the voice of the Spirit in you to pray for the saints around you.

We have in our local church in northwest Chicago an example of miracle working prayer. A man named Mike Moffat, around 30 years old, father of two, was given two weeks to live. He needed heart surgery, a kidney transplant and a liver transplant. Within a day or two of a time of prayer and fasting for him he got word that he would have surgery on his heart. By the end of the week he suddenly had a liver and a kidney doner. I gave him the new nickname: Lazarus. . received the prayers of the saints. God heard our prayers and has sustained our brother.

I want you to understand that God uses our prayers. You may say, if God is sovereign why do I need to pray? Because in God's sovereignty he has chosen to use secondary means. He has chosen to accomplish his will through the requests of the saints. Therefore, if you do not pray, God will accomplish his will another way. We do not serve a God of fatalism. You need to understand that. God uses secondary means, like the things you do, in order to accomplish his will. This does make him less sovereign; it demonstrates how gracious and kind God is to use broken people like us. But there is another reason to rejoice. Not only in the prayers of the saints, but also in the help of the Holy Spirit.

### Rejoice in the Help of the Holy Spirit

**Philippians 1:18b-19** | Yes, and I will rejoice, [19] for I know that through your prayers and the help of the Spirit of Jesus Christ this will turn out for my deliverance.

God promises to sustain you through as well through the help of the Spirit of Jesus Christ. What a precious title for the Holy Spirit. This was Paul's help, and this is your help. God's grace is sufficient for you, and that sufficiency manifests in your life through the ministry of the Holy Spirit. The Holy Spirit works in you both conviction and comfort. God is working on our behalf through both human and divine means. The divine means is the Holy Spirit.

Dear saint, you have been sealed with the Holy Spirit (Eph 1:14). The Spirit in you is God's mark of ownership. He's not abandoned you. He is the Helper. He is your Comforter. He is here to help you grow in Jesus. He is continually giving you either comfort in *righteousness* or conviction of *sin*. Respond to him continually. That's your help. He's always helping you – never condemning you. There is no condemnation (Rom 8:1), but you need to respond to his ministry in you. Rejoice child of God. Through every circumstance and everything that occurs in your life is God the Holy Spirit is communicating with you. Yield to his ministry. What is he doing, but making you conformed to the image of Jesus? The blood of Christ has accomplished it, and the power of the Spirit that raised Jesus from the dead is working in you. Receive the help of the Spirit of Christ. Rejoice in his help! You are not alone. You are never alone!

### Rejoice in Your Final Deliverance

Paul says because of the prayers of the saints and the help of the Holy Spirit, "this will turn out for my deliverance" (1:19b).

**Philippians 1:19** | This will turn out for my deliverance,

The Christ-centered life is built on joy. Paul says, "Yes, and I will rejoice" (1:18b). I'll rejoice because no matter what happens, I will finally one day be delivered. I will cross over the River Jordan to the Land of Canaan where I will live with my Lord Jesus Christ. It's a long journey on this side of the Promised Land, but I'll get there.

The journey of this life in the flesh is long and tedious, but I have a promise that God's working in me for my deliverance through the saints' prayers and through the help of the Holy Spirit. I am not alone. I am never alone. God is with me. The saints are praying for me at all times. Jesus is making this happen in heaven through his ministry of intercession.

## THE CHRIST LIFE IS THE PURPOSEFUL LIFE (1:20-21)

### A Clarifying Purpose

So many people struggle with direction for their life. How do they know what is wise, what is God's will? Paul didn't have that problem. Knowing and loving Christ gave deep clarity to the purpose for his life. Paul says in 1:21, "For me to live is Christ..." That is a purpose in life that brings clarity.

> **Philippians 1:20-21** | As it is my eager expectation and hope that I will not be at all ashamed, but that with full courage now as always Christ will be honored in my body, whether by life or by death. [21] For to me to live is Christ, and to die is gain.

Paul begins by saying he wants to live his life in such a way that he will not be ashamed at the Lord's return. That's his "eager expectation and hope." The language of hope here is a settled conviction. Hope in the Greek mind is not wishful thinking, but a settled and sure expectation. Everything he did in life was with the end in view. Paul walked in the presence of the living Christ with an expectation that Christ could return at any moment. It was his enthusiastic expectation.

When I was a child, I always enthusiastically awaited the first snow of winter in Chicago. I never knew when it was coming, but there was never a doubt that it would indeed come. That hope, was not wishful thinking, but a settled hope that it would definitely come. Only the timing was uncertain. It had snowed every winter from the beginning of my life. It never disappointed. Those first flakes of the winter season are always large and bring wonderment to the soul. So it is with the child of God, we eagerly await the coming of our King Jesus. It's not a questionable expectation—not if, but when! And it is far more certain even than the winter snow in Chicago.

Paul hope painted everything else with the color of the second coming. His language of expectation is one that has the second coming always in the mind of Paul. This has the idea of "watching something with the head turned away from other objects." Paul's attention is wholly occupied with one thing, to the exclusion of others.[41] Paul has one single passion: to live a life that honors Jesus Christ.

## A Magnifying Purpose

Paul says, I'm going to "honor Christ in my body, whether by life or by death." Some translate the word "honor" as "magnify." That's a helpful illustration. Sometimes we tend to magnify lesser things in our lives, and we find ourselves entrenched in anxiety, frustration, and even despair. Not Paul. His purpose magnified Christ to the point where he had an enthusiastic and eager expectation and hope. His purpose brought an exhilaration to his life. Whatever difficulty in life or even events that brought him to the point of death, Paul could always say: God is bigger. Honoring Christ was the express motive of his life. Christ's sovereign power and guidance of his life brought him great hope.

Christ is already all in all. He is everything. But so many people are blind to his majesty. It is the Christian's duty to open their eyes and magnify Christ to them. With Paul, we must magnify him to the world. "For me to live is Christ and to die is gain." As magnificent as Christ is, in reality he is diminished in the hearts and minds of the world. They don't see reality. So daily, I'm going to open up reality to the hearts and minds of the lost by magnifying Christ. In every little thing, I'm going to demonstrate the greatness and glory of Christ in my life.

## An All-Consuming Purpose

Christ is worthy of magnifying with our whole heart and life. Therefore, we sign on with Paul's creed in 1:21, "For me to live is Christ and to die is gain..." Everything I do is Christ in me and Christ for me. Why do I hunger so much for holiness? For me to live is Christ. Why do I care about advancing the gospel? For me to live is Christ. Why do I constantly yield my life to Christ to do what he wants? For me to live is Christ! Everything I do is for Christ. Everything he brings in my life is for the magnification of Christ. Hallelujah.

Paul says, "For me to live is Christ and to die is gain..." When I die, I meet Christ. When I die, I have no more sin or sorrow. When I meet Christ, I can cast my crowns before him. The world cannot take what is most precious to the Christian. You can take my life, but then: "to die is gain." To die is to gain all of heaven, all of Christ. That's what heaven

---

[41] Motyer, *Message of Philippians*, 86.

is. It is gain. Not because of the streets of gold or the river of life or the cities with music that is beyond anything I've ever heard. It's not heave because of the marriage supper or the trees with 12 different kinds of fruits. Heaven is heaven because of Christ. I want to be in heaven because he is there! He is my "exceeding great reward" (Gen 15:1). For the saint, death is never to be feared. Death is an entrance into perfect life without sin. Death is gain since sin's penalty is removed, sin's power is defeated, and sin's presence is banished.

## THE CHRIST LIFE IS THE LONGING LIFE (1:22-24)

> **Philippians 1:22-24** | If I am to live in the flesh, that means fruitful labor for me. Yet which I shall choose I cannot tell. [23] I am hard pressed between the two. My desire is to depart and be with Christ, for that is far better. [24] But to remain in the flesh is more necessary on your account.

Paul is learning contentment, to continue to live in this body of flesh, on this rebellious sinful earth, but he is determined to live out God's purposes. We will live here one day on a renewed earth, but right now we are waiting for Christ to wipe out all sin from the world at his second coming. As a Christian, your ultimate citizenship is not in this earth. You are just passing through. You are a citizen of heaven. In Philippians 3:20-21, Paul says, "our citizenship is in heaven, and from it we await a Savior, the Lord Jesus Christ, [21] who will transform our lowly body to be like his glorious body, by the power that enables him even to subject all things to himself." This world is not our home. We long to be with Christ. We don't look for full satisfaction in this life. We can only enjoy the good gifts God gives us in this life in relation to our faith in Christ. We fear God and we enjoy his good gifts. But this is not our long-term home.

### We Long for Spiritual Fruit

In God's perfect plan, we are here on this earth only temporarily. The main reason we remain here on earth is for what Paul describes as "fruitful labor."

> **Philippians 1:22** | If I am to live in the flesh, that means fruitful labor for me.

If I'm going to be camping out here on earth, then I need to see spiritual growth in my life. Christ has delayed his coming because he wants us to bear spiritual fruit. That's a massive part of the Christ-centered life. The Christian is not comfortable in this present rebellious world. The popular culture resists glory of Jesus Christ. We are called to work hard and give all our effort and labor to bear fruit from the lives who will be raised from death to life.

## We Long to be Present with Christ

If I'm going to be camping out here on earth, then I need to see spiritual growth in me and in you and all around. That's a massive part of the Christ-centered life.

**Philippians 1:23** | I desire to depart and be with Christ, which is far better.

Wouldn't you agree? It's so much better to be without sin, without sickness, and all the effects of sin and rebellion. It's so much better to depart and be with Christ. I love the word "depart." It means to be "unloosed" from your burdens (*analuó* = I unloose for departure). This word was used by three different people groups in antiquity. It was used when *sailors* would unloose the moorings from the dock when they were ready to sail from one port to the next. It was used of *soldiers* when they would depart from one campsite to another. We are just camping out in this life. A camping tent is a good description of our physical body. We are so preoccupied with our tents. Like our bodies, a tent gets old. It wears out (2 Cor 5:1). And then it was used of *farmers* when the yoke was lifted from the work animal at the end of the day. The animal was unloosed from the harness. Jesus used this analogy to encourage us to allow Him to rule our lives (*cf* Mt 11:29). When our yoke is removed, we get to enter the kingdom of heaven (cf Mt 25:21, 23). Dear child of God, to be loosed from the burdens of this life is far better than remaining here. We all long to depart to be with Christ, though it is necessary to remain here on earth for the evangelization of sinners and the sanctification of the saints.

### Death Will Be an Encounter

Our departure to be with Christ will be an encounter. It is not the departure that makes the death of a believer sweet; it is the arrival! Heaven is not about what's there; it's about who's there. Of course, there will be family and friends, but the main attraction is our intimate, face-to-face encounter with Jesus. Heaven's main attraction is God, not stuff (*cf* Jn 14:3; 2 Cor 5:8; 1 Thess 4:17). The stuff is just the wrapping paper. God is the gift!

### *Death Will Be Much Better*

Meeting Christ in death will be so much greater than anything in this life. Paul says in 1 Cor 13:12, "we see in a mirror dimly, but then face to face...." Right now, life has so many heartbreaks and difficulties. It's like trying to see through a broken mirror. But one day we will see Christ face to face. Paul saw heaven for a moment, and it was too much for him to even explain (*cf* 2 Cor 12:1-4). Truly, "eye has not seen nor ear heard" the glories of heaven. As Paul says, departure from this earth is far better for all of us.

## We Long to Camp Out

I love the language here. To remain means to "camp out" a little longer. The longing is not for camping out, but for greater fruit for the Philippians account. Paul says we are just "camping out" on this old earth awaiting the new creation. Paul says: it's necessary to camp out a little longer.

> **Philippians 1:24** | But to remain in the flesh is more necessary on your account.

Remember Paul is a tentmaker. The word "remain" is from his tentmaking vocabulary. It literally means to "camp out." This life is a temporary campout. I don't mind sleeping on the ground for a night or two, but I'm always ready to sleep in my own bed. I don't mind the rustic facilities, but I'm so glad for the comfort of my own home. I like camping. But I like it for about a day or two. Maybe a week if we are hunting. But then, I need to get back home. Some of you ladies, your idea of a good camping trip is roughing it at a hotel or motel for a weekend. No matter who you are, camping is only good for a short amount of time, but then you are ready to go home.

Paul was good with camping out because he saw it as necessary for the growth and sanctification of the Philippians. Right now we are just camping out, but soon we will be home. We long for home, but for now it is necessary that we be on earth, camping out for a little while longer so that we can grow and change into the image of Christ. We need to grow in our relationship with the Lord and fulfill God's kingdom purposes of evangelism and discipleship. He would have his heaven full.

Remember, we are to live a life that is incarnational for sinners, just like our Savior did. Jesus "camped out' on this earth for a short time in order to rescue sinners. We are carrying on Jesus' rescue mission. We are the ones to run into the burning buildings of people's lives. That's why we remain camping out.

## THE CHRIST LIFE IS THE GROWING LIFE (1:25-26)

### Growth in Joy

> **Philippians 1:24-25** | But to remain in the flesh is more necessary on your account. [25] Convinced of this, I know that I will remain and continue with you all, for your progress and joy in the faith.

The reason for Paul to stay *"camping out"* on earth is for the Philippians growth and progress in joy in the faith. Paul is "convinced" that remaining on earth will result in the sanctification of the saints. We should all be enthusiastically expectant of this.

It's easy for us to be discouraged with so many circumstances of life, but Paul will not allow himself to go there. He is focused on the Philippians' growth in joy. Paul is convinced that it is better for the overall plan of God to be "all there" while he's on earth. He's not a bystander but is engaged in the Christian life with "fullness of joy" (Psa 16:11).

Joy is one powerful aspect of the fruit of the Spirit (Gal 5:22-23). Indeed, "for the kingdom of God is not eating and drinking, but righteousness and peace and joy in the Holy Spirit" (Rom 14:17). Joy is a major experience in the Christian's life. That doesn't mean we don't lament (the Psalms help us to weep over the brokenness of this life). Jesus said, "Blessed" or "happy" are "those who mourn" (Mt 5:3). The point is the Christian's joy does not come from the circumstances of this life, but the beauty of Christ, which never changes. Peter tells us that though you don't see Christ right now, "you believe in him and rejoice with joy that is inexpressible and filled with glory" (1 Pet 1:8). The Christian breathes the air and atmosphere of glorified joy. We are "seated in the heavenly realm" ruling and reigning with Christ (Eph 1:3).

## Growth in Glory

**Philippians 1:26** | So that in me you may have ample cause to glory in Christ Jesus, because of my coming to you again.

Paul wants to remain in the flesh in order to magnify Jesus in the saints. When they saw Paul they could only give glory to God. Here was this self-righteous sinner, now humbled. Glory is all about what Jesus has done. He's done it all! Living for the glory of Christ is the only life worth living.

One of my dearest friends is Ahmed Joktan. He is the son of the Meccan mufti in Saudi Arabia (like a cardinal or archbishop in Islam). He is cousins with five of the jihadist 9/11 hijackers. God saved him, and every time we see each other, I have "ample cause to glory in Christ Jesus" when I see how God can save anyone. Let us glory in Christ for the work of salvation and sanctification that he is doing in each one of us. He will complete that work (1:6).

### Conclusion

During the civil war, there were so many millionaires in the south. They all had confederate money. When the North won, all those millionaires became bankrupt. That's how people are without Christ. They think they have so much, whether it be money, reputation, security, popularity in this life. But there's coming a day when we die. For me to live is Christ and to die is gain!

Life in Christ is amazing. I wouldn't have it any other way. But when we depart, that's when all we've done for Christ will come to be so valuable. And those who do not have Christ will all be bankrupt. For those in Christ, in life, we are rich, and in death we are rich in the Lord. For the lost, you finish and lose everything.

# 6 | PHILIPPIANS 1:27
## WALK WORTHY OF THE GOSPEL

*Only let your manner of life be worthy of the gospel of Christ, so that whether I come and see you or am absent, I may hear of you that you are standing firm in one spirit, with one mind striving side by side for the faith of the gospel.*
PHILIPPIANS 1:27

When I was a child we moved to Louisiana, and I had to walk according to a different culture. To be accepted and appreciated, I had to learn that new culture. I had to learn how to say ya'll. I had to learn how to eat crawfish. I had to learn how to swim with water moccasins and alligators. I learned a new culture. I walked according to the atmosphere of that culture. In a sense I had a new culture and citizenship in Louisiana. I was now south of the Mason Dixon line. In Philippians 1:27, we are taught that we have a new culture and a new citizenship. We are growing each day more and more, learning to walk worthy of that citizenship in the New Jerusalem.

Paul lays the foundation in Philippians 1:21, "For me to live is Christ and to die is gain" (1:21). What an amazing life philosophy! Paul now begins to tell us how to live a Christ-centered life, a humble life, worthy of the gospel from 1:27 through chapter 2 and verse 18. Paul has told us: to live is Christ, and now he tells us how to live the Christ exalting life. This passage is both a threshold and a launching pad. You pass the threshold into a building, a new place. You enter in. We need to enter into the Christ exalting life. Paul is commanding us to enter in. But then it is a launching pad. He takes us to new places with Christ.

> **Philippians 1:27-30** | Only let your manner of life be worthy of the gospel of Christ, so that whether I come and see you or am absent, I may hear of you that you are standing firm in one spirit, with one mind striving side by side for the faith of the gospel, [28] and not frightened in anything by your opponents. This is a clear sign to them of their destruction, but of your salvation, and that from God. [29] For it has been granted to you that for the sake of Christ you should not only believe in him but also suffer for his sake, [30] engaged in the same conflict that you saw I had and now hear that I still have.

We are presented with two things here: you have to choose daily to walk worthy, and second that worthy life brings conflict and difficult consequences that might frighten you. We are called to choose to walk worthy no matter what the difficulties.

## THE EXHORTATION TO WALK WORTHY (1:27A)

### An Important Exhortation

Paul begins with a plea. It's hard to see in our English translation with the word "only," but Paul is saying: what I'm about to tell you is the most important think you need to remember as you live the Christian life.

> **Philippians 1:27a** | Only let your manner of life be worthy of the gospel of Christ.

Sometimes we use the word *only* to simply introduce a new thought. There are other times when we use the word *only* as a way to describe singularity: like only child. Here Paul is using this word to underscore the weight of supreme importance. It is sometimes translated, "above all else" (NLT, CEV). This is something that should singularly describe a Christian's life: "Only let your manner of life be worthy of the gospel of Christ..." (1:27; *cf* Gal 2:10, 5:13). *'This one thing and this only."* Nothing else must distract or excuse them from this great objective; above all, living out the gospel must be their all-embracing occupation and focus.[42]

If you go back and look at the previous verses in chapter 1, Paul has said not to be overly concerned about him since his difficulties and imprisonment are not setting the back the cause of Christ, but advancing it, working out for the furtherance of the gospel. We learned that no matter what we are going through in life, however hard or confusing, God will use it to advance the gospel. Christ will build his church, and the gates of hell will not prevail against it. He then gives the motto of every Christian: "for me to live is Christ and to die is gain" (1:21).

And now as a good disciple-maker, he wants the Philippians to live this way too. He says whether I die, or whether I live, let this one thing be your concern. He says: this is of supreme importance. Above all, more important than anything else you do: "Only let your manner of life be worthy of the gospel of Christ..." (1:27). Walk worthy saint of God. Christ is worthy. Exalt him in your life. Exalt him in how you live.

You may remember when you came of age, 12 or 13 years old, and mom and dad said, *"Whatever you do,* don't answer the door for strangers." Or, *"Whatever you do,* you need to be in bed by 9pm." This is of supreme importance. Above all, this is important. That's the sense Paul introduces this section. Above all, walk worthy of Christ. Exalt Christ in your life. He's going to tell us how to do that from here through chapter 2:18.

### A New Mindset

Paul says: "Only let your manner of life be worthy of the gospel of Christ..." (1:27). The word, "let your manner of life be" (πολιτεύεσθε)[43] is one word in Greek. We get our word "politic" from this word. It means to live out as a citizen. And here it's a present imperative, a continual command. Above all else, what you should be constantly doing is living out the gospel as a heavenly citizen. It's the same root word as Philippians 3:20 when Paul says, "Our citizenship is in heaven." Let your political mindset, how you operate, be geared toward your heavenly home. In other words, the key to walking worthy is adapting to a

---

[42] Motyer, *Message of Philippians,* 92.

[43] Kurt Aland et al., *The Greek New Testament, Fourth Revised Edition (Interlinear with Morphology)* (Deutsche Bibelgesellschaft, 1993), Php 1:27.

new homeland. You have a new heavenly citizenship. You need to adapt to your new homeland. Christ is your home. Abide in him and he in you. Christ is your culture.

## A Divine Imperative

When Paul turns his attention to the Philippians, he does not plead with them. He does not beg or entreat them. Instead, in the full consciousness of his authority as an apostle, the Spirit of God breathes out Scripture through Paul and commands us to walk worthy of the gospel. He is not asking them, he is giving a command that says: if you truly belong to Christ, then submit yourself to his way of living.

When the letter was brought to the Philippian church, perhaps by Epaphroditus (2:25) and this letter was read before the congregation, they knew it was from God. It was a divine imperative. "Only let your manner of life be worthy of the gospel of Christ..." (1:27). Paul was binding their consciences to these words. We cannot live whatever way we want. We must live a life in submission to Christ. He died and rose again. I deserve hell, but now I belong to him.

This command is a present imperative tense (in Greek). In other words, we are to make this our constant goal. It's just as the 1st question in the Westminster Catechism: What is the chief end of man? To glorify God and love him forever. Above all else we are to live a life that points to the glory and worthiness of Christ. It's not to be lived out only on Sunday, but *every day.*

Let me pause here and ask you by way of application, what is your response to God commanding you to do something? When you hear the voice of God in Scripture, what is your response? Nothing is more effective in uncovering the state of the human heart than our instinctive reaction to a word from God. Your reaction to God's command reveals your heart. What is your reflexive reaction in the presence of a word from God that comes as a command? Few things are a more accurate indicator of the state of your heart.

### *The Unrepentant Sinner*

If you sit here this morning as an unrepentant, unregenerate man or woman, boy or girl, then nothing more quickly brings to the surface the state of your soul and your standing with God than a command from God. Almighty God says, "This you must do!" And you think you can ignore it. In the language of Pharaoh, you say: "Who is the LORD that I should obey him?" (Exo 5:2). *"Who is this God that wants to tell me how to live? I'll just ignore him. I'll just act as if I've never heard God's voice."* That kind of reaction to God's voice exposes a heart of stone. The state of the unbeliever is hardened and opposed to God. We are all born this way: dead in sin, with a stony heart. God's commands are not important to the unbeliever. The unconverted person can take or leave what God says. The lost person is not committed to a life of hearing and obeying God's word because by nature, he's at war with God. "The mind-set of the flesh [*the lost person's nature*] is hostile to God because it does not submit to God's law. Indeed, it is unable to do so" (Rom 8:7, CSB). Furthermore, the Bible tells us that every lost person on the planet knows God but is pushing down and suppressing the truth of God's glorious existence (Rom 1:18-20).

I wonder, what was your instinctive reaction when I said, this is not only of crucial importance, but to walk worthy of the gospel is a divine imperative? It's weighty. God is saying: *I have a right to regulate and direct your life*. What is your reaction to that? Do you groan? Do you push against his commands? Are you at your core uncomfortable with God's sovereign right as King to direct you? If so, face what you are: a rebel against a God of love. An enemy of God. And in that condition, under the wrath of Almighty God, unless you repent and believe the gospel. When we become children of God, the state of our heart is changed to one of love and joyful obedience. Where is your heart. God's divine imperatives are lovingly embraced by his children. He has revealed his infinite love is such a way, that we are compelled by joy to follow whatever he says to do.

### *The Self-Righteous Sinner*

When the self-righteous sinner hears God's commands, he might delight to hear it and add it to his list of things to do. He might look at others like the Pharisee and say, "I thank you that I'm not like that sinner over there. I know and try to follow God's commands." When the self-righteous person hears God's command, he looks at it as another rung in his self-made ladder to heaven. Every precept or rule is another step of his ladder in which he himself can climb into heaven. He is utterly self-deceived, thinking his own performance is the basis of a right standing with God. When such a person hears a divine imperative, many times he has a reaction that seems to be very positive. "Wonderful, now I know something else that will make me right with God."

We all have this self-righteousness in us, and it blinds us. Self-righteousness is like eating from a nice plate but never cleaning it. You pile on good food to a plate crusted with dry and decaying food that you never washed off. So you have good food that is mixed with the hardness and crustiness of a dead and decaying heart of pride. The heart is hard and cannot receive God's commands in the way they were intended. The humble saint knows we can never come into God's presence in the filthy rags of our own righteousness.

### *The Humble Saint*

When the Christian hears the divine imperative, he or she melts. We have the presence of God indwelling us. The Spirit speaks and convicts when the word is preached or read or listened to. The humble saint hears the command to "walk worthy of the gospel" and treats sin as deadly. It is our sin that put Jesus on the Cross. The humble saint *takes sin seriously*. Treat it as the thing that it is. All sin receives the wrath of God. We take God seriously when he says he hates something. He hates sin. Sin destroys.

Imagine that in front of your house were a four-lane highway. Imagine that for a year, the highway was uninhabited. It was safe to play on. Your kids play on it. Neighborhood kids are all over the highway. No problem, right? But then one day a sign goes up. On such a date traffic will commence. That day comes and your children are no longer safe on the highway. You would do whatever it takes to keep a dear child from losing their life right? How much more important is your soul and their soul? Are you willing to do whatever it takes to walk in a way that is worthy and that will not soil the glorious reflection of Christ in your life?

## A Glorious Gospel

We are called to walk worthy of the gospel, the good news that we need a Savior, and God has sent us the Savior we need. he says, "I am the way." He's not a way or a good way, he's not the best way, but the only way! He's the way, the truth and the life, and no one comes to the Father except through him. Walking worthy of the gospel means believing the gospel. The good news begins with bad news: you are a helpless unworthy sinner. You need a Savior.

Walk worthy. That's what Paul says. Receive it. What an honor. What a privilege. Christ is worthy. Revelation 5:12, "Worthy is the Lamb that was slain to receive power and riches and wisdom and might and honor and glory and blessing." He's worthy of your life. He's worthy of your total commitment. He's worthy of your serious and radical sacrifice. He's worthy of your time and your life. He's worthy of every second of every day. He's worthy of your love. He's worthy of your strength. Give him your life. If you are young, he's worthy – serve him your whole life. Start young. If you are old, it's not too late! It's never too late! He's worthy.

## WAYS TO WALK WORTHY (1:27B)

Paul is a clear-headed preacher and a wise pastor. He doesn't just present the principle that Christ is worthy of your life. He actually tells us in what ways Christ is worthy. He doesn't just tell us to walk worthy. He tells us how. He gives at least three ways we are to walk worthy.

> **Philippians 1:27** | Only let your manner of life be worthy of the gospel of Christ, so that whether I come and see you or am absent, I may hear of you that you are standing firm in one spirit, with one mind striving side by side for the faith of the gospel.

### Walk in Consistent Obedience

The first way Paul intimates that we walk worthy is consistent obedience. Paul begins by saying: "whether I come and see you or am absent, I may hear of you that you are standing firm..." (1:27b). If you are aiming for a life worthy of the gospel, the apostle points to a life of obedience. There is a pattern of life that does not depend on human accountability. The fact that Christ is King and omnipresent and indwelling us through the Spirit, is enough to motivate the Christian to a consistent pattern of obedience. What is that pattern? It involves *first*: a consistent pattern of obedience to Christ. Paul says I desire to know – whether in person or by someone else visiting you (like Epaphroditus) who observe your pattern of life—I want to know that you are standing firm in consistent obedience. Live out the love of Christ. Live out your devotion to Christ. He is worthy.

### A Cosmic Consistency

Paul exhorted the Philippians in a way which would have appealed to them. What he said, literally, was: "Exercise your citizenship worthily for the gospel of Christ." Our consistency comes from a cosmic focus: we are citizens of a heavenly kingdom. We can be so focused on meaningless things, but we need to lift our heads up to the heavens.

> If then you have been raised with Christ, seek the things that are above, where Christ is, seated at the right hand of God. ² Set your minds on things that are above, not on things that are on earth.
> —Colossians 3:1-2

> Lift up your heads, O gates! And be lifted up, O ancient doors, that the King of glory may come in. —Psalm 24:7

Lift up your head to the New Jerusalem, child of God. That's where your citizenship is. This way of speaking would have been easily understood by the Philippians. Philippi was a Roman 'colony', a title seen as one of the coveted prizes of the Roman empire. 'Colonial' status meant that the people of Philippi were reckoned as Roman citizens. Their names were on the rolls at Rome; their legal position and privileges were those of Rome itself. They were a homeland in miniature. But all this is also true of them spiritually as men and women in Christ. Grace has made them citizens of a heavenly city; in their far-off land they are an outpost of the heavenly homeland, the New Jerusalem; heaven's laws are their laws, and their privileges, its privileges. The life *worthy of the gospel* where the exalted Christ, the exalted Lamb who was slain, forms the focal point of all life.[44]

### A Growing Consistency

Paul says whether I am present or absent, I want to have a report that you are living a consistent life, worthy of the gospel you claim to believe. What does this mean? It means that as the people of Philippi faced their trials and temptations, and as we and face our trials and tests, and frustrations and fits and frames of mind, we would consistently be choosing to obey this command to live a life worthy of the gospel. Paul's hope was though all the trials and tests come, it would be reported to him that the Philippians are living lives worthy of the gospel.

---

[44] Motyer, *Message of Philippians*, 93.

Where is our hope? In ourselves? No! Our emotions and circumstances are sometimes like a roller coaster. We change. But there are changeless things in this universe you can anchor your soul to. Is the hope of the gospel changeless? Yes! Is Jesus Christ's position as King of kings changeless? Indeed! Anchor yourself to that. God's promise to give you sufficient grace to live a consistent Christian life is changeless as well. There is a consistency in the believer's growth. It's not the same rate for everyone. It's not perfection. It's not that there are no ups and downs. There are dry periods and times when our growth is arrested and stunted. But the overall pattern of gospel living is clear: Paul says: "Only let your manner of life be worthy of the gospel of Christ," that is, "Let it be *consistently* worthy (1:27), that whether I drop in to see you or Epaphroditus travels to Rome to give me a report in this rented house where I am imprisoned, that I may hear of your consistent obedience. That is what will gladden my heart. Amidst all the changes in society, changes in your circumstances, all of the ups and downs in your emotional state, and all the changes that life constantly brings – among all that, I want to hear above all else, that you are a consistent people." We are far from where we ought to be, but we are also so far from where we once were. We were dead in sin, now we live. We were blind, now we see. John Newton, author of *Amazing Grace*, said it this way:

> I am not what I ought to be, I am not what I want to be, I am not what I hope to be in another world; but still I am not what I once was, and by the grace of God I am what I am.

Are you consistently growing in your character? Are you more humble when you are right? Is it your attitude in an argument with your spouse or close friend that you are like the one who is wrong? When you are accused of some fault, do you say, "I'm the problem. It's me O Lord." Spurgeon said, "If anyone thinks ill of you, do not be angry with him; ... If you have your moral portrait painted, and it is ugly, be satisfied; for it only needs a few darker touches, and it would be still nearer the truth." When you are accused, realize you are much more sinful in God's sight than in man's sight. Are you growing in your reliance of the grace of God in trials? Are you growing in self-denial and seeing consistent victory in Christ? The pattern of your growth and obedience is to be consistent.

### A Militant Consistency

How desperately this world needs to see Christians who are consistently reflecting Christ. Are you committed? Are you all in? We are to "endure hardness as a good soldier of Jesus Christ" (2 Tim 2:3). A soldier can't be allured by civilian life. "No soldier gets entangled in civilian pursuits, since his aim is to please the one who enlisted him" (2 Tim 2:4). Or are you controlled by something other than the lordship of Christ? We live in the generation of feelings. Everyone is led by the rudder of their emotions. The mark of our culture is hedonism and narcissism and serving self. And you cannot allow this world's culture to put its imprint on you. If you let self dictate whether or not you serve God, then the mark of your life will be inconsistency. What about you? Are you predictable? Do people see a godliness in you that is consistent? Father, mother, do your children see in you a consistent humility? Are you consistent in the right ways? Is there a growing kindness? Is there an increasing love for the all the brothers and sisters, not just the one's that are easy to get along with? Is there a consistency in your service for Christ? Are you helping in one area of the church, and you are comfortable, but are you ready to grow in another area of ministry? You need to be willing to stretch and grow in your service.

### A Persevering Consistency

As a Christian, when you feel like giving in the towel and quitting, it is the Spirit who comes and brings a militaristic resolve never to quit. He comforts us. He puts a divine and holy ambition to persevere no matter how hard it gets. Consistency is the mark of grace in our lives. By God's grace we can "stand firm" in the hope of the gospel. No matter what comes, we can say with Job, "Though he slay me, yet will I trust in him" (Job 13:15). We "press on toward the goal" of knowing Christ (Phil 3:12-13). "Having put my hand to the plow, I will not turn back." That's Paul's great passion and concern for the Philippians. It's the burden of these pastors and elders. We long for your consistent character in the gospel.

We avail ourselves of the means of grace, not because our flesh feels like it, but because we must. The very happiness of our soul depends on it. But our flesh, the sinful, selfish part of us, constantly fights against our best motives. The spirit is willing but the flesh is weak. So we go to pray, because God told us, "Men ought always to pray and not to lose heart" (Lk 18:1). So we pray whether we feel like it or not. And soon we do feel like it. Soon we are delighted in prayer. We meet with the congregation for fellowship and preaching not because we feel like it. God commands us not to neglect meeting together for worship, but to do so more and more as we see the Day of Christ approaching. We fellowship and worship not because we feel like it, but because God commands it. And once we are here, we are so glad we are so glad we've come. We don't always feel like doing what we ought to do. The flesh is weak. But once we do obey we are so glad we did. The joy of the Lord is our strength. We meet him in the midst of obeying him. We don't wait for a certain feeling to obey God. We obey. We are to walk worthy, and the first way Paul says we can do that is consistency. He wants to see Christians standing firm in the gospel.

But now we come to the second mark of the worthy walk: fearing God. This is the heart of the passage. The pattern of obedience is not only to be consistent, but it is to be carried on in the fear of God. The external mark is consistent growth and obedience, but the inward engine is a heart fears God and melts before his presence.

## Walk in the Fear of God

Paul says: it's not about human accountability that makes us walk worthy. Whether we have human accountability or not, we walk worthy of the gospel. We have a far deeper motive for walking worthy of the gospel: We fear God. We are aware of the presence of God. It's not about Paul's apostolic presence that motivates the Philippian believers. It's the fear of God.

> **Philippians 1:27** | Only let your manner of life be worthy of the gospel of Christ, so that whether I come and see you or am absent, I may hear of you that you are standing firm in one spirit, with one mind striving side by side for the faith of the gospel.

Paul was aware of the danger that his presence as a man of God might greatly influence the measure of the Philippians' obedience to the revealed will of God. Whether Paul was there or not, he wanted to see them "standing firm" and "striving side by side" because of the fear of God. He comes back to this theme in verse 12 of the next chapter:

> Therefore, my beloved, as you have always obeyed [*consistency*], so now, not only as in my presence but much more in my absence, work

out your own salvation with fear and trembling, ¹³ for it is God who works in you, both to will and to work for his good pleasure.
—*Philippians 2:12-13*

You see what he is saying? Your walking worthy of Christ is not mainly due to human accountability. It's a much deeper motive: You are aware of the God who is working in you! You are so aware of this you tremble and fear.

### *Adam in the Garden*

It's not our human accountability that transforms us, it is the living God. If our striving for a life worthy of the gospel is material altered by our spiritual guides, we have yet to walk in the fear of God. You cannot walk worthy of the gospel without an acute sense of the presence of God. There is a fullness in God that is forfeited by sin. We saw this in the life of the first man. When he sinned, and paradise was lost, the most important thing that was lost was Adam's communion with God. He was out of delightful submission to the will of God.

When Jesus died and said, *Tetelestai*, "It is finished," God ripped the veil from top to bottom and opened paradise again. We can worship him now within the veil. We are interdependent in the Body of Christ, but human accountability is not what is most important. We need to have the powerful and glorious presence. At times we seem to lose the fear of God. When I come from my devotions and come to breakfast, and my wife burns my pancakes, and I make some snide comment, I have left the presence of God behind. If I go to work, and I start hating my job or my boss or a co-worker, and I'm filled with annoyance with someone created in the image of God, I've stopped fearing God. Remember the words of Solomon in Proverbs 9:10, "The fear of the Lord is the beginning of wisdom and the knowledge of the Holy One is understanding."

### *Joseph in the Old Testament*

Joseph in the Old Testament knew the fear of God. When he was tempted by Potiphar's wife, and she daily tempted him and said, "Lie with me" what was his response. Here is a man living in the fear of God. Listen to him: "How then can I do this great wickedness and sin against God?" (Gen 39:9). The fear of God is an expression that describes an experience of the awe and majesty of the living God. We can know concepts, but God wants us to know him personally.

## Walk in Unity

The next thing we see flows from the first. Unity comes from the fear of God because God's fear promotes a deep and profound humility in our hearts. "The sacrifices of God are a broken spirit; a broken and contrite heart, O God, you will not despise" (Psa 51:17). Unity always comes from humility. Paul's goal is for them to walk together, standing firm in the gospel and serving together side by side in the gospel.

> **Philippians 1:27** | Only let your manner of life be worthy of the gospel of Christ... with one mind striving side by side for the faith of the gospel.

### Unity Flows from the Holy Spirit's Work

We already have this unity, but we need to guard it. It was given to us as a gift from the Holy Spirit when we were born again (Eph 4:1-3). Proud people don't serve together. Proud people fight. Humble people have the humility to serve together with "one mind striving side by side for the faith of the gospel." Disciples of Jesus do life together. We are no possessive of any ministry. We are glad to serve wherever needed. This humble attitude comes from a fresh vision of his holy presence. Ask him to humble you. It's what we need. You are either humble as a child of God or you will be humbled. "God resists the proud but gives grace to the humble" (Jas 4:4).

### Unity Flows from Hard Work

"Standing firm" is military language. Paul wants to hear that they are "standing firm in one spirit." There is a place in our lives where we do not bend. We are standing firm in the gospel. To walk worthy of the gospel goes against this world. There is so much coming against us.

Philippi is a Roman colony. That's a high privilege. They value the citizenship privileges given in that status. Philippi was also a military town, heavily populated both by active-duty troops and by retirees from service in the Roman legions. Some of the church's Philippi's members would have been active and retired soldiers and would associate vivid combat memories with Paul's words. If the military works hard at keeping in unison. Putting their shields together. Following commands of the general, so we as Christians should stand firm in one spirit, the Holy Spirit. We should follow his commands in the word and in through his voice in our conscience.

Steadfastness is an Olympic term. Then Paul says we are to work hard at unity as an athletic team does. "...with one mind striving side by side for the faith of the gospel." The word "striving" is derived from a root that sometimes refers to athletic competition. Not far south of Philippi is Achaia. Before the Olympics came to Athens, they began in Achaia. This was a town known for their athletic teams. Everyone does their part, but they all work together.

"Side by side" is a military term. Ancient Greek athletics developed out of military training for combat, as we still see today in sports such as the javelin, the hammer, the discus, and wrestling. Here, Paul is thinking in terms of mortal combat. The Roman soldiers had to march "side by side" together in war. He paints the picture of an advancing line of Roman legionnaires, their long shields forming both a seamless wall before them and a "roof" over their heads against the enemy's arrows and spears. His point is: "Don't let the opposition divide you! Instead, let the pressures from your opponents draw you together in a deeper and stronger unity! Paul will develop this theme more fully in 2:3 – "Do nothing from rivalry or conceit, but in humility count others more significant than yourselves" (2:3). He's going to show us how to do that in chapter 2, we are to imitate Christ who being in the form of God humbled himself and chose not to submit himself to becoming a man! It's hard work to be unified! Walk worthy "...with one mind striving side by side for the faith of the gospel." It's a battle.

In a war you don't have time to look at your own self of lick your own wounds. You march forward together helping each other. This is military language. You leave no one behind! You'll have to battle your flesh. You'll have to battle wrong thoughts about people. You'll have to instruct yourself and renew your mind (Eph 4:22ff). It's hard work to stay unified. Brothers and sisters, we are to be advancing, side by side for the faith of the gospel.

### *Unity Flows from Our High Calling*

We stand firm like a soldier. We strive side by side like athletes. Why? For the faith of the gospel. What is the gospel? It is the Good News of the substitutionary atonement. It's so simple a child could understand: Jesus died for my sins. That's the gospel. God's wrath is satisfied. My hell is paid for. Christ died and rose again for my justification.

What is faith? Faith is trust. Faith is not twelve steps – it's one step: surrender. It's a total trust and surrender to the fact that Christ, who is exalted God would humble himself to die in my place for my transgressions. Now this high calling isn't just individual, it's corporate. We have a responsibility for one another. I am responsible to walk with you side by side and serve together for the faith of the gospel. Your burdens are my burdens and my burdens are yours. Together is a wonderful word. As we learned early, it is the Spirit of God that put us together. Let us rejoice and serve along side one another, exalting Jesus Christ!

## Conclusion

Walk worthy saints because Christ is worthy. He is exalted. Recognize that. He is worthy of your life and energy and all that you are and have. Walk in consistent obedience. Walk in his fear. And in humility let's walk and serve together side by side for the gospel.

# 7 | PHILIPPIANS 1:27-30
## THE COURAGE TO SUFFER

*For it has been granted to you that for the sake of Christ you should not only believe in him but also suffer for his sake.*
PHILIPPIANS 1:29

Can I ask you a question? Are you encouraged in your walk with God? You ought to be. Yet so often we live in fear. That is not the will of God. So often we do not walk worthy of the gospel because we are afraid. I think of Simon Peter. In fear he denied the Lord three times. But something transformed him. With faith he saw the risen Lord, and he became courageous! All the apostles were transformed by faith after the resurrection, and they became tenacious for the gospel. The love of God invaded them, and they were transformed.

What is it that makes us courageous? I believe the Bible answer is faith. That's what God told Joshua. And 365 times, God tells us "Fear not"! It's always "fear not, and trust in me." Don't lean to what you see but look to me. Get your reality from me. If you lack courage, it's because you lack focus. Where does courage come from? And how do you get it when you need it, when some fear towers over you and threatens you, and you feel like cowering and fleeing into some place to hide? It

Let us consider what it means to walk worthy and how exactly we attain that. I want to walk worthy of that high call in Christ. I need courage. Christ is our mighty champion. He's already triumphant. How can we have the courage to walk worth? Four pillars of courageous faith that will give you strength as you suffer for Christ: faithfulness, forcefulness, fearlessness, and favor.

> **Philippians 1:27-30** | Only let your manner of life be worthy of the gospel of Christ, so that whether I come and see you or am absent, I may hear of you that you are standing firm in one spirit, with one mind striving side by side for the faith of the gospel, **28** and not frightened in anything by your opponents. This is a clear sign to them of their destruction, but of your salvation, and that from God. **29** For it has been granted to you that for the sake of Christ you should not only believe in him but also suffer for his sake, **30** engaged in the same conflict that you saw I had and now hear that I still have.

As we guard our unity in the Spirit, there will always be intense spiritual opposition. We will indeed suffer. Live up to your heavenly citizenship. "Live as citizens of heaven in a way that is worthy of the gospel of Christ." Live up to your heavenly calling. Live up to your union with Christ. Live in the power of Christ. Be lifted up by grace to walk according to that high calling. Yet, the moment you begin living for Christ, opposition comes. Paul says don't be "frightened in anything by your opponents" (1:28a). "Don't be intimidated by your enemies."

Paul commands us to walk worthy of the gospel. A literal translation would be: "Live up to your heavenly citizenship, worthy of Christ's gospel." You are united with Christ. Walk worthy of your union. You are a member of God's family. Walk worthy. You are adopted. Walk worthy! You are one with Christ. Walk worthy. When Christ died, you died with Christ. All your sins are fully propitiated. The wrath of God is satisfied for every transgression today, yesterday, forever! You are fully forgiven by our compassionate and tender heavenly Father. When Christ was resurrected, you were raised with him by the Spirit. Keep getting to the higher ground of the holy life. This is a gift from God. He has given you "everything you need" for life and godliness. When Christ ascended to the Father's right hand, you ascended with him. You are "seated in the heavenly places" (Eph 2:5). Now you must set your mind on heavenly things, not on things on the earth (Col 3:1ff). When Christ comes again, you will be glorified like him. Walk worthy of the death, resurrection, ascension, and second coming of Christ. Can we walk worthy of these great realities even if we are suffering terribly? Yes! And we do that first with a focus on faithfulness.

## HAVE COURAGE TO SUFFER WITH FAITHFULNESS (1:27)

**Philippians 1:27** | Only let your manner of life be worthy of the gospel of Christ, so that whether I come and see you or am absent, I may hear of you that you are standing firm in one spirit, with one mind striving side by side for the faith of the gospel.

I'm convinced that what the world needs is to see a Christian whose character is bold and courageous, who is living a consistent life of holiness, whose life manifests sheer faithfulness! Christians in America are comfortable. We have forgotten Christ's call for us to take up our cross and suffer. Paul says to the Philippians, you need to be united like soldiers, "standing firm in one spirit." We need to be united like athletes, with "one mind striving side by side for the faith of the gospel." We are to be faithful to Christ in all things.

To be faithful means to be loyal, constant, staunch, steadfast, resolute mean firm in adherence to whatever one owes allegiance. For the Christian, this firm adherence is not from our own power, or faith in ourselves, but we are filled with faith in another's power. We are filled with faith in Christ who has infinite power. The faithful one is the faith-filled Christian!

### Faithfulness is Manifested by Spirit

Notice Paul says: "Stand firm in one spirit" (1:27c). Hold your ground in one spirit! How is that possible? How can people with such differences, with so many different ideas to be "in one spirit"? How can you please all the people all the time? If you've ever thought of trying it, don't do it. It's impossible. It was Abraham Lincoln who said, "You can please some of the people all of the time, and you can please all of the people some of the time, but you can't please all of the people all of the time." And if you can't please all the people all the time, how are you going to keep everybody in one spirit of unity? I'll tell you: there's only one way. When one Holy Spirit is allowed to be and do what he wants to be and do in every one of our spirits, then we will strive side by side together. That's what Paul is asking for. It's my spirit abandoned to the Holy Spirit. It's realizing the Christian next to me is in exactly the same place. "Stand firm in one spirit." Faithfulness! The Spirit will bring it.

The faithfulness that characterizes the Christian flows from my surrender to the Holy Spirit. This is the kind of unity and faithfulness the Spirit of God produces in the heart of the child of God.

## Faithfulness Marks the New Birth

Faithfulness is a fruit the Spirit (Gal 5:22-23). The faithful, consistent life is a gift that comes from resting in the Spirit of Christ. All believers will experience the faithfulness that comes out of a new heart. Remember what was prophesied 2600 years ago. It was prophesied in Ezekiel that the Spirit would come and take out our "heart of stone" and put in a "heart of flesh" in the gospel times that we are in, and it has happened (*cf* Eze 36:25-27). God's word is true. We are seeing God's faithfulness to his word right now. God promises to give you a faithful heart. It's not something you can work up. It's a miracle of God's revealed word to your heart. You believe, and you are changed. He put in us a faithful heart. He joins us to a body of believers with faithful hearts.

## Faithfulness Moves Us to Victory

Paul tells us "stand firm"! The athlete rejoices in a win. The soldier rejoices in victory. We have the victory through our Lord Jesus Christ. Hold your ground! Be united in your battle: fight the good fight as God's army. "The gates of hell shall not prevail," so go forward no matter what and build Christ's church. When I think of the fruit of faithfulness that the Spirit produces, I have to remember one of David's three mighty men named Eleazer.

> He was with David when they defied the Philistines who were gathered there for battle, and the men of Israel withdrew. [10] He rose and struck down the Philistines until his hand was weary, and his hand clung to the sword. And the Lord brought about a great victory that day, and the men returned after him only to strip the slain.
> —*2 Samuel 23:9-10*

Eleazer was with David when they battled against the Philistines. The Bible says that the battle was so fierce that the rest of David's battalion withdrew, but Eleazer kept fighting against 800 men! They had to pry that sword from Eleazer's hand. He lost all vision for everything else except one thing: faithfulness. He knew he had the victory because of the Lord. What courage in his great and mighty God he had! What a mighty man not just for David, but a mighty man of God. His fellow soldiers came to take the spoil, but only after Eleazer cleaned the Philistines' house (so to speak)!

The courage to remain faithful always comes from faith in another. You are powerless, but God is infinite in power. Is there this faithful tenacity to move forward in your life? What are you ceding to the enemy of your soul? What have you given up on in your life of holiness? We are called never to give up, but to be faithful. Don't you know that the Lord can "restore the years that the locusts have eaten"? Don't you know that God can "make beauty from ashes"? You need to look in faith to the one who makes us faithful. Jesus says, "Without me, you can do nothing" (Jn 15:5). The prophet Zechariah said, "Not by might, nor by power, but by my Spirit, says the Lord" (Zech 4:6). The Lord said to Paul, "My grace is sufficient" and "when you are weak, you are really strong... my strength is made perfect in your weakness."

### *Scriptural Examples*

God can take a puny David and defeat a prideful Goliath! How? David had a great God who can defeat giants! God can take a "has bin" named Moses and turn him into a prophet through which the entire Egyptian army is defeated. How? Moses had a great God who made Moses one of the most faithful man in the Old Testament. Simon Peter, what a big mouth he had! What an unstable personality! God can take a bumbling Simon Peter and turn him into a faithful apostle who preaches Pentecost. God can take *you* wherever you are, and whatever you are going through and make you faithful. How? Through faith in his power, God can make you strong. We have no power without the Lord. "Unless the Lord build the house, they labor in vain who build it" (Psa 127:1). "The joy of the Lord is my strength" (Neh 8:10) "I can do all things (context: in all situations) through Christ who strengthens me" (Phil 4:13). I know you hear God's voice right now, Christian. Jesus said "My sheep hear my voice, and they follow me" (Jn 10:27ff). God is talking directly to you today, and you need to stop trying to live in the power of your own faithfulness.

### *Applications*

So, you say, how can I lay this foundation of courage in my life? Surrender to the power of our great God! He is able! Surrender and rest in him! That's where faithfulness comes from! Whatever it is that keeps your from consistency, God's got you. That's where you have to begin. God's bigger than your flesh, the world, and the devil. "Greater is he who is in you than he who is in the world" (1 Jn 4:4). God wants you to be faithful in every area of your life. It's going to take courageous faith to be faithful. It's not about small you, but our great God! Perhaps you've neglected the greatness of God in your life. I'm calling you to step up and step out in reliance on your great God! Step out on faith and be faithful in your quiet time with God: in prayer, and in the word. Be faithful in pursuing your spouse if you are married. Be faithful in your purity. Be faithful in giving God the firstfruits of all that he gives you, in tithes and offerings. Be faithful in your finances. Don't cheat the IRS. Don't cheat God either. Be faithful in assembling together at church, small groups, home fellowships. Be faithful brothers and sisters to walk with integrity, according to your heavenly citizenship. What this world needs to see is Christians who are ruggedly faithful to the Christ they say they believe in. We need to follow him faithfully, not in our own power or pride, but in weakness and humility. "He must increase, and I must decrease" (Jn 3:30). That's the secret to faithfulness.

## HAVE COURAGE TO SUFFER WITH FORCEFULNESS (1:27)

**Philippians 1:27** | Only let your manner of life be worthy of the gospel of Christ, so that whether I come and see you or am absent, I may hear of you that you are standing firm in one spirit, with one mind striving side by side for the faith of the gospel.

Forcefulness comes so easy for some and hardly at all for others. Stand firm. Don't move! Don't give any ground to the enemy! We have to be forceful and disciplined. Forcefulness is not always looked upon well, but we must insist on being forceful, living from a heart of conviction, and moving in the power of the Spirit.

### Pictures of Forcefulness: Soldiers & Athletes

Paul says we are to be "striving together for the faith of the gospel." What does it mean, striving side by side? It's the word we get our English word, "athletics". It has to do with wrestling. Paul says, "I want to see all of you, like soldiers, holding your ground with one spirit." At the end of his life, Paul says, "I have fought a good fight, I have run the race,

I have kept the faith" (2 Tim 4:7). Paul tells the Philippians: I want to see you lined up like athletes: wrestling and winning against the forces of darkness. We need to be weapons in God's hands, ripping people from the fires of hell. "The gates of hell will not prevail" because Christ said, "I will build my church."

We need to be like athletic fighters and not give in to the philosophies and fears of this world. There needs to be a forceful presentation of the gospel of Christ where it's needed most. In the Olympic games that Paul is referring to, the wrestling event was quite different. The wrestlers lined up shoulder to shoulder and battled against the other team. At the given signal, they went at it, one united front against another. The only way the gospel is going to get to the uttermost parts of the earth so that every creature hears the gospel, is when everyone in the local church realizes we are competing on the same team. We cannot do this alone. We must insist on unity and togetherness. Put aside all differences among you. Cover offenses with love. Put the great looming glory and love of God before you!

Like an athlete wrestler, we need to deny self for the entire team. An athlete is a person who denies self. We have to have the courage to say no to worldliness and no to personal ambition. Our ambition must be for Christ. We must be forceful with ourselves because of love for Christ. Jesus in order to follow him, you have to daily attend your own funeral: If anyone desires to come after me, let him deny himself, and take up his cross daily, and follow me (Lk 9:23).

An athlete is a person who trains. On Olympic teams, they are to train together. An athlete is a person who willing to cut out unnecessary things. There's a courage to it. There's a competition. There's a drive, a forcefulness we must have. We must deny self like an athlete. "An athlete is not crowned unless he competes according to the rules" (2 Tim 2:5). Paul says:

> Do you not know that in a race all the runners run, but only one receives the prize? So run that you may obtain it. [25] Every athlete exercises self-control in all things. They do it to receive a perishable wreath, but we an imperishable. [26] So I do not run aimlessly; I do not box as one beating the air. [27] But I discipline my body and keep it under control, lest after preaching to others I myself should be disqualified. —*1 Corinthians 9:24-27*

## The Power of Forcefulness

Forcefulness is necessary personally, but also corporately. Forcefulness can be seen as a negative thing. Why is it necessary for Christian conduct? Because you must have a tenacity and a forcefulness when it comes to unity. Paul says, "I want to see the same kind of abandonment and self-denial an athlete has for the unity of the gospel!" But it's not merely on an individual level. "With one mind striving side by side for the faith of the gospel" (1:27). Have the same discipline that an athlete would have. The ancient wrestler-athlete had to be forceful when it comes to unity. There must be a grittiness. There must be a firmness when it comes to unity. We are going forward together. We are not leaving anyone behind. We must fight side by side together against the enemy.

# HAVE COURAGE TO SUFFER WITH FEARLESSNESS (1:28)

Fear is a very real experience for all people because of the fall, but God does not intend for any of his children to be fearful, though we often are. You must not live in fear because fear destroys unity.

## Courage is a Sign for the Saved

**Philippians 1:28** | And not frightened in anything by your opponents.

God never tells us to be afraid of anything, except to fear the Lord. And that fear of God is not a servile fear, but an awe and reverence for the greatness and goodness and majesty of God. God calls us to an audacious faith and courage. Remember the words of God to Joshua? "Have I not commanded you? Be strong and courageous. Do not be frightened, and do not be dismayed, for the Lord your God is with you wherever you go" (Josh 1:9). Or remember the words of Isaiah. This ought to breed courage in us:

> But now thus says the Lord, he who created you, O Jacob, he who formed you, O Israel: "Fear not, for I have redeemed you; I have called you by name, you are mine. ² When you pass through the waters, I will be with you; and through the rivers, they shall not overwhelm you; when you walk through fire you shall not be burned, and the flame shall not consume you. ³ For I am the Lord your God, the Holy One of Israel, your Savior. I give Egypt as your ransom, Cush and Seba in exchange for you. —*Isaiah 43:1-3*

Indeed, we are told by John the apostle that "all cowards shall have their part in the lake of fire" (Rev 21:8). This infers that all of God's people have the courage that is gifted to us by the Spirit, else it would not be an evidence of the new birth.

## Courage is a Sign for the Lost

**Philippians 1:28b** | This is a clear sign to them of their destruction, but of your salvation, and that from God.

The word Paul uses for "clear sign" is interesting. It was used by Caesar to determine the fate of a gladiator. At the Roman Colosseum, if a gladiator was seriously wounded or threw down his weapon in defeat, his fate was left in the hands of Caesar. The emperor could give him the "thumbs up" or "thumbs down." That's what this clear sign originates from. In other words, as Christians go forth into the world, their fearless unity, their love for one another, is a "clear sign" – literally a "thumbs up" or "thumbs down" for the eternal destiny for all around. Paul put it this way: when we go out into the world, "we are a living letter, known and read by all men" (*cf* 1 Cor 2:15-16).

Hear what Paul is saying. Don't be frightened by your enemies/opponents. You are giving off an aroma that makes some of them want to persecute you and even kill you. You are a signpost for God to those who are lost, a warning sign that they are perishing. Some are going to "see your good works and glorify your Father who is in heaven." Others are going to hate you and mob you. There will be both rioting and rejoicing. Paul was attacked by a mob at Thessalonica. He was again attacked by a mob at Ephesus. He had to be lowered down a wall in a basket in Jerusalem because people wanted to kill him. At the end of the day, your example of Christlikeness is meant to warn and awaken the lost to come to Christ.

The fact that you are being oppressed by the enemy on all sides is a sign of what's coming. It's a harbinger of the future. For the lost, their hatred of Christ a sign of their destruction, but for you persecution is a sign of your salvation. Although it seems now that the church's opponents have the upper hand, their current persecution of believers, whether severe or mild, is a harbinger of a radical reversal to come. It is actually "a clear sign" of the enemies' own impending destruction and of believers' eventual rescue by God himself (1:28).

## HAVE COURAGE TO SUFFER WITH FAVOR (1:29-30)

We can have courage to walk worthy because the battle is won, and the winning of it does not come from us. It clearly comes from God. "It has been granted" speaks of God's gifts of grace. We might say that each one of us is truly "blessed and highly favored." Spiritually speaking, we are embarrassed with riches.

"Has been granted" is from charizō, which is from the same root as the noun *charis* (grace) and literally means "to give, render, or grant graciously." In his sovereign grace, God gave believers the marvelous gift of faith to believe in him (*cf* Eph 2:8-9). We have everything we could ever need in Christ (2 Pet 1:3; Psa 23:1). We are enriched. We have an unlimited spiritual arsenal to fight the enemy. We are indeed blessed with every spiritual blessing in Christ. Paul says to the Philippians, we have been enriched in two ways. Here Paul mentions two gifts. One is obvious. The other is a surprise.

> **Philippians 1:29-30** | For it has been granted to you that for the sake of Christ you should not only believe in him but also suffer for his sake, **30** engaged in the same conflict that you saw I had and now hear that I still have.

### We are Favored with the Ability to Believe

Faith is a gift from God, so no one should boast (Eph 2:8-9). Because of man's inability to please God, this gift of faith is an obvious necessity. There is a pattern of worthy conduct that characterize heaven's citizens (Phil. 1:27). Yet the gospel is not a set of responsibilities to be fulfilled. It is good news to be believed—the joyful report of a mission accomplished on our behalf despite our unworthiness and helplessness. The ability to believe in Christ is one of two gifts of grace that come from God, according to this text (1:29–30). These two gifts—faith and suffering—are Paul's explanation of his concise but momentous assertion that our final salvation will be "from God" (1:28). In Christ, the Christian is infinitely blessed with every spiritual blessings (Eph 1:3-9). Consider how infinitely blessed we are to be chosen in Christ from the foundation of the world.

Rejoice in your election! God has chosen you. It is not there to ask whether or not you are elect. That is a futile question. Ask yourself, is Christ the only Savior? Could I forsake him and go back to the world?

Who gave you that faith to keep you? What a gift! If you have the faith to believe in Christ's atonement for your sins, then God has graciously opened your eyes. This is God's electing grace. Before we could ever choose him, he chose us. Indeed, "we love him because he first loved us" (1 Jn 4:4, KJV). Further, Jesus said in John 6:37, "All that the Father gives me will come to me, and whoever comes to me I will never cast out." The giving precedes the coming. The Father must give us to the Christ. You were given to the Father in eternity past, long before you ever believed. We are to walk worthy, but there is nothing to boast in. Your faith comes from the Father. It's a gift. "It has been granted to you to believe in Christ."

## We are Favored with the Ability to Suffer

We can have courage because the battle is won, and the winning of it does not come from us. It clearly comes from God. "It has been granted" speaks of God's gracious gifts. We are not surprised by the first gift: faith, but certainly suffering is a gift we would want to give back!

> **Philippians 1:29-30** | For it has been granted to you that for the sake of Christ you should not only believe in him but also suffer for his sake, [30] engaged in the same conflict that you saw I had and now hear that I still have.

Paul says, we are "engaged in the same conflict" as he is. Remember Paul was imprisoned and beaten with Silas in Philippi. But that suffering was a gift. Paul and Silas sang in the jail that night and the walls of the prison shook with an earthquake of joy and fell down. We rejoice in suffering because we are counted worthy to suffer for Christ. There are various ways we suffer in the Christian life. There is the suffering of persecution. "Yea, and all that will live godly in Christ Jesus shall suffer persecution" (2 Tim 3:12). As you bring the word of the gospel to the world, you will suffer. They will reject you. There will be some rioting, but there will also be rejoicing! There is the suffering of trials. "Count it all joy, my brothers, when you meet trials of various kinds,3 for you know that the testing of your faith produces steadfastness" (Jas 1:2-3). It's when troubles come that your endurance has a chance to grow! There is the suffering of God's compassionate chastening. "Whom the Lord loves, he chastens" (Heb 12:6). Sometimes God lays us up to draw us closer.

Your suffering is a gift from God! You are going to suffer so much in this life, and there is a reason for that. It is so show that you are "going to be saved" (1:28), "and that from God" – that is, by God himself. You are so weak. Your suffering is so great. There is no way you could save yourself. God's going to make that clear through the gift of suffering.

Why does God call suffering a gift? Think about what suffering does to us. It humbles us. Job said, "Though he slay me, yet will I trust in him" (Job 13:15). James said, "Count it all joy, my brothers, when you meet trials of various kinds, for you know that the testing of your faith produces steadfastness" (Jas 1:2-3). Suffering builds faith. It helps you draw near to God. It strips you of everything so that you will draw near. It humbles you. It produces strong and steadfast faith.

There is satanic attack daily. You are not home yet. You are in a war zone. Where is your focus? You need to focus on your heavenly home with Christ in his new creation. It is a fatal mistake to assume that God's goal for your life is material prosperity or popular success as the world defines it. The abundant life has nothing to do with material abundance. Faithfulness to God does not guarantee success in a career or even in ministry. Never focus on temporary crowns.

Paul was faithful, yet he ended up in prison. John the Baptist was faithful, but he was beheaded. Millions of faithful people have been martyred, have lost everything, or have come to the end of life with nothing to show for it. But the end of life is not the end!

> For we fix our attention, not on things that are seen, but on things that are unseen. What can be seen lasts only for a time, but what cannot be seen lasts forever. —*2 Corinthians 4:18, GNT*

When life gets tough, when you're overwhelmed with doubt, or when you wonder if living for Christ is worth the effort, remember that you are not home yet. At death you won't leave home — you'll go home.

## Conclusion

You need to have courage to walk worthy. No matter what happens, courage comes from faith in a big God. If you lack courage, you need to refocus and recalibrate. Turn your eyes upon Jesus. He's the one who chose you and he's the one who holds you.

In the 1940s, children across America would have to go through wartime drills. In schools everywhere they would have wartime tests where the alarm would go off, warning of a possible approaching bomb. The children would have to get under their desks or go to a shelter. They were never quite comfortable.

Dear saints, we are not home yet. We will suffer on this earth. But let us rejoice that we are counted worthy to suffer for Christ. We are counted worthy in Christ to go through every trial, every difficulty for a goal. That goal is that we would know the nearness of God, know his majesty and fear, know the conviction and comfort of the Holy Spirit, and as a result, be transformed. Walk worthy saints, even in the midst of your suffering. If you lack courage, refocus on Christ. Turn your eyes on our victorious Savior and King!

# 8 | PHILIPPIANS 2:1-11
## EVERY KNEE SHALL BOW

*Therefore God has highly exalted him and bestowed on him the name that is above every name, so that at the name of Jesus every knee should bow, in heaven and on earth and under the earth, and every tongue confess that Jesus Christ is Lord, to the glory of God the Father.*
PHILIPPIANS 2:9-11

Do you ever feel stuck? There's a behavior that you've tried to stop, but you just can't seem to do it. There's a negative thought-pattern that you have attempted to move on from, but nothing you try ever works. There's a relationship that you want to repair, but despite all your best intentions, nothing seems to make things better. You want to change, but you feel... stuck.[45] When we think of the church at Philippi, we usually think of it as Paul's sweetheart church, with a message of joy, and that's true. But there were several places of "stuckness" that needed to be undone.

When Epaphroditus brought a generous gift from the church in Philippi, and good news of the church's concern for Paul, he also

---

[45] Timothy S. Lane, *Unstuck: A Nine-Step Journey to Change That Lasts* (Epsom, UK: The Good Book Company, 2019), 2.

brought the bad news of a possible division in the church family. Apparently, there was a double threat to the unity of the church; false teachers coming in from without (Phil. 3:1–3) and disagreeing members within (4:1–3). What Euodia ("fragrance") and Syntyche ("fortunate") were debating about, Paul does not state. Perhaps they both wanted to be president of the missionary guild or the choir!

Paul knew what some church workers today do not know, that there is a difference between unity and uniformity. True spiritual unity comes from within; it is a matter of the heart. Uniformity is the result of pressure from without. This is why Paul opens this section appealing to the highest possible spiritual motives (2:1–4), that of honoring the triune God and seeing Christ humbled to the lowest place, and then exalted to the highest place (2:5-11). Where are you stuck? The pathway to getting unstuck is seeing the glorious Christ in all his glory.

> **Philippians 2:1-11** | So if there is any encouragement in Christ, any comfort from love, any participation in the Spirit, any affection and sympathy, [2] complete my joy by being of the same mind, having the same love, being in full accord and of one mind. [3] Do nothing from selfish ambition or conceit, but in humility count others more significant than yourselves. [4] Let each of you look not only to his own interests, but also to the interests of others. [5] Have this mind among yourselves, which is yours in Christ Jesus, [6] who, though he was in the form of God, did not count equality with God a thing to be grasped, [7] but emptied himself, by taking the form of a servant, being born in the likeness of men. [8] And being found in human form, he humbled himself by becoming obedient to the point of death, even death on a cross. [9] Therefore God has highly exalted him and bestowed on him the name that is above every name, [10] so that at the name of Jesus every knee should bow, in heaven and on earth and under the earth, [11] and every tongue confess that Jesus Christ is Lord, to the glory of God the Father.

As we look at Philippians 2:1-4, I am reminded of Peter's words in 1 Peter 5:6, "Humble yourselves, therefore, under the mighty hand of God so that at the proper time he may exalt you." You could summarize these verses as "Get low so God can exalt you and use you." As Paul writes the Philippians, he wants them to grasp how to be humble like

Christ. In 2:5-11, Paul then shows us Christ's journey of humiliation to exaltation. It is a journey we are all called to follow.

Someone might say: You know I just can't be humble. That's just not who I am. It's not in my personality. My dad had a hot temper, and I have one. I'm just being myself. If I act humble, I will squelch who I am. We all have the command and the ability to be humble. The command is in verse 5: "Have this mind among yourselves," that is, the mind of Christ. He humbled himself though he was God. In verses 1-4 Paul tells us we have the ability to be humble because we are bornagain.

## THE POWER FOR HUMILITY (2:1-4)

We have the ability to be humble because we have been regenerated. Have you been touched by grace? Then you'll be able to have a gospel humility, gospel transformation, gospel fruitfulness, and gospel friendships. That's what we are going to talk about through Philippians 2. It's all about what the gospel produces in our lives. We won't be stagnant. We won't be untouched. If we've been touched by God and touched by grace, people around us will know. Your family and friends will see it. With God's touch comes gospel growth and gospel blessing.

Paul begins by letting us know the obvious: we need to live in the blessing by placing our focus on the triune God, and not on ourselves. That's usually the secret to contentment. Don't focus on your singleness if you are single. Don't focus on your marriage if you are married. Don't focus on your job primarily or your bank account or //you fill in the blank//. Get your heart focused on the triune God who loves you.

### Look to the Truine God

Focus on God. The triune God. That's where Paul goes. He focuses on what every true and genuine believer experiences. He basically says: if you are a born again believer you will be committed to the triune God and to the church. He gives four gospel assumptions: you are committed to God the Father, Son and Holy Spirit and you are committed to the church. These are gospel realities. He says:

> **Philippians 2:1-2a** | So if there is any encouragement in Christ, any comfort from love, any participation in the Spirit, any affection and sympathy, [2] complete my joy by being of the same mind.

This is a similar trinitarian formula that Paul uses in other places. Paul constantly invokes the triune God. For example, he blesses the Corinthians in a similar way. "The grace of the Lord Jesus Christ and the love of God and the fellowship of the Holy Spirit be with you all" (1 Cor 13:14).

### We are Encouraged by the Son's Sacrifice

**Philippians 2:1a** | So if there is any encouragement in Christ.

Christ spoke of our unity being like the unity between the Father and the Son. "Holy Father, keep them in your name, which you have given me, that they may be one, even as we are one. 12 While I was with them, I kept them in your name, which you have given me" (Jn 17:11-12). Are you discouraged with life? Are you frustrated? Fighting? Despairing? Don't be proud. Humble yourselves in the presence of Christ. Be encouraged that he died for you. Christ is God the Son. He has all the attributes of deity because he is God. "Is there any encouragement in Christ"? Yes! There is if you are born again. When Paul says if, he's saying, if there is any encouragement in Christ, *and there certainly is if you are born again.*

### We are Comforted by the Father's Love

**Philippians 2:1b** | So if there is ... any comfort from love.

Then Paul asks is there "any comfort from love"? He does not supply what love or where it is coming from, but because of the other Trinitarian formulas in Scripture, it seems obvious that this is referring to the comfort we receive from God. Aren't you comforted by the love of God? He chose you before the foundation of the world. He predestined you to be conformed to the image of his Son. He loved you with an everlasting love. Doesn't that comfort you? Focus on the unmerited love and favor you are receiving right now by God the Father. You have the love of the Father – just as he said to his son this is my son in whom I am well pleased. That's what God says about you because of Christ.

### We are Enriched by the Spirit's Fellowship

**Philippians 2:1c** | So if there is... any participation in the Spirit.

Paul wants us to know that since we are united to Christ, we participate in the very harmony of the Trinity. Paul asks is there "any participation in the Spirit"? Here the word is "fellowship" or in Greek, *koinonia*. The idea is "sharing in the presence of God." If you are a true believer, you share in the presence of God through the Holy Spirit. You are united to the living God. You are one with the Father and Son and Holy Spirit.

So think of it now. Is there "any encouragement" in Christ's sacrificial atonement for you? Is there any comfort from God's everlasting, electing love for you? Is there any deeply satisfying fellowship in the Spirit? In other words, are you experiencing the triune God as a born-again believer? Paul mentions one more thing. It's a beautiful thing. He has us focus on the church's affection and sympathy.

### We are Supported by the Church's Sympathy

**Philippians 2:1d-2a** | So if there is... any affection and sympathy, ² complete my joy by being of the same mind.

Paul asks, "Is there any affection and sympathy" for the brothers and sister in Christ's church? Here Paul appeals to the divine compassion and mercy that came from Christ himself to us at salvation and now passes through us to others.[46] Are you as committed to God's forever family as Christ is, laying your life down and holding the church up? Are you totally committed to the body of Christ? Paul says the best thing you can do to reflect the triune God is to be one with each other as you are one with the triune God. There are hints of Jesus' high priestly prayer in John 17, in his plea to the Father for the unity of his people. Paul here joins that plea.

Of course, these are four gospel assumptions. Ok Paul says, if these four commitments are genuine because that's what God does in your heart as a believer – he puts those commitments there – if these things are true and present, then fulfill my joy and be unified.

## Love the Body of Christ

Paul says, if the gospel has truly taken root in your life, then complete my joy by carrying out three practical gospel responsibilities that will enrich your unity and fellowship with the body of Christ.

---

[46] Hughes, *Philippians*, 75.

### Be Harmonious Together

**Philippians 2:2** | Complete my joy by being of the same mind, having the same love, being in full accord and of one mind.

*We must be one in mind.* These believers were to be "like-minded" and to have "the same mind." This has to do with agreement in doctrine and creed. They were to hold to the same creed and embrace the same tenets of truth that they had been taught from the very beginning. No matter what liberal, free-thinking theologians may say, there is no spiritual unity without doctrinal oneness. When it comes to fundamental doctrines, A. T. Robertson said Christians should be "like clocks that strike at the same moment."

*We must be one in heart.* The world needs Jesus. Christians are to have the "same love", not loving the same things but possessing the same love. They are to show that God's love is flowing in them and through them. Love God and one another and the lost world because of our need in Christ.

*We must be one in soul.* The phrase "of one accord" literally means to have "joint souls." We ought to all have the same soul when it comes to service for Christ. We have the same destiny in heaven and should be working together on earth. We are to be soul brothers, in harmony with all God's people!

### Be Humble Together

**Philippians 2:3** | Do nothing from selfish ambition or conceit, but in humility count others more significant than yourselves.

Each one of us is responsible for the unity of the body. If we do not take ownership over our own spirits and dispositions, there will be no unity in the body. Paul challenged each one that he or she was not to do anything "through selfish ambition or conceit." This is a warning against a competitive, selfish spirit. Selfish ambition is a work of the flesh, according to Galatians 5:19–20, and is behind the petty squabbles and fights in so many churches today.

Besides the Lord Jesus Christ, Paul himself stands out as one of the true examples of this humility. During his third missionary journey, he referred to himself as "the least of the apostles" (1 Cor 15:9). Later, during his first Roman imprisonment, he described himself as "the least of all the saints" (Eph 3:8). Toward the close of his life, he wrote to Timothy and confessed that he considered himself the chief of sinners (1 Tim 1:15). These were not statements of false piety but represented Paul's attitude toward himself as he viewed the totality of the body of Christ. There was no pride or arrogance about his many accomplishments. He truly considered others better than himself. Harmony, humility, and now let's see how helpfulness are all signs of unity.

### Be Helpful Together

**Philippians 2:4** | Let each of you look not only to his own interests, but also to the interests of others.

If a Christian values his brother highly and is practicing the spirit of humble-mindedness, he will naturally be looking for ways to help others. Are you one who has a diligent hand and a servant's heart? Christ, when he wanted to show humility, he put on a servant's towel. For the "Son of man came not to be served but to serve and give his life a ransom for many" (Mk 10:45). Those who heed these words of Paul have the larger view of life. The view that seeks one's own things tends to narrowness, selfishness, bigotry, smallness, and meanness of soul. The view that seeks to promote the interests and well-being of others leads to largeness of life both here and hereafter.[47]

One thing I love about Christ's church is the servant's attitude I see in healthy congregations. Don't be afraid to be all in. I love to see believers discipling each other and lifting each other's burdens in your local church. Truly humble people are "self-forgetful" and are not concerned with being possessive over a ministry or taking things personally when criticism may come. Because we do not look to our own interests, we have thick skin and a big, tender heart as we see and meet the needs of others.

## THE PATHWAY TO HUMILITY (2:5-8)

Have you been touched by grace? Then you'll be able to have a gospel humility, gospel transformation, gospel fruitfulness, and gospel friendships. That's what we are going to talk about through Philippians 2.

---

[47] J. Phillips, *Exploring Philippians*, Php 2:4.

**Philippians 2:5-8** | Have this mind among yourselves, which is yours in Christ Jesus, ⁶ who, though he was in the form of God, did not count equality with God a thing to be grasped, ⁷ but emptied himself, by taking the form of a servant, being born in the likeness of men. ⁸ And being found in human form, he humbled himself by becoming obedient to the point of death, even death on a cross.

## Have the Mind of Christ (2:5)

We are called to have the mind of Christ. Wow. Live with Christ's mindset, because, look at this: it's already yours. It belongs to us by family right. We've been adopted into God's family.

**Philippians 2:5** | Have this mind among yourselves, which is yours in Christ Jesus.

To demonstrate how we are to walk with the humble mind of Christ, Paul gives us what most Bible teachers believe to be an ancient hymn of the early church in verses 6-8, rightly referred to as "The Christ Hymn". In all of Scripture, these verses stand unparalleled in their majesty. We see the great position of Christ and how he laid that glory aside for a robe of humble humanity. If Christ was willing to humble himself in this way, how much more should we be willing to humble ourselves? Let us be like Christ. Let us put on his mind! As Paul S. Rees says:

The occasion and meaning of this eloquent outburst are simple and clear. "Don't forget," cries Paul, "that in all this wide universe and in all the dim reaches of history there has never been such a demonstration of self-effacing humility as when the Son of God in sheer grace descended to this errant planet! Remember that never—never in a million æons—would he have done it if he were the kind of deity who looks 'only to his own interests' and closes his eyes to the 'interests of others!' You must remember, my brethren, that through your union with him, in living, redemptive experience, this principle and passion by which he was moved must become the principle and passion by which you are moved."[48]

---

[48] Paul S. Rees. *The Adequate Man* (Westwood, NJ: Revell, 1959), 43.

## Consider the Humility of Christ (2:6-8)

Now Christ says to us in so many places: "Follow me." He says "Go and make disciples out of all nations!" So if we are learners and disciples of Christ, then we need to follow his journey. We are united to him, so let us follow him.[49]

### He Relinquished His Place (2:6a)

Look at the prominence that Christ enjoyed before the foundation of the world.

> **Philippians 2:6** | Who, though he was in the form of God, did not count equality with God a thing to be grasped.

Who is Jesus? He was "in the form of God." The Word "was" means to live or exist or to be. This is not a transitive verb. There's an act of being and existing here. Jesus existed in his very nature as God. The word "form" is *morphe* or "by very nature" Jesus is God. It is directly parallel in the Greek to "equality with God." This verse is talking about Christ's pre-existence. That is before the world began, Christ existed because Christ created the world.

> In the beginning was the Word, and the Word was with God, and the Word was God. ² He was in the beginning with God. ³ All things were made through him, and without him was not any thing made that was made.   —*John 1:1-3*

*Jesus claimed pre-existence with the Father*, co-equality in power and glory. In his high priestly prayer in John 17, Jesus prays: "Father, glorify me in your own presence with the glory that I had with you before the world existed" (Jn 17:5). Before the world began, Jesus shared in the glory of the Father. Now if any one of us would pray that way it would be downright blasphemy. It would be lunacy. But it's not blasphemy or lunacy because Jesus is deity! Look at the exalted position Jesus relinquished!

*Jesus claimed to be without sin*. Listen to him in John 8. He said, "Can any of you prove me guilty me of sin? If you cannot, why won't you have faith in me?" (Jn 8:46). Wouldn't that be something for a man, 33 years of age, come along and declare: "Who of you have ever

---

[49] The six-step outline is adapted from David Jeremiah. *Count It All Joy: Discover a Happiness That Circumstances Cannot Change* (Elgin, IL: David C. Cook, 2016) 90-92.

seen me commit a sin"? If I said that you all would jump up pretty quickly and say, "I have." If you don't know me then ask my wife and children. They'll tell you. I'm a sinner. You're a sinner. But Christ, though he was "tempted in every way, just as we are, yet he did not sin" (Heb 4:15, NIV). He hungered and thirsted. He was tempted. He was a man, just like you. But he did not sin. He was fully man. But he was more than that.

*Jesus claimed to be God.* Once in a while you might meet someone who will try to convince you that the Bible does not teach that Jesus is God. But the Bible consistently affirms what Paul was telling the Philippians: No one has seen God at any time. Jesus said ... "He who has seen me has seen the Father" (Jn 14:9). John said, "No one has ever seen God; the only God, who is at the Father's side, he has made him known" (Jn 1:18). Paul said, "He is the image of the invisible God, the firstborn over all creation" (Col 1:15). And, "in him [*Jesus*] all the fullness of God [*fullness of divinity, of a divine nature*] was pleased to dwell" (Col 1:19). Paul says to Timothy, "And without controversy great is the mystery of godliness: God was manifested in the flesh" (1 Tim 3:16). Jesus said, "Before Abraham was, I am" (Jn 8:58).

Who is Jesus? He claimed to the Great I Am who existed before Abraham and who appeared to Moses. Listen to Christ: "Before Abraham was, I am. [*I am in eternal existence*]." No wonder the leaders got angry and tried to throw stones at Jesus when he claimed pre-existence in John 8. No wonder they gathered stones in the Temple to stone him (Jn 8:59). No wonder they tried to kill him and eventually crucified him. He stood up and said, "I am God." Was he? Was he who he claimed to be? He never had a formal education. Yet 2000 years later billions are talking about him.

Some said he was a lunatic. Was he mad? He claimed to be God! Was he mad? Some said he was a liar from the devil. They said, "You're nothing but a liar and a devil." He made a claim of equality with God. Is he a liar? Was he trying to deceive the crowds? Jesus Christ is not a lunatic. He's not a liar. He then, must be Lord of all. He raised the dead. He did things only God could do. He made the blind to see. The elements of the wind and the sea obeyed him. They obeyed their Master because he created them.

Who is Jesus? That's the question. We can't escape him. He's everywhere. Our greatest philosophers write about him. Our greatest historians write about him. Our greatest poems are about him. The greatest music sings his praises. Our greatest architecture is dedicated to him. Time itself is divided by him.

Who is Jesus? He had all the characteristics of a man. He was fully man. Yet he is more than a man. What man can say that he existed before he was born. Jesus is the eternal self-existent one. He is the uncaused cause of everything. By him all things were created.

Jesus' birth was not the beginning of his existence. Jesus sexists from everlasting to everlasting. He's the first and the last, the beginning and the ending, the Alpha and Omega. He planned it all, he executed it all, and all things are maintained by the word of his power and will. What mere man can control the laws of gravity. Christ is God. He controls the seasons. He brought this polar vortex of negative 50 below and he'll bring it up this week to 50 above. And one day he'll burn it all up.

But he relinquished that place. He gave up the outward manifestation of his deity. And though he continued to be God of all, he robed that fact in the likeness of sinful humanity, yet without any sin. Jesus relinquished his place and left heaven and came down here.

### He Refused His Privileges (2:6-7a)

Jesus had every right to continue in the exterior manifestation of his glorious person, but he chose to let that robe of glory go and put on a robe of lowly humility. Look at the prominence that Christ enjoyed before the foundation of the world. Before he came into this world the Bible says he refused his privilege.

> **Philippians 2:6-7a** | Who, though he was in the form of God, did not count equality with God a thing to be grasped, [7] but emptied himself.

Though Christ continued to be God, he refused to hold on to the outward glory as God. The word "a thing to be grasped" carries with it the idea being "held on to for one's own advantage" (as the NIV translates it). He refused to hold on to his outward glory for his own advantage but divested himself of that glory by veiling himself with human flesh in order advance others. He's God, but he doesn't count his privileges as deity as something to be held on to and guarded at all costs.

Paul goes even further: "he emptied himself" (2:7a) J. B. Phillips translated the phrase this way: *"He stripped himself of all privilege."* Christ divested himself not of his deity, but of the outward and independent use of his divine attributes. Instead, he submitted himself fully to the Father and used his divine attributes as directed by his Father. His food, as he said, was "to do the will" of his "Father who sent" him.

God the Father planned that his Son would be robed and divested of his outward glory that people on earth wouldn't recognize him. Isaiah said, "he had not beauty that people would desire him" (Isa 53:2). He wasn't displaying the glorious nature of his being. He divested himself of the outward manifestation of his glory except at the Mount of Transfiguration when his clothing shine because he was unveiling his glory to his inner circle of Peter, James, and John.

### He Restricted His Presence (2:7b)

**Philippians 2:6-7a** | He... emptied himself, by taking the form of a servant, being born in the likeness of men.

Christ took on the nature of a slave. When Christ took on the "form of a servant [slave]," he adopted the *nature* and *being* of a slave. The sovereign became the subject. He did this by taking on a human nature. This taking on was an emptying, as Christ so dramatically demonstrated when he stripped himself in the Upper Room and washed the disciples' feet. Christ did not *exchange* the form of God for the form of a slave. Rather he *manifested* the form of God in the form of a slave.[50]

One of the most overlooked aspects of our Lord's coming to earth is the restriction that it placed on his presence. When we read of Christ "taking the form of a bondservant, and coming in the likeness of men," do we understand that Jesus gave up his unbounded universal freedom, instead being confined in a human body that in turn was confined to a country no bigger than Palestine? When we are told that Jesus took the form of a bondservant, the same word is employed that describes Jesus as being in the form of God. Jesus was in the form of God and He took upon himself the form of a bondservant. His human nature was authentic in substance and reality. C.S. Lewis said it this way:

> The Eternal Being, who knows everything and who created the whole universe, became not only a man but (before that) a baby, and before

---

[50] Ibid., 84–85.

that a fetus inside a Woman's body. If you want to get the hang of it, think how you would like to become a slug or a crab.[51]

### He Realized His Purpose (2:8)

The descent bottoms out as we read about Christ's purpose of dying and giving his life to atone for the sins of the world.

> **Philippians 2:8** | And being found in human form, he humbled himself by becoming obedient to the point of death, even death on a cross.

The death of Jesus Christ was not an accident. It was in the program of God from before the foundation of the world. Nearly one-third of the material in the Gospels is devoted to his days in the shadow of the cross, because the very purpose for his coming was his death. The writer of the book of Hebrews made it very clear that our Lord was made man for one supreme reason: "But we see Jesus, who was made a little lower than the angels, for the suffering of death … that he, by the grace of God, might taste death for everyone" (Heb 2:9). "Inasmuch then as the children have partaken of flesh and blood, he himself likewise shared in the same, that through death he might destroy him who had the power of death, that is, the devil" (Heb 2:14). Paul sums it up for the Corinthians. "For he made him who knew no sin to be sin for us, that we might become the righteousness of God in him" (2 Cor 5:21, NKJV).

## THE PRACTICE OF HUMILITY (2:9-11)

We have a great motivation to be humble here today: Jesus is Lord! He has no competition. Because of Jesus humble death on the cross, death is defeated, and Jesus is exalted. We should live a life of devotion, reverence, and worship for our Lord Jesus Christ. He is worthy that each of us should bow the knee and proclaim him as Lord.

### The Father Exalts Christ

> **Philippians 2:9** | Therefore God has highly exalted him and bestowed on him the name that is above every name.

---

[51] C.S. Lewis. *Mere Christianity* (New York: Collier Books, 1952), 154-155.

Look back to Christ's resurrection. He defeated death. God exalted him and gave him a name above every name. This great doctrinal passage is a systematic Christology. Here we learn of Christ's preexistence, his incarnation, his humiliation, his crucifixion, and now his ascension and exaltation.

The ascension of Christ at the end of forty days is clearly documented by Luke in Acts 1:9–11. Liberal scholars like to say the ascension was just a story told to express the way the church felt about Jesus at the time of his death. But Luke's record is an eyewitness account of the ascension of our Lord into heaven. In fact, Luke employed five different terms for "sight" to assure the historicity of this event. We are told that the disciples "watched," that he was "taken up ... out of their sight," that they "looked steadfastly toward heaven as he went up," that the angels asked them why they were "gazing up into heaven," and that they were told that the same Jesus would return to earth in like manner "as you saw him go into heaven."

## All People & Angels Exalt Christ

> **Philippians 2:10-11** | So that at the name of Jesus every knee should bow, in heaven and on earth and under the earth, [11] and every tongue confess that Jesus Christ is Lord, to the glory of God the Father.

The ascension was the beginning of his exaltation, for Christ is now seated at the right hand of the Father in heaven. Paul looked beyond this day, however, to a yet future day when every knee will be made to bow before him, and every tongue will be caused to confess that he is Lord to the glory of God the Father. At the mere mention of his name, everyone above the earth will bow, including all the good angels and all the redeemed who have died before Christ returns. Everyone on the earth will bow, including all human beings. Everyone under the earth will bow, including all the inhabitants of hell and all the evil angels. And in that moment, the cycle will have been completed. The One who was humiliated will be exalted. The One who was brought low will be raised up high and revealed to be the King and God of all creation.

## All Confess Christ as Yahweh

> **Philippians 2:11** | And every tongue confess that Jesus Christ is Lord, to the glory of God the Father.

All will make the universal confession: Jesus Christ is Lord. This comes from Isaiah (45:23), and it refers to Yahweh. Paul's language is unmistakable. All kings and presidents all flesh, both rich and poor will bow with all angelic beings, and we will all confess that Jesus Christ is Yahweh.

Peter put it this way: "Therefore humble yourselves under the mighty hand of God, that he may exalt you in due time" (1 Pet 5:6). James said, "Humble yourselves in the sight of the Lord, and He will lift you up" (4:10). Three times in his ministry Jesus spoke on the text: "Whoever exalts himself will be humbled, and he who humbles himself will be exalted" (Mt 23:12; Lk 14:11; 18:14). Since Christ humbled himself, we must be willing to humble ourselves, and as we continue to live in humble obedience to his will, we can anticipate our moment of exaltation some future day.

Before God can bless us, we need to be completely humbled. We need to see the majestic exaltation of Jesus and take the low position as he did. Consider some Scriptures. "When pride comes, then comes disgrace, but with humility comes wisdom" (Pro 11:2). "Pride brings a person low, but the lowly in spirit gain honor" (Pro 29:23). "Humility is the fear of the Lord; its wages are riches and honor and life" (Pro 22:4). "Humble yourselves, therefore, under God's mighty hand, that he may lift you up in due time" (1 Pet 5:6). "If my people, who are called by my name, will humble themselves and pray and seek my face and turn from their wicked ways, then I will hear from heaven, and I will forgive their sin and will heal their land" (2 Chron 7:14). "Wisdom's instruction is to fear the Lord, and humility comes before honor" (Pro 15:33).

## Conclusion

Christ is exalted! Bow the knee before him. No other mind should be in the Christian but the mind of Christ. We should all be robed in humility and meekness before him. He is King of kings. We are his humble servants. We are God's children. If you are without Christ, turn to him now. Whether you do it now or when it is too late, you will still have to bow before your Creator and God, Jesus Christ. Every knee shall bow, and every tongue will confess that Jesus Christ is Lord.

# 9 | 1 PETER 2:12-13
## HOW CAN I CHANGE?

*Work out your own salvation with fear and trembling,
for it is God who works in you, both to will
and to work for his good pleasure.*
PHILIPPIANS 2:12-13

Have you ever set out to help someone, not really knowing what you were doing or how you were going to do it? Have you ever tried to tackle some gnawing problem in your own life but didn't have a clue about how to get started? Christopher Columbus experienced this problem when he set out to find a westward passage to Asia. Because he had little idea about what he was doing, someone proposed the following award in his memory for those who emulate him. I had to laugh when I heard of the parodied "Christopher Columbus Award."

> Citation: This award goes to those who, like good old Chris, when they set out to do something, don't know where they are going; neither do they know how to get there. When they arrive, they don't know where they are, and when they return, they don't know where they've been. (Source Unknown)

Tragically, many Christians set out in life with little more understanding of what they are doing than had Mr. Columbus. While he possessed no accurate charts to lead him to Asia, the journey that we take as believers was very carefully mapped out for us by the Captain of our salvation. [52]

> **Philippians 2:12-13** | Therefore, my beloved, as you have always obeyed, so now, not only as in my presence but much more in my absence, work out your own salvation with fear and trembling, [13] for it is God who works in you, both to will and to work for his good pleasure.

Paul's pattern in all his letters is to explain doctrine, and how it leads to duty and doxology. Paul says: Christ humbled himself for you. He was obedient unto death for you. He is exalted and ruling the world for your good. Therefore: what? Because Christ is your substitute and saves you from the wrath of God, and because he is your Lord: King of all kings and Lord of all lords: therefore... "work out your own salvation in fear and trembling" (2:12b).

Information should always lead to transformation. Is Jesus exalted on high? Is that seen in your life? If what happens on Sunday doesn't change our Monday, then our Sunday doesn't matter. We are not here just to sit and soak, but to live changed and abundant lives because of Jesus Christ. Seeing the glory and wonder of his cross and sacrifice for me changes everything. Seeing his exaltation in heaven changes and transforms me. I no longer want to worship the things that are in this world. I want to worship him.

Christ died and rose again not only for our justification, to make us right with God, but for our sanctification—to make us conformed into his image. Let's get on the edge of our seats and be ready to live differently. Let's be changed into Christ's image.

Christ laid aside his divine prerogatives. He emptied himself of his right to defend himself. Remember he said, "Are you not aware that I can call on my Father, and he will at once put at my disposal more than twelve legions [*50 to 100K*] of angels?" (Mt 26:53). He refused to defend himself or stand up for his divine rights as God, but instead was obedient to the Father, even unto death on a cross.

---

[52] Jim Berg, *Changed Into His Image* (Greenville, SC: JourneyForth, 1996).

## SPIRITUAL GROWTH IS PERSONAL (2:12)

This is your own salvation. It's your walk of sanctification. This is different than justification. In justification, we are passive, dead in trespasses and sins. In sanctification we are very much alive and applying the redemption we have in Christ to life. Christ did it all in justifying us. Now we cooperate with God in our sanctification. Having been made alive, we work out our salvation by the grace and power of God working within us. God's work in us results in hard work through us.

### A Transcendent Labor

> **Philippians 2:12** | Therefore, my beloved, as you have always obeyed, so now, not only as in my presence but much more in my absence, work out your own salvation with fear and trembling.

Spiritual growth is a personal submission to the sovereignty of God. Paul wasn't concerned with the Philippians pleasing him. He wanted them to please God when there was no one around. He wanted them to practice the presence of God.

God is sovereign. He's put you where he's put you in order for your maximum growth. We believe this right? This is the truth of Romans 8:28-29, "And we know that for those who love God all things work together for good, for those who are called according to his purpose. 29 For those whom he foreknew he also predestined to be conformed to the image of his Son." Some days the state you are in is hard. I'm not talking about the cold winters in Illinois. I'm talking about marriage or singleness. It's hard to be single. You feel left out in a couple's world. But let me remind you that Jesus was single. Paul was single. Being single is hard in some ways. Yet Paul says it's better to be single so you can dedicate yourself to unhindered service for Christ. Well, maybe you say, if I was only married to a really godly spouse, I'd be able to better grow. Nope. That's not how it works. If you are not growing now, you won't grow if you are married. The same could be said about married people. I'd grow if I had a better spouse. Nope. Sorry. God gave you the spouse he gave you for maximum growth. God is sovereign, and the only way we can grow is by practicing the presence of God. It's not about pleasing people or pastors. It's all about pleasing the Lord.

What exactly does it mean to work out our salvation? It means the degree to which you yield to the indwelling Spirit impacts the work he'll achieve through you and the changes he will affect in your life. You need to yield and choose to cooperate with the Spirit. Paul says in Galatians 5:16, "Keep in step with the Spirit." God's Spirit transcends our thoughts, our heart, our every action.

## A Strenuous Labor

**Philippians 2:12b** | Work out your own salvation...

Spiritual growth is a strenuous labor. It requires hard work. Are you going to add to your faith or not? Christ asks the question, "Why do you call me 'Lord, Lord,' and not do what I tell you?" (Luke 6:46). In other words, salvation always results in the believer working hard, following the Lord in obedience. Peter says in 2 Peter 1:5, "make every effort to add to your faith..." Growing in godliness is hard work. There is no place for laziness. We must exert ourselves to obedience with diligence. The believer is anything but passive in sanctification. And because our eyes have been opened to the absolute joy in Jesus, we know there is no happiness outside of growth. Look how Peter describes spiritual growth. It's enlightening.

> His divine power has granted to us all things that pertain to life and godliness, through the knowledge of him who called us to his own glory and excellence, ⁴ by which he has granted to us his precious and very great promises, so that through them you may become partakers of the divine nature, having escaped from the corruption that is in the world because of sinful desire. ⁵ For this very reason, make every effort to supplement your faith with virtue, and virtue with knowledge, ⁶ and knowledge with self-control, and self-control with steadfastness, and steadfastness with godliness, ⁷ and godliness with brotherly affection, and brotherly affection with love. ⁸ For if these qualities are yours and are increasing, they keep you from being ineffective or unfruitful in the knowledge of our Lord Jesus Christ. ⁹ For whoever lacks these qualities is so nearsighted that he is blind, having forgotten that he was cleansed from his former sins. ¹⁰ Therefore, brothers, be all the more diligent to confirm your calling and election, for if you practice these qualities, you will never fall. ¹¹ For in this way there will be richly provided for you an entrance into the eternal kingdom of our Lord and Savior Jesus Christ. —*2 Peter 1:3-11*

This is hard work. If we don't work hard, Peter says we'll be ineffective, unfruitful, so nearsighted we are blind. We'll could even forget we are cleansed from our former sins. Instead, we need to work hard and practice these qualities so that we never fall and backslide.

Spiritual growth is compared to an athletic event. Paul said, "train yourself for godliness" (1 Tim 4:7). "I have fought the good fight, I have finished the race, I have kept the faith" (2 Tim 4:7).

Spiritual growth is compared to a battle or war. "Therefore, take up the full armor of God, so that you will be able to resist in the evil day, and having done everything, to stand firm" (Eph 6:13). Paul says, "I have fought the good fight" (2 Tim 4:7). "Endure hardness like a good soldier of Jesus Christ" (2 Tim 2:3, KJV).

Spiritual growth is like working a mine, a field. Paul says: "work out your own salvation." Interestingly, the word translated "work out" was the same Greek term popularly used for "working a mine" or "working a field." In each case there were benefits that followed such diligence. The mine would yield valuable elements or ore. The field would yield crops. All the properties are there to prosper, but you have to work it. Paul's point is clear: As we work out our salvation, we everything we need to grow in Christlikeness.[53] God's given us the seed, but we need to water it and work it so it will grow. God's given us the mine, but we need to retrieve the precious metals to enjoy their riches.

In another place Paul says: "Him we proclaim, warning everyone and teaching everyone with all wisdom, that we may present everyone mature in Christ. For this I toil, struggling with all his energy that he powerfully works within me" (Col 1:28–29). Paul toils. Paul struggles. If we would do good for others, so must we. Do you ever wonder how to exercise spiritual power? Maybe people will tell you, "Eat this." "Say these words." "Pray this prayer." "Read this author." "Have this experience." "Go to this conference." "Look inside yourself." But no! Spiritual power is exercised in strenuous self-giving service for others. The word for struggling in Colossians 1:29 can also be translated as "agony." Which is to say, agony rather than ecstasy is the way to spiritual power. Do you want to know the power of God and a faith that works? Then give yourself over to the struggle of working for the good of others, even as Christ himself worked and struggled for our good. True Christian faith is not lazy faith. It is faith that works, like Paul's.[54]

---

[53] Charles R. Swindoll. *Laugh Again* (Nashville: Thomas Nelson, 1991), 97.
[54] Mark Dever. *Discipling* (9marks: Building Healthy Churches) (Wheaton: Crossway, 2016), 30-31.

## A Personal Labor

**Philippians 2:12b** | Work out your own salvation...

Spiritual growth is a personal responsibility. When Paul says "work out your own salvation" he's referring to an aspect of our salvation that we might call "sanctification" or simply *spiritual growth*. We are called to work hard at our own spiritual growth. Paul says you are called to "work out your own salvation." It's intensely personal. God put his Spirit in you. The living God has indwelt you. Your mom and dad can't live this out for you. Your pastor, your spiritual leader, your teachers cannot live this out for you. It's on you. Work out at your own salvation, your progressive spiritual growth. It's personal. It's your personal responsibility. No one else can walk with God for you. This is your walk. So, work, because God works in you.

It's your responsibility alone to grow in Christ. Listen, there are people that you will look to in the Christian life, that will let you down. There will be others that you really want to help you, but they are unavailable. Ultimately, your growth in Christ is your responsibility.

You cannot tie your growth in Christ to anyone else. Pastors are great. Godly examples are fantastic. Teachers are heroic. Parents who love Jesus are indispensable. But at the end of the day, you must trust in Christ and in Christ alone. "There is one mediator between God and man, the man Christ Jesus" (1 Tim 2:5). And salvation comes by him and him alone.

Here's the point: if you are not changing, it's not anyone else's fault. If you are not growing and changing, it's on you. Spiritual growth is your responsibility. If you aren't growing, you can't blame it on anything but you. I'm not growing because I'm single. If I only had a spouse. I'm not growing because of my marriage. If I only had a better spouse. I'm not growing because of my church. If I only had a better pastor. I'm not growing because of my job. If I only had a better job. I'm not growing because... you get the idea, right? Spiritual growth is your responsibility. You are called to "work out your own salvation." It's a personal commitment.

I think about my responsibility to grow in relationship with my wife. It's personal. Just imagine that Jill and I are getting ready for date night. And I say, "Jill, I know it's date night, but I'm going to have William take my place. He'll be just as good as me I promise..." Which one of you could take my place? No, no, no! That's not really how it works. The relationship can only get better and grow if I take personal responsibility to shepherd Jill and care for her and listen to her. It's intensely personal. I've got to commit for it to flourish.

It's the same way with God. No one is going to grow for you. If you are not growing in your walk with Christ, it's not anyone else's fault but yours. Sure other people can help you, but you are ultimately responsible for your growth. Growth has to be a priority in your life whether on not that person you've depended upon is there or not. You have to make this decision to prioritize your walk with God to "work out your own salvation." Ultimately Christ will build his church. Your ultimate shepherds are not on the elder team at your local church. As elders and pastors we do our best, but we are all sinners. There is only one truly Good Shepherd, and his name is Jesus Christ. Christ is the vine and you are the branches. You must be sure you are connected to the vine. You must be sure you are walking closely with him.

## A Practical Labor

Here is a few suggestions on how you can grow. Now realize that you cannot do any of these things in your own power. It is the Spirit of God in you that works as you strain and agonize toward a goal. It is not our own power that can do anything. Jesus says, "Without me you can do nothing" (Jn 15:5). We must struggle, as Paul said, "with all his energy that he powerfully works within me" (Col 1:29). With that in mind, be Spirit-filled in some of the following activities. Read the word – choose a topic or a book study or a Bible plan but get into the word! Get involved in ministry – don't just sit on your spiritual gifts. Use them! Pray – pray privately. Join the prayer mid-week prayer meeting. Fellowship – join a small group. Have church folk over to your home. Bring a meal to a sick person. Start a journal to record your spiritual growth – take notes for sermons and teachings. Record answers to prayer. Disciple a young believer – some of you know the Bible so well, but much of your knowledge is wasted. Find a new believer and begin praying for them. Have them over. Go through a book of the Bible together. Go through a basic discipleship study with an elder or spiritual leader.

## SPIRITUAL GROWTH IS PROGRESSIVE (2:12)

**Philippians 2:12-13** | Therefore, my beloved, as you have always obeyed, so now, not only as in my presence but much more in my absence, work out your own salvation with fear and trembling, <sup>13</sup> for it is God who works in you, both to will and to work for his good pleasure.

Wayne Grudem says in his very helpful Systematic Theology:

Sanctification is a progressive work of God and man that makes us more and more free from sin and like Christ in our actual lives.[55]

We are to "grow in grace, and in the knowledge of our Lord and Savior Jesus Christ" (2 Pet 3:18). Paul says growth is a process. "And we all, with unveiled face, beholding the glory of the Lord, are being transformed into the same image from one degree of glory to another. For this comes from the Lord who is the Spirit" (2 Cor 3:18). To continue to grow you need to daily be "renewed in the spirit of your minds" (Eph 4:23).

Why do we need to work out our salvation? Isn't it already "worked out"? Didn't Christ do that on the cross? Isn't our salvation finished? Yes, from God's perspective, our salvation is finished. Christ gave the victory shout from his cross: "It is finished!" In that sense we are complete in Jesus. But we need to see our salvation from a bird's eye view: past, present, and future.

Theologically, we can speak of our salvation in the past, present and future. The Bible says "by grace you have been saved." That's *justification*. The Scripture also says you are "being saved" – day by day you are being conformed to Christ's image. That's *sanctification*. One day, when Christ returns, your salvation will be complete, and you will be given a renewed, immortal body that cannot sin, like Christ's glorious body. That's *glorification*. Calvin said, "salvation is taken to mean the entire course of our calling, and that this term includes all things by which God accomplishes that perfection to which he has determined us by his free election."[56]

---

[55] Grudem, *Systematic Theology*, 746.
[56] Silva. *Philippians*, 118-119.

## Justification: An Event

We considered Christ humbling himself to the point of death on the cross – he was obedient unto death. It is finished. My justification is complete. I'm saved. I'm completely righteous in Christ. Nothing can separate me from the love of God in Christ. That's glorious news. Can I ask you, have you been born again? There is a sense in which our salvation is an event. It is a line of demarcation. You pass from death unto life. You are transferred from the kingdom of darkness to the kingdom of his glorious Son. You turn from idols to serve the living God. You are born-again. That's an event. That's our justification. We trust in Christ's work on the cross, and sin is finished for us. He made an end of sin for us. There is now no penalty for sin, no condemnation. We are perfectly holy and righteous before God. We are adopted into his family. Now we can never work for this. We have to receive the perfect work of Christ by faith. Justification is not at all by human effort, but by the free gift of God.

## Sanctification: A Journey

But there is a part of our salvation that is unfinished and incomplete because it is a process. The penalty for sin is removed, but the power of sin is being removed as a process. There is a salvation that God has worked in us, but now he wants to work it out of us. We call that progressive sanctification. It doesn't happen overnight. We are "being saved." We are "predestined to be conformed into the image of God's dear Son" (Rom 8:29).

So the second part of our salvation is a work deep in our hearts through the Holy Spirit. As many are purchased by the blood of Christ will be, throughout their lives, renewed in the spirit of their mind. The Spirit of God in regeneration indwells the Christian and creates in him or her a new nature. But the old nature is never completely eradicated. It stays around like a little monster that terrorizes us. We have to put it to death by choosing to obey God's word and rely on the Spirit's infinite power in us. There is a fierce battle every day for the Christian. It's hard work. That's what this text is all about. The seed that the Spirit plants in us is his own presence, and He is perfect. But the process is not perfect. It takes place at different speeds for people.

So when we are born again, we are like a baby or like a tree, and we need to grow! Our new nature has all the elements of perfection, but it needs to be (as our text says) "worked out with fear and trembling." There is a seriousness and a sweat and a deep divinely authored commitment that God gives every Christian to grow in Christ.

God has already worked in us first and given us everything we need in his Spirit and in a new heart and a new nature to overcome the old nature. No longer can sin ever have complete and total dominion over us. Even in Christians who backslide, they never stop hearing the voice of the Spirit and their own conscience. So as we look at these verses, Paul is not telling us to work out our justification that we have already obtained by Christ's blood. Christ did it all. We can add nothing to that. We are perfectly righteous before the throne of God in heaven because of Jesus. But what we are talking about is your inner spiritual life. God has wrought something powerful and eternal in you. That's something that can never be undone. You are loved and perfect before God's throne. But now you have to take what God has done in you and "work it out."

## Glorification: Our Final Destination

And one day Christ will come, and we will be perfected in his likeness. I can't wait for that day! That's called glorification. It's our final destination. When you look at Romans 13:11, Paul says that our salvation is nearer to us now than when we first believed. What does that mean? It is nearer to us now than when we first believed? It doesn't mean that we are still working on our salvation, trying to earn it. That is not what it means. Instead, what it means is the future glorification, culmination of our salvation, is still to come, and we are now closer now than when we first believed. I am guessing, by the nature of the fact that you are breathing this moment, that you haven't experienced that final facet of salvation, but it could be today. For all who have been born again, I remind you that there is coming a day when we will see his face, and we will be reconciled to God in his fullness forever.

We are talking about our sanctification. And the real question is: as a Christian, how can I change? Now if you are not a Christian, you cannot change in any meaningful eternal way. You are dead in your trespasses and sins. But if you are a new creation in Christ, you will be growing and changing every day. Your spiritual growth is progressive. We all know you can't pay anyone to get in shape for you. You can't pay someone to eat right for you. No one can exercise for you. You can be very rich and very out of shape. Paying someone else to exercise doesn't get you in shape. If they could pay someone to exercise for them, they would. It doesn't work that way. Same goes for our spiritual life. It's your soul. It's your life. It's your vitality. How strong do you want to be in your walk with God?

God's given you the all the tools you need for spiritual growth. Work out your own salvation, for God is working in you. God's given you everything you need to for spiritual growth. You are blessed with "every spiritual blessing" in Christ Jesus (Eph 1:3). You have "everything for life and godliness" (2 Pet 1:3). You have been made to be "partakers of the divine nature" (2 Pet 1:4). "Those who seek the Lord lack no good thing" (Psa 34:10).

You may not progress at the rate of everyone else, but every Christian will grow. It's a promise. We need to recognize that there are different speeds of progress in growth in the Christian's life. Growth is not always at the same speed. There are many falls and times when a Christian grieves the Holy Spirit along the way. We cry out all along the way, "Wretched man that I am! Who will deliver me from this body of death?" (Rom 7:24). And that is the whole point. A genuine Christian is constantly aware of his sin. He is constantly clinging to Christ as the only Savior and way of escape.

## SPIRITUAL GROWTH IS PRAISE-DRIVEN (2:12).

Working out our salvation is easier when we are supervised, but Paul says we can't rely on human supervision alone.

> **Philippians 2:12-13** | Therefore, my beloved, as you have always obeyed, so now, not only as in my presence but much more in my absence, work out your own salvation with fear and trembling, [13] for it is God who works in you, both to will and to work for his good pleasure.

### The Focus of Our Praise

Paul says your spiritual growth is not about my human supervision. He says: whether I'm with you as an apostle or away, whether I live or die, in my presence, but much more in my absence, "work out your own salvation with fear and trembling." Why fear and trembling? Because it's God who you are focusing on. There is an awe and wonder that God is working in us. It's for "his good pleasure." It's because God is always present. We are aware of his presence with us. Human supervision alone is not enough because we are wayward. "All we like sheep have gone astray..." (Isa 53:6). We are, as the hymn says, "prone to wander." We need the active ministry of the Holy Spirit in us.

Anyone remember gym class? You remember Physical Education class? Get going with some calisthenics. The gym teacher says, "Do 30 jumping jacks." And you get going and start trying to do them. While the teacher is there you there doing them, but when the teacher goes around the corner, you stop. For some Christians, that's their Christianity.

Sunday morning comes around. We are praising God. We are in the word. We are in prayer. Monday morning, Tuesday morning... not happening. The pastor's not there to help you. Hopefully you have some people in your life to propel you forward spiritually, but you can't ultimately depend on that. That's why Paul says, "but much more in my absence, work out your own salvation with fear and trembling..." All the more, you need to focus on God with "fear and trembling"! It's hard to grow spiritually when no one's around, but perhaps the most important part of your walk is what happens when no one's around to remind you. No one else can walk with God for you.

Ultimately my most powerful motivator for spiritual growth has to be the glory of God. My motivation cannot be to be approved by my spouse or my church. My motivation can't be to change my situation or change another person. My motivation has to be the glory of God. "Whether you eat or drink, or whatever you do, do all to the glory of God" (1 Cor 10:31). We can't grow by focusing on people. We must focus on God. Look at Christ's example. Look at the majesty of God. Enjoy the comfort of the Holy Spirit as he speaks to you and guides you through the word. If you start looking at people, you will become bitter and despairing, and you will lose focus.

Isaiah got a vision of God, and he preached to a whole nation, even though they were disobedient. When you get a vision of God, and an awareness of God's presence, you overcome your sinful desires. You cannot listen to your flesh. Your emotions, Ephesians 4 says are deceitful. Your heart still lies to you. You can't trust your heart. That's why if you want to grow spiritually you need the word of God. You've got to get an awareness of God.

## The Fear of Our Praise

Growing Christians have an awareness of God's presence. There is a seriousness. It's a priority not because of Paul who may or may not be with them. It's a priority because God is always with us. That's the reason there is this awe and seriousness.

> **Philippians 2:12-13** | Therefore, my beloved, as you have always obeyed, so now, not only as in my presence but much more in my absence, work out your own salvation with fear and trembling, [13] for it is God who works in you, both to will and to work for his good pleasure.

The fear of the Lord is the beginning of wisdom. A growing Christian understands that there is an awareness of God that breeds fear, but not slavish dread. The fear of God is an awe and reverence for God. The question is asked in Hebrews 2:3, "How shall we escape if we neglect such a great salvation?" Christians understand and treasure Christ. They fear not honoring him. They tremble at that. Paul is not advocating a slavish terror, but a wholesome self-distrust. The Christian should fear lest his will not be continually surrendered to Christ, or lest the carnal traits of character should control the life. He must fear to trust his own strength, to withdraw his hand from the hand of Christ, or to attempt to walk the Christian pathway alone. Such fear leads to vigilance against temptation, to humility of mind, to taking heed lest we fall.

## SPIRITUAL GROWTH IS PREDESTINED (2:13)

> **Philippians 2:12b-13** | Work out your own salvation with fear and trembling, [13] for it is God who works in you, both to will and to work for his good pleasure.

### God's Plan Reaches Beyond Time

Why do I say your salvation is predestined? God made this promise in so many places in Scripture. You are saved by grace through faith, "not of works." Yet... "God has foreordained your good works that you should walk in them" (Eph 2:10). "You are predestined to be conformed to the image of God's dear Son" (Rom 8:30). "God chose you before the foundation of the world that you should be holy and without blame before him" (Eph 1:4). The Apostle Peter said: We are "elect...according to the foreknowledge of God the Father, in the sanctification of the Spirit, for obedience to Jesus Christ" (1 Pet 1:1-2).

## God's Plan Requires Your Cooperation

So how can I change? The answer: you cooperate with the grace of God. The only way you can work out your salvation is if God is working already in you. You work out what God is working in you. When you were born again, you were given the down payment of your salvation: the Spirit of God. You got your first installment of heaven (Eph 3:14). The Greek word for our work and God's work is the same. We get our word "energy" or "energize" from it. God energizes your work. His Spirit indwells you.

## God's Plan Guarantees Your Growth

A true child of God is "predestined to be conformed to the image of God's Son" (Rom 8:29). The Apostle Paul was comforted by God's promise to sanctify his people. "I am sure of this, that he who began a good work in you will bring it to completion at the day of Jesus Christ" (Phil 1:6). Paul also said, "Now may the God of peace himself sanctify you completely, and may your whole spirit and soul and body be kept blameless at the coming of our Lord Jesus Christ. 24 He who calls you is faithful; he will surely do it" (1 Thess 5:23-24).

Long ago, God made a promise to guarantee your spiritual growth. He told the Prophet Ezekiel: "I will give you a new heart, and a new spirit I will put within you. And I will remove the heart of stone from your flesh and give you a heart of flesh. 27 And I will put my Spirit within you, and cause you to walk in my statutes and be careful to obey my rules" (Eze 36:26-27). King David said, "The steps of a good man are ordered by the LORD, and He delights in his way. 24 Though he fall, he shall not be utterly cast down; for the Lord upholds him with His hand" (Psa 37:23-24). God works out what he has already worked in you. What has he worked in you? A new heart. He's put his Spirit in you. Now, your "body is the Temple of the Holy Spirit" (2 Cor 6:19).

He works in you by his Spirit so that you can have total victory in any area of your life. Once you have trusted Jesus as Savior, you can begin living out what He's given you, which is his abundant life. If you've given your heart to him, the Holy Spirit now indwells you—he is with you forever. It is God's Spirit working in and through you that empowers you to live out your salvation.

## God's Plan Rejects Laziness

There is great tension in spiritual growth. Our justification is all God. We are dead in our trespasses and sins. He has to raise us from the dead. But once we are alive in Christ, we are to apply that redemption. That's spiritual growth. Let me show you the tension in the Scriptures. If my sanctification is predestined, why do I need to work it out? The answer: God is working out his sovereign plan through you. The point is, because you have a new heart with new desires, you *want* to work out his plan through your life.

### *Tension in Evangelism*

Jesus says, "I will build my church..." right (Mt 16:18)? But then he tells us to build and to "Go into all the world and preach the gospel to every creature" (Mk 16:15) and "make disciples of every nation" (Mt 28:20). Paul says, "God gives the increase..." but that's not how evangelism works. We don't sit around saying: well God gives the increase. No, we strategize and go and preach. "Some plant. Some water. God gives the increase." God gives the supernatural growth (1 Cor 3:6-8).

### *Tension in Sanctification*

It's that way in our spiritual growth. We plant and water every day through prayer, the word, fellowship, instruction and teaching in the word. And God has to speak. To understand the principle of working out our salvation, remember what we learn from Ephesians 2:8-10. It says there that our salvation is "not of works," but that we are "created in Christ Jesus" as a new creation "for good works". Do you see the balance? God plants a seed in us, but we are called to water it. As we water it, God gives the supernatural growth. Paul says, "I am the least of the apostles, unworthy to be called an apostle, because I persecuted the church of God. 10 But by the grace of God I am what I am, and his grace toward me was not in vain. On the contrary, I worked harder than any of them, though it was not I, but the grace of God that is with me" (1 Cor 15:9-10). Paul worked so hard, but the power and ability to work came from God. We see the same thing here in Philippians 2:12-13. You have to "work out" what God has already "worked in" you. Work out your spiritual growth. Cultivate the life of Christ in you. God is working right along with you.

## Conclusion

This is your own salvation. It's your walk of sanctification. No one else can walk with God for you. This is your walk. Be encouraged to work, because God is working in you 24 and 7. One hundred per cent of the time, God is working in you his will and his good pleasure. We are called to "work out" what God has "worked in"! Amen!

I love remodeling. Years ago, we remodeled our church's parsonage. It was completely dilapidated and destroyed. What a joy that one of our deacons got a group of guys from Leopardo construction in Chicago to volunteer. Over the course of a month. The materials were supplied, and we worked hard to remodel the entire place. What a reconstruction project. We supplied the materials, but Leopardo supplied the workers. They went according to the plans of our architect which were formulated before they even began to work.

The Father is our architect. Jesus provided all we need through his death to reconcile us to God and grant us all the power we need through the Holy Spirit. The Lord has sent his Holy Spirit to remodel your life. He's given you everything to transform you. He wants you to participate. He's the great architect. Are you following him? Are you working out what God has already worked in you?

# 10 | PHILIPPIANS 2:14-18
## BE AN INFLUENCER!

*Do all things without grumbling or disputing, that you may be blameless and innocent, children of God without blemish in the midst of a crooked and twisted generation, among whom you shine as lights in the world.*
PHILIPPIANS 2:14-15

Imagine what it would be like to live in complete darkness. We sometimes fear in modern times what might happen if the electric grid was attacked or if it failed. But think about this. The electric lightbulb wasn't invented until 1882 and wasn't in widespread use until 1900. In 1925, less than a hundred years ago, only half of the homes in the U.S. had access to electricity. I think we agree that being in darkness is a terrible thing. We are grateful for modern electricity. But how much more grateful are we for spiritual light? Having a connection to God in your spiritual darkness makes all the difference.

Light is essential to our existence on the earth; most of us know that. Light is needed for the process of photosynthesis for plants. We need it to navigate through our lives. There are objects in front of us. Daniel 12:3 says, "Those who are wise will shine like the brightness of the heavens. And those who lead many to righteousness, like the stars, forever and ever." Physical light might be the greatest physical influencer of the world. If that is so, spiritual light is even more important.

We are called in Philippians 2 to influence the world. Four illustrations are given: life, light, word, and sacrifice. Paul says live the life. Shine as the stars. Speak the word. Give yourself as a sacrifice. We are called to influence the world to come to Christ and see people converted and transformed. You are a part of this if you are a Christian.

God fills us with his Spirit to grow his church. We are to help and love and disciple one another. But we must break out. We must not hide our lights under a bushel. The light shines, and the darkness cannot overcome it. You are not only to disciple one another. You are to make disciples of all nations. We've got to break out of the realm of this church and shine our lights in the world. That's what this passage (Phil 2:14-18) is all about. We are not just in this world to become intelligent Bible scholars. We are called to make disciples. True disciples of Christ make other disciples.

> **Philippians 2:14-18** | Do all things without grumbling or disputing, $^{15}$ that you may be blameless and innocent, children of God without blemish in the midst of a crooked and twisted generation, among whom you shine as lights in the world, $^{16}$ holding fast to the word of life, so that in the day of Christ I may be proud that I did not run in vain or labor in vain. $^{17}$ Even if I am to be poured out as a drink offering upon the sacrificial offering of your faith, I am glad and rejoice with you all. $^{18}$ Likewise you also should be glad and rejoice with me.

It's interesting that after some of the highest and holiest verses in the Bible (2:1-11), Paul's application is "stop complaining." We are naturally bent inwardly. Dear friends, the world will never be reached if we are self-focused. Satan's plan for us is to remain focused on our own hurts. If you can't get over your hurts, you will never get a heart for the world. Stop complaining and fighting. Absorb the hurts and serve! "Serve the Lord with gladness" (Psa 100:1). Lay down your life for the world.

The most sobering reality in the world today is that people are dying and going to hell today. Your family. Your friends. Your children. They may be going to hell. If you don't do something, they will depart from you forever. You will never touch them and hold them. Jesus' marching orders were for us to go!

> Go into all the world and proclaim the gospel to the whole creation.
> —Mark 16:15

> Go out to the highways and hedges and compel people to come in, that my house may be filled. —*Luke 14:23*
>
> Go therefore and make disciples of all nations. —*Matthew 28:19*

God says to Isaiah, "Who will go for us?" (Isa 6:8). "How shall they hear without a preacher?" (Rom 10:14). "Faith comes by hearing and hearing by the word of Christ" (Rom 10:17).

We are going to see four activities we can do to bring the gospel beyond the boundaries of your local church and your family.

## WE LIVE THE LIFE (2:14-15)

We are to be different from the world. We are to glow in the dark. It doesn't help if you shine the light right into people's faces. It also doesn't help much if you shine your light into the light. Before you do anything in evangelism, you have to live a life of contentment in God. You have to understand the joy of the Holy Spirit.

### An Appreciative Life

**Philippians 2:14** | Do all things without grumbling or disputing.

Complaining is a contradiction of Christian joy. Complaining stops your spiritual growth. It stops the witness of your life to the world. It hinders the gospel. This comes right after Paul says: work out all that God is working in you. Complaining stops the process. We are to be positive, hopeful people. Yes, we confront sin and error in our lives, but we have the good news. We never have anything to complain about.

Complaining sees only the little idol in front of you. "I want something" and if you don't get it you complain. It demonstrates a cold, self-centered heart. Complaining stops the work of God. It also stops our light from shining. Once you start complaining, you've stopped reflecting Jesus. Jesus said we are not to hide our light under a bushel. That's what complaining does. It stifles the work of the Holy Spirit.

> You are the light of the world. A city set on a hill cannot be hidden.[15] Nor do people light a lamp and put it under a basket, but on a stand, and it gives light to all in the house. [16] In the same way, let your light shine before others, so that they may see your good works and give glory to your Father who is in heaven. —*Matthew 5:15-16*

There was a man driving his car. A woman was driving behind him in another vehicle. They were at a stoplight. When the light turned green, the man in the lead car did not look up. He was looking down, maybe at his phone. But he didn't go. It's green. But his car didn't go. The lady in the car behind him did see it. And she let him know that she saw by honking the horn. She honked her horn. But the guy in the lead car didn't budge, didn't move, didn't look up. So she honked it again.

She's getting a little mad at this time, rolled down her window and yelled. Nothing happened. But just when the light turned yellow, right before it turned red, he looked up, noticed it, and zoomed through the intersection, leaving the woman to go through another whole light cycle. Well now, she's fuming. And she rolls her window down, puts her arm out, and gives a certain gesture. I don't need to go any further than that. She yells some very choice words, ranting, raving, pounding the steering wheel. And just then, she noticed a police officer with a gun pointed saying, "Ma'am, I want to see both hands. I'm going to open the car door with your hands up. I want you to get out of the vehicle."

So she gets out of the vehicle. The police puts her arms behind her, puts her in handcuffs, and takes her to jail. She's in a cell for two hours. After two hours, that same police officer lets her out and says, ma'am, I'm very sorry for the misunderstanding. But you just have to know that, as I was listening to the words you were saying and I was watching the gesture you were making, and I was watching you ranting, and raving, and going through those contortions, and I had also noticed on the back of your vehicle the What Would Jesus Do? Bumper sticker, and the little Chrome fish that's on your trunk, and the Follow Me to Sunday School license plate holder. Naturally, I assumed that you had stolen the car. Fair enough, right? The message on the back of the car was very different from the message coming from inside the car.

Grumbling and complaining do not add to the light. The wording here is very similar to Exodus when the children of Israel were complaining against God. Complaining is whining selfishly. That's adding darkness to the darkness. We are called to shine the light by giving hope. What does complaining do? Does it edify? Does it help people be conformed to Christ's image?

Complaining is calling too much attention to the darkness without any solution. We are gospel people. We are good news people. Complaining is nothing but the bad news. If we call attention to a problem, we as Christ's people give the good news.

Complaining is the opposite of rejoicing. We are not to be grumbling against our brothers and sisters or questioning the wisdom and care of God. It is the opposite of working you're your salvation in God's strength. Christians should be the most joyful human beings on the planet. We are not getting what we deserve.

We should "rejoice in the Lord always, and again I say, rejoice" (Phil 4:4). When we complain we are questioning the goodness of God. "Whatever we do, it should be "all for the glory of God" (1 Cor 10:31). When we see something wrong, Christians are to be a part of the solution. Sometimes Christians are like a person with limburger cheese stuck up their nose. Everything stinks. Instead, we ought to be the most hopeful people. We are those who have the aroma of Christ. We believe Christ can do anything since he raised us from the spiritually dead.

We are to be "good newsers" not complainers. The fruit of the Spirit does not include complaining. Complaining is the fruit of impatience and self-centeredness. We should notice problems, but our attitude should be always hopeful.

## A Hopeful Life

**Philippians 2:14** | Do all things without grumbling or disputing.

The Bible commands us to be hopeful Christians, not complainers. "All things work together for good!" (Rom 8:28) is still a part of our Bible. "For I know the plans I have for you, declares the LORD, plans to prosper you and not to harm you, plans to give you hope and a future" (Jer 29:11). "He who did not spare his own Son but gave him up for us all, how will he not also with him graciously give us all things?" (Rom 8:32).

Something happened last year, called an eclipse. We could see that an object much, much, much smaller than the sun could actually block the Earth from the rays of the sun. So it passed between the Earth and the sun blocking the rays. And in some places, it was a total eclipse. It's marvelous to see that. Now, what happened last year, that eclipse, must never happen with us. We must never block the glory of the son, S-O-

N, the Son of God. In all of his radiance and glory, we by our lives must never diminish that glow. But we should reflect that glow.

Complaining keeps us from using our spiritual gifts. When you see a problem, it's never ok to complain. It's time to love and to disciple. What does complaining point to? It points to an eclipsed heart. Complaining points to a heart that is not willing to do what it takes to make disciples.

## A Happy Life

Paul begins by saying how different Christians should be. We are not ones who are complaining. As Christians, we have the ability and opportunity to be God-focused instead of self-focused.

**Philippians 2:14** | Do all things without grumbling or disputing.

We as Christians have nothing to complain about. We bring to light things that need change, but never for the sake of being negative. Christians ought to be positive people. We ought to be the most joyous people on the planet. Complaining reveals a discontented soul. A healthy Christian has a heart that is always full of praise!

We are called to a certain attitude of service in all the things we do. As we are working out what God has worked in, we are to have a level of joy and gladness. "Serve the Lord with gladness" (Psa 100:1). "The joy of the LORD is my strength" (Neh 8:10). "Let everything that has breath praise the LORD! Praise the LORD!" (Psa 150:6)

We are like "lights" in a dark world. This begins by having a life free from complaining and filled with gratitude. The "all things" that the Christian is to "do" is a broad, all-inclusive statement that encompasses all things that God calls us to do in our lives—at home, work, school, church, and play, and in all areas of marriage, parenting, friendship, and ministry. There is nothing in our lives that is not touched by an attitude of blessing and not complaining.[57]

We are not self-focused but others-focused. We have *nothing* to complain about. We live a life with the aroma of Christ because we want those who are stranded in sin to find life and liberty in Jesus Christ. We will take aggressive, God-sized, impossible steps of faith that he might do more and more and more.

---

[57] Steven Lawson. *Philippians For You: Shine with joy as you live by faith* (Blue Ridge, VA: The Good Book Company, 2017), 111.

When you get your eyes on what God can do, you live a very happy life. It's not about what we can do, but what God has done. That's why Christians no they have nothing to complain about.

## A Blameless Life

> **Philippians 2:15** | That you may be blameless and innocent, children of God without blemish in the midst of a crooked and twisted generation, among whom you shine as lights in the world.

Blameless means we have a good outward testimony. Innocent means we have a godly inward character. Both your outward testimony and inner life are godly. That's how you shine. We as Christians want to shine as lights in a dark world. We go to church. We hear the truth. We drink it down and eat it up. But we are not just intelligent heathens. No, we are transformed believers. We are born again to newness of life. And we know that it's not just the preacher who has the hot mic. You as a Christian have a hot mic 24/7. People see how you live. Christians live blameless, bright lives in the world.

We are those who live upright lives of holiness because Christ lives in us. We don't want to sin. We don't need to sin. We have the power not to sin. When we live in holiness, we are not only happy, but we are blameless. People ought to look at your life and say: why do you follow the rules? Why do you get the permit for your house when others sneak around the permit payment? Why do you punch out on break when everyone else milks the clock? Why do you obey the traffic laws? Why do you Christian young men guard your purity and the purity of the girls around you? It's because we as Christians believe Christ is with us through the Holy Spirit, and therefore, we live blameless lives. We practice the presence of God. Why do we live lives of such carefulness? Because Jesus Christ has raised us to new life. We can't afford to present a cheap Savior. He gave all so that we could be transformed. We don't have a pretend gospel. Our message really is good news!

Now the next point that Paul makes is, instead of complaining about the darkness, shine your light!

## WE SHINE THE LIGHT (2:15B)

> **Philippians 2:15b** | Children of God without blemish in the midst of a crooked and twisted generation, among whom you shine as lights in the world.

We shine as lights in this dark world. The spiritual and moral darkness of the surrounding society may give the impression that *you* are the misfits. But that is only the darkness talking. God has made you the new norm. You are the new creation. God is making you into beacons of light, reflections of Jesus who is the Light of the World (Jn 8:12), in a midnight sky. The darker the social setting around you, the brighter your Savior shines through you." We are to fulfill our place as lights in the world. Lights are used to make things evident. Lights are used to guide. Lights are used as a warning. Lights are used to bring cheer. Lights are used to make things safe.[58]

> Let your light shine before others, so that they may see your good works and give glory to your Father who is in heaven. —*Matthew 5:16*

## Shine Amidst Sinners

**Philippians 2:15b** | Children of God without blemish in the midst of a crooked and twisted generation, among whom you shine as lights in the world.

We are like ships on the ocean. To be effective, we have to keep the ocean out. We are called to be "fishers of men", but in order to be effective we have to keep our boat in the ocean but keep the ocean out of the boat.

A Christian lives a life that is distinct from the world in several ways. We are to keep the ship in the ocean and the ocean out of the ship, so to speak. If you have a boat, you can't tread water. You've all heard the story of the Titanic. It's was the unsinkable ship until it hit an iceberg. It's only unsinkable if you keep the ocean out of the ship. The simple way to state this is that we are to influence the world without being influenced by the world. Listen to Jesus' high priestly prayer:

> I do not ask that you take them out of the world, but that you keep them from the evil one. [16] They are not of the world, just as I am not of the world.[17] Sanctify them in the truth; your word is truth. [18] As you sent me into the world, so I have sent them into the world.
> —*John 17:15-18*

How effective is a boat on dry-dock? It's sad to see a boat on shore. A lot of Christians are like boats on shore who are highly equipped to

---

[58] David Guzik, *Philippians*, David Guzik's Commentaries on the Bible (Santa Barbara, CA: David Guzik, 2013), Php 2:14–16.

catch fish, but never go out to the ocean. There's no fishing going on. There's no effectiveness. Sometimes we are insulated at church discipling each other in the gospel. We should do that but that's not our full mission. We are called to reach the world and make disciples of all nations. We need to get off the shore and get into the ocean of lost people. With boldness and love we need to shine the light of Christ. You will not be happy as a Christian if you are insulated, gazing at your belly button. What are some ways we can be inwardly focused in an unhealthy way?

## Shine as Stars

> **Philippians 2:15b** | Children of God without blemish in the midst of a crooked and twisted generation, among whom you shine as lights in the world.

This necessitates interaction with non-believers. You are children of God who are living without blemish "in the midst of a crooked and twisted generation" and you are among them shining "as lights in the world." You cannot reach people who don't know Jesus if you don't know people who don't know Jesus. Who are you loving? Who is your light shining upon? "Not *lights* merely, but luminaries, *heavenly bodies*."[59] This seems to be in reference to Daniel 12:1-2.

## Stay Bright!

How do Christians get spiritually dim so suddenly? Some who shined so bright are now barely shining at all. They are present at church, but maybe their heart is somewhere else. Be careful not to allow yourself to have a slow fade from being on fire to a barely burning light. Consider some warnings not to let your light go out. How does our light slowly go out?

Over focus on theology without application. Healthy theology should always lead to doxology and evangelism. We ought to be praising our God and proclaiming our God to the nations. I enjoy a good debate, but if that debate doesn't end with us marveling and praising God to the point where our hearts are broken for the nations, we can turn even good theology into idolatry. Don't do that. The point of the

---

[59] Ibid.

study of God is to bring you to a place of praise and to equip you to reach lost people all around you.

Always learning, never discipling. If you are constantly studying but never teaching, you've got a problem. Every true disciple of Christ is a disciple maker. The word "disciple" means "learner." So you should be learning so that you can teach others.

Always preaching, never praying. Always walk in the reality that you are the temple of the Holy Spirit.

Confessing sin far more than praising God. You should be praising God and interceding 90% of the time and confessing sin about 10%. Holiness requires confession of sin, but hyper-scrupulousness never helped anyone.

Focus on the shame of the past instead of the joy of now. We can experience shame in any area of life, but we don't have to let it keep us company or define us in the future. Shame should be something we learn to walk through and come out on the other side of, remembering that mistakes and failure are often among our greatest teachers. Remember no matter what that you are being conformed into the image of Christ (Rom 8:28-30). Rejoice in the Lord always because he's loving you through every circumstance, sin, trial or victory.

Letting the judgment passages define you more than the grace passages. Many people who are not growing have a wrong view of God. They think God is there to punish them. We must always read the Bible allowing the grace passages to overshadow the judgment passages. The law is never there to merely condemn us (Jn 3:16-18) but to lead us to Christ (Gal 3:24).

Dear saints, look deeply into the grace of God. The more you gaze into his beauty, the brighter your light will shine.

## WE SPEAK THE WORD (2:16)

**Philippians 2:16** | Holding fast to the word of life, so that in the day of Christ I may be proud that I did not run in vain or labor in vain.

Along with the metaphor of stars shining in the sky is the holding forth or display of the word of God. It means both to grasp and to display. Paul labored more than all the other apostles. He worked harder, went farther, suffered more than all the rest. Of course, it was all by the grace of God. But he says, he's not just laboring for the Philippian believers to have Bible knowledge. The goal is for them to make disciples that he may be proud of what Christ has done in them at the day of Christ.

## The Power of the Word

What's Paul's pride and glory on the day of Christ? It's disciples who are making disciples. What makes disciples to be so strong and fruitful? It's the power of the word of God.

> **Philippians 2:16** | Holding fast to the word of life, so that in the day of Christ I may be proud that I did not run in vain or labor in vain.

As believers live in a dark world, Paul says that they must be "holding fast the word of life" (2:16). "Holding fast" (*epecho*) more correctly carries the idea of "holding on by holding forth." It carries the idea of "putting something on display."[60] The concept is not merely that we would have a tenacious grip on the gospel but would also extend it to others. We must always be presenting the gospel of Jesus Christ to others with whom we have contact. Healthy disciples are those who make disciples.

### *The Word's Supremacy*

The Bible here is called the "word of life." It is the only way the disciple can change into the image of Christ. It rests supreme above all other methods of change. The disciple (learner, follower) of Christ has an unbreakable connection with God through his word. God's word gives life in so many ways. First there is the word's power to regenerate. We have been "born again… through the living and abiding word of God" (1 Pet 1:23; Jas 1:18). Then there is the word's power to transform us. God's word keeps us from sin (Psa 119:11) and changes us into the image of Christ (2 Cor 3:18). There is the power of God's word to protect us as an offensive spiritual weapon called the "sword of the Spirit." God's word has the power to renew your mind, change your heart, and tear down strongholds. It will cast down sinful reasonings. The word has the power to give life as we feed on it day and night (Psa 1:1-3), and as we receive it as our food and spiritual milk (Mt 4:4; 1 Pet 2:2). It will transform your behavior from the inside out.

---

[60] From Mounce: "to hold out, present, exhibit, display."

### *The Word Spoken*

And here in Philippians 2:16, Paul says we "hold fast" to the word of life. It is literally "on display" in our life and on our lips. Paul asks, "how are they to hear without someone preaching" (Rom 10:14). That means we can't be content with just knowing the power of the word. We must proclaim it. We must hold it forth and "speak the truth in love" (Eph 4:15). It's merciful to warn sinners of hell and invite them to heaven and eternal life in the new creation.

The Bible, and specifically the message of the gospel that gives life if we preach it. This Bible alone is powerful, "living and active" (Heb 4:12) and imparts spiritual life. God says, "My word does not return void" (Isa 55:11). "Faith comes by hearing and hearing the Word of Christ" (Rom 10:17). "The gospel is the power of God unto salvation" (Rom 1:16). The word of life is so powerful that it gives us eternal life.

## The Purpose of the Word

Why do we hold fast and hold forth the word of life? What's the purpose of the word? Paul tells us that he's preparing a people for the day of Christ, when Jesus returns in power and glory, and all people, great and small, appear before the tribunal of Christ.

> **Philippians 2:16** | Holding fast to the word of life, so that in the day of Christ I may be proud that I did not run in vain or labor in vain.

We all prepare for important events. The athlete prepares for his competition. The mother prepares dinner for her family. The builder prepares the foundation so he can build a structure on it. The teacher prepares the lesson for her class. Some people even hire a preparer for tax day! All things are worth preparing for, but nothing is more important than preparing to meet the Lord face to face on the day of Christ.

> He has set a day when he will judge the world with justice by the man he has appointed. —*Acts 17:31*

> God will bring every deed into judgment, including every hidden thing, whether it is good or evil. —*Ecclesiastes 12:14*

> It is appointed unto men once to die, but after this the judgment. —*Hebrews 9:27*

There is coming a day John says when people will be "calling to the mountains and rocks, 'Fall on us and hide us from the face of him who is seated on the throne, and from the wrath of the Lamb'" (Rev 6:16). But for believers, it will be quite different. The apostle John says that the day will be infinitely glorious. Transport yourself there as you listen to John's words describing what the day of Christ will be like for all of God's people.

> And I heard a loud voice from the throne saying, "Behold, the dwelling place of God is with man. He will dwell with them, and they will be his people, and God himself will be with them as their God. [4] He will wipe away every tear from their eyes, and death shall be no more, neither shall there be mourning, nor crying, nor pain anymore, for the former things have passed away." [5] And he who was seated on the throne said, "Behold, I am making all things new." —*Revelation 21:3-5*

We are all looking forward to that day when we see Jesus. But as believers, we often forget that even though it is a great day of rejoicing, it is also a day of examination. There is no condemnation (Rom 8:1), but our good works and gospel fruit will be examined by Christ, and we will be rewarded. That's what Paul is talking about when he speaks of "running" or "laboring in vain."

> According to the grace of God given to me, like a skilled master builder I laid a foundation, and someone else is building upon it. Let each one take care how he builds upon it. [11] For no one can lay a foundation other than that which is laid, which is Jesus Christ. [12] Now if anyone builds on the foundation with gold, silver, precious stones, wood, hay, straw— [13] each one's work will become manifest, for the Day will disclose it, because it will be revealed by fire, and the fire will test what sort of work each one has done. [14] If the work that anyone has built on the foundation survives, he will receive a reward. [15] If anyone's work is burned up, he will suffer loss, though he himself will be saved, but only as through fire. —*1 Corinthians 3:10-15*

As believers, we don't just want to "be saved, but only as through fire." We want to have golden crowns to cast at the Savior's feet. Christ did all the work for us to be saved, but he calls on us to bear fruit that we may glory in what Christ has done through us. Being saved "only as through fire" does not mean the believer has no fruit, but the fruit is weak. It's "wood, hay, and straw." This speaks to our heart motives behind our fruit. God is not simply looking for outward works, but he "looks on the heart" (1 Sam 16:7).

## The Practice of the Word

**Philippians 2:16** | Holding fast to the word of life, so that in the day of Christ I may be proud that I did not run in vain or labor in vain.

Paul says the word of God is important because it brings glory to Christ on judgment day. Unless the Philippians are holding forth the word of life and putting it on display to others, Paul says: my ministry of discipleship is in vain. It's a failure. Paul knows he will have invested his life well if those he has ministered to continue to be faithful witnesses of the word. Paul only thinks himself successful if the Philippians are reproducing themselves by making disciples with the word of life. We all must be those who not satisfied with merely hearing the word, but being doers, practitioners of the word (Jas 1:21-25).

On that last day, God will review every minister's work. He will reward them according to their faithfulness. The bottom line is that we are to be making disciples, putting the word of life on display for others. We are to be holding fast the word by holding forth the word. We are called to be fishers of men. If we just gather our boats on dry land and compare our fishing equipment, we are failures. This is what Paul is saying. "My pride, my joy on the day of Christ is you making disciples."

Same goes with us. If we at our local church are merely a theology factory, we have failed. We need rich theology, but if we are here just showing off our Bible equipment to each other, we are failing at the mission. The mission is not to make disciples of each other. Yes, do that. Mentor each other. If you don't, you will fail at the larger mission. But don't just be content edifying each other. Yes that's absolutely vital, but go beyond that and reach others for Christ.

Our mission is missions. Our mission is Christ's mission: make disciples of all nations. Make disciples of every creature. How can we do that. Here are some ways we can all make disciples. *Reach*: share your testimony. Share the gospel. The first thing you teach is the gospel to anyone who doesn't know it. This means the whole world. *Read*: if you are a mom or dad, start reading the Bible out loud with your family. *Teach*: discipleship is teaching. Teach the Bible to anyone. Teach what you know. Be willing to correct and rebuke. Discipleship means we stand up in love for Bible principles. This begins in the home and spreads to our friends and acquaintances. *Model*: be open about what you are learning with other believers. Be open about your failures and your repentance with your close circle of peers and mentors. Be hopeful to those younger in the faith that the word is sufficient. *Love*: iron sharpens iron. All this is done in humble love. We are not showing off knowledge. Our goal is always to give hope and to edify the body in love. *Forgive*: "Love covers a multitude of sins" (1 Pet 4:8).

Let me mention that if you are saved you should be doing some form of all of these. There is always someone that doesn't know what you know. If you know that Christ is Lord and Savior, you know so much more than the great majority of the world. Shine your light! Speak the word!

## WE SACRIFICE FOR THE KINGDOM (2:17-18)

### Resolve to Sacrifice

> **Philippians 2:17** | Even if I am to be poured out as a drink offering upon the sacrificial offering of your faith, I am glad and rejoice with you all.

One of the greatest ways to be an influencer for the kingdom is to pour your life into others. The Bible demands all Christians everywhere to participate in life-on-life discipleship. That's the theme of the book of Acts. Paul was glad to pour his life into the lives of everyone around him. Paul was resolved to be poured out as a drink offering for the Philippians. A drink offering was a God-ordained sacrifice that was poured on top of an animal sacrifice (Exo 29:38-41). Wine was poured either in front of or upon the burning animal. As the wine vaporized, the steam rose upward. This symbolized the rising of the sacrificial offering to God. So, Paul's life is being poured out upon the lives of the Philippians. Their hearts and souls are being mixed together in the gospel.

Paul was glad to pour out his life as a sacrifice for all the believers. He was joyful. Paul was under house arrest in a rented house in Rome. He had a Roman soldier chained to him. The Philippians knew he could be put to death at any time. He was glad to give his life for the cause of Christ. How about you? Do you know the Christian life is a life of sacrifice? Jesus is worthy of your sacrifices.

## Rejoice in Sacrifice

**Philippians 2:18** | Likewise you also should be glad and rejoice with me.

Paul says, "Rejoice with me" for the honor of sacrificing for the kingdom. That's discipleship. The Philippians might have been terribly sad, since Paul is writing this letter from prison. But Paul says, "It's an honor, and you should rejoice with me! Be glad when I sacrifice for the kingdom." Saints, it's a joy to sacrifice for the kingdom, isn't it? It's a joy we all share. Few commands could be more practical for our Christian lives. Rejoice when it hurts to serve God. Be glad when you are stretched to the limit. Don't complain. "Be glad and rejoice with me," Paul says. Ministry can be hard and grueling, but there is no room for complaining—only rejoicing and more sacrifice. Why? Because we get to boast in Christ at the end of the day. When we see Jesus, we won't be complaining about how hard it was and licking our wounds from ministry. No, we will be rejoicing and amazed that God could use such poor sinners such as ourselves to do such amazing work. Rejoice that you are a tool in God's hand!

Even if you cannot rejoice in your circumstances, you can rejoice in the Lord and his sacrifice for you. The Father gave his best offering as payment for your sins (Rom 8:32). You can rejoice in God's high and holy standard met by the blood of Jesus. You can rejoice in God's limitless goodness. You can rejoice in God's amazing grace. You can rejoice in God's perfect sacrifice. You can rejoice in God's abundant supply. Jesus paid it all. What a sacrifice!

### Conclusion

Be an influencer. Today, that word might have very different meaning. People want to be "influencers" through social media for the latest styles and comedy. They want to be influencers of music and even politics. But the Lord is calling us to be a very different kind of influencer. Live the life of Christ. Shine the light of Christ. Speak the word of Christ. And display the sacrifice of Christ. That will prepare people for the day of Christ far more than any self-consumed social media post. Influencing people for heaven is hard word. It will entail far more than a paragraph on Twitter or a pic on Instagram. God wants you to pour your life out into another life today. Shine, speak, live the life of Christ. That's the best way to have fruitful labor that will bring God glory in the day of Christ.

# 11 | PHILIPPIANS 2:19-30
## MODELS OF MINISTRY

*I hope in the Lord Jesus to send Timothy to you soon, so that I too may be cheered by news of you. For I have no one like him, who will be genuinely concerned for your welfare.*
PHILIPPIANS 2:19-20

When we speak of ministry, we are talking about the hard work of discipleship. What is discipleship? The word disciple means "learner." To make a disciple is teach and model Jesus so that they become like Jesus. Discipleship is the teaching and modeling in life to help people become more like Jesus. Dietrich Bonhoeffer said, "Christianity without discipleship is always Christianity without Christ." We can't wait until we've got everything perfect with our lives. Every Christian here needs to make disciples now. Listen to Francis Chan to describe the nitty gritty of discipleship.

> With discipleship, your problems are not just your problems—ultimately, they belong to the church body that God has placed you in. You are called to encourage, challenge, and help the other Christians in your life, and they are called to do the same for you. If you wait until

all of your own issues are gone before helping others, it will never happen. This is a trap that millions have fallen into, not realizing that our own sanctification happens as we minister to others.[61]

At the end of Philippians 2 (vs 19-30) we have a beautiful description of three ordinary men doing world changing ministry. Again, ministry is the work of discipleship. We are all called to do it. We are called to make disciples of all nations. That's why we come to know three men who are men of great joy and who love making disciples. Let me introduce you of three ordinary models of extraordinary joy for ministry: Paul, Timothy, and Epaphroditus.

> **Philippians 2:19-30** | I hope in the Lord Jesus to send Timothy to you soon, so that I too may be cheered by news of you. [20] For I have no one like him, who will be genuinely concerned for your welfare. [21] For they all seek their own interests, not those of Jesus Christ. [22] But you know Timothy's proven worth, how as a son with a father he has served with me in the gospel. [23] I hope therefore to send him just as soon as I see how it will go with me, [24] and I trust in the Lord that shortly I myself will come also. [25] I have thought it necessary to send to you Epaphroditus my brother and fellow worker and fellow soldier, and your messenger and minister to my need, [26] for he has been longing for you all and has been distressed because you heard that he was ill. [27] Indeed he was ill, near to death. But God had mercy on him, and not only on him but on me also, lest I should have sorrow upon sorrow. [28] I am the more eager to send him, therefore, that you may rejoice at seeing him again, and that I may be less anxious. [29] So receive him in the Lord with all joy, and honor such men, [30] for he nearly died for the work of Christ, risking his life to complete what was lacking in your service to me.

In our study we see three models of joyful Christian ministry—Paul: a model of selflessness, Timothy: a model of service, and Epaphroditus: a model of sacrifice.

## PAUL: A MODEL OF SELFLESSNESS (2:19-21)

The apostle Paul had a selfless spirit that drove his joy in ministry. When you lose focus on yourself, and you have a big vision of God and

---

[61] Francis Chan. *Multiply: Disciples Making Disciples* (Colorado Springs, CO: David C. Cook, 2012), 55-56.

his plan moving forward, you are truly joyful. God is in the business of moving mountains. He's in the business of raising the spiritually dead. He loves doing the incredible and unfathomable in people's lives. It's easy to be selfless when your eyes are focused on a big God. We serve a great God, amen?

Some of you know that I have a twin sister. I also have two twin brothers who are 12 years older than me. My twin sister loves horses. We always had friends in the Wilmington and Kankakee area that had a horse ranch. We loved riding horses. When we were 9 years old, my sister and I moved to Louisiana. For our first horse ride in the bayou the spooked and took off wildly. My sister lost the reigns, and the horse ran wild for what seemed like forever but was likely 15 minutes. I remember we had to chase the horse with the car until a horse trainer was able to grab the horse and halt it. In those moments we were thinking very carefully and clearly about how to rescue my sister. That's selflessness. Paul the apostle modeled it for us.

There's a clarity to our vision when we completely forget ourselves and concentrate solely on the task before us. It's an energizing feeling to be so focused on someone else that there is no thought of our own welfare, predicament, or problems. Though it seems ironic, it's a blessed state, far more meaningful than when we are obsessed with our own trials and tribulations. Paul is the model of a selfless servant of Christ. He's so concerned about others that is not overcome by his own difficulties and sorrows. We see this in verse 19.

## The Joy of Selfless Ministry

Paul is under house arrest, and what is his joy? Keeping his best friend and ministry partner with him? No. What would make him rejoice is seeing the Philippian believers encouraged by Timothy.

> **Philippians 2:19** | I hope in the Lord Jesus to send Timothy to you soon, so that I too may be cheered by news of you.

This is what makes Paul joyful: a selfless spirit. Seeing others happy in Christ cheers Paul's soul. Paul is ready to pour himself out like a drink offering for the faith of the Philippians (2:17-18). Life in Christ is worth risking everything. It's worth being radical. No matter what happens you win. "For me to live is Christ and to die is gain" (1:21).

### Radical Selflessness is Seen in Paul

The extreme to which Paul adhered to this selflessness is, in fact, shocking to modern sensibilities. The great apostle tells the Romans that he wishes he could cut himself off from salvation if in doing so he might save Israel (Rom 9:3). Again, let's not quickly pass over this. Paul was fully aware of the total horrors of hell—the physical pain, the emotional angst, the spiritual alienation—yet still he proclaims, "I wish I could be damned in hell for all eternity, if in my damnation the rest of the people of Israel could be saved."[62]

Here is Paul 800 miles away from Philippi, and the one he calls "my son" and says, "I have no one like him" (2:20a) and "you know Timothy's proven worth" (2:21a) and yet he says: "I'm going to send him to you, just as soon as I know my fate" (2:23). Paul's going to die within three years. He'll be released for a year or so and then back to a deeper darker prison (the infamous *Mamertine prison* in Rome). Here's the point: in Paul's hour of need he sends his most valued partner Timothy to Philippi to care for them. He's going to send the only one he trusts to the people he loves: the Philippians. Paul is selfless: focused on the needs of others.

Selflessness starts first at the cross of Jesus. It's at the heart of being a Christ follower. "For they all seek their own interests, not those of Jesus Christ" (2:21). If you want to see Christ's interests, you have to look at the cross. He gives his life away. Discipleship is a selfless endeavor. It's going to mean giving your life away in teaching and modeling Christ for others. This selfless sacrifice should give you joy!

### Joy is the Mark of True Discipleship

There ought to be a joy about our ministry. We all have favorite flavors. Some of you like sweet. Some of you like savory. Some of you like spicy. Some of you like mild. If Christians have a flavor, it would be joy! Do you have a joyful spirit in your ministry?

The great Methodist missionary to India (called the Billy Graham of India), E. Stanley Jones, said, "When I met Christ, it was as though I had swallowed sunshine."[63] Isn't that a great statement? He was

---

[62] Gary Thomas. "The Joy of Selflessness." Gary Thomas Ministries. April 28, 2016. Accessed March 01, 2019. http://www.garythomas.com/free-resources/the-joy-of-selflessness/.

[63] E. Stanley Jones. *The Way* (Nashville: Stone & Pierce, 1946), 70.

speaking of the joy that he experienced in meeting Jesus Christ. And then there was C.S. Lewis, a person that we've all probably read, that great British scholar, who said, "Joy is the serious business of heaven."[64] While I believe that joy is sometimes quite fleeting on earth. Do you find ministry a hassle or a joy? What greater business is there in heaven or on earth? When one sinner repents, all heaven rejoices! Shouldn't we be rejoicing?

## The Hard Work of Selfless Ministry

Selfless ministry is hard work. Paul didn't just bury his talent. He didn't bury the treasure of the gospel. He was constantly raising people up and turning them into leaders. We are all called to do the hard work of discipleship, investing in each other. Paul did that with Timothy.

> **Philippians 2:20-21** | For I have no one like him, who will be genuinely concerned for your welfare. [21] For they all seek their own interests, not those of Jesus Christ.

Timothy was uniquely in tune with the Philippians because he'd been around Paul so much. He had a "father-son" relationship with him. Do you know how much time it takes to raise up disciples? We are called to duplicate ourselves. Paul did that with Timothy.

### Metaphors for Discipleship Imply Work

Consider how much work discipleship is. The Scriptures compare it in many ways. Discipleship is like a father-son relationship. With them from cradle to maturity. You know why Timothy was selfless when everyone else was "seeking their own interests"? Because Paul was selfless. Timothy has a huge heart of compassion because his father in the faith has a huge heart of compassion. Making disciples is far more than a program. It's like a father-son relationship. It takes a lot of time. It is the mission of our lives. It defines us. A disciple is a disciple maker. How much work does a father or mother put into a child? You've got to clothe them and keep them clean and do everything for them at first. You are with them at all their important milestones.

Discipleship is like being a fisherman (*cf* Mt 4:19). A fisherman must fish at all hours. Sometimes you fish all night till people start re-

---

[64] C.S. Lewis. *Letters to Malcolm: Chiefly on Prayer* (San Diego: Harvest, 1964), 92-93.

sponding to the Holy Spirit. We are not only fishers of men in evangelism but in discipleship. We have to keep going after people. We could add to this a similar picture of the shepherd going after the sheep. Discipleship is like being a slave of all (Mk 9:35). A servant has no rights. We give up our rights. We work all hours. Discipleship is like a bearing a cross. "If anyone comes to me and does not hate his own father and mother and wife and children and brothers and sisters, yes, and even his own life, he cannot be my disciple. Whoever does not bear his own cross and come after me cannot be my disciple" (Lk 14:26-27).

We as disciples are the salt that is constantly preserving people's lives with truth. We are the light that is constantly shining into the darkness of confused souls helping them see and follow Jesus. As disciples we are like a body that works together. Like a bride that is always faithful to her groom. Like a temple that perpetually is inhabited by the living God. All of these metaphors imply the constancy of the work of discipleship. We don't just do discipleship on the Lord's Day. Discipleship is not a program. It's a life. We live life together.

### Models for Discipleship Require Work

Why was this tiny church having a global impact all the way to Rome? They weren't a mega-church. They understood the joy of ministry. It takes every member involvement. Every member needs discipleship. What are some practical ways we can do discipleship? Let's consider several.

Establish a discipleship group. Be in contact with at least one or two other person every day (Heb 10:24-25). Everyone should have a little discipleship group. We'll call it D-group for short. Who's in your D-group?

> And let us consider how to stir up one another to love and good works, [25] not neglecting to meet together, as is the habit of some, but encouraging one another, and all the more as you see the Day drawing near.  —*Hebrews 10:24-25*

Surely these verses are not only referring to meeting together on the Lord's Day, but also more and more privately. With text messages, cell phones and video chats, we should be in continual contact discipling one another throughout the day. Pick at least one or two people for your D-Group. Usually, these start organically.

Pray. Prayer takes hard work. Jesus said that we "ought always to pray and not lose heart" (Lk 18:1). Pray for specific needs for your D-group throughout the day. Abide and shine. Make sure you are meeting with God, abiding with him. The goal of discipleship is to know God better and help others know him better (Phil 3:10). Being a disciple of Jesus means that we are being transformed into his image. God wants to change us so much that it intrigues others.

Do life together. Do lunch. Men, do basketball, or something. Ladies, do whatever women do. Invite each other to your home. Worship, fellowship, pray at your church together. Reach out. Invite people to church. Give out gospel tracts. Give your testimony. Pick up your phone. Be approachable. Be cheerful when you answer the phone. Call fellow believers. Pick up when they call. Follow through. Don't just start this. Finish it. Persevere together.

## The Reward of Selfless Ministry

Look at verse 25 and consider the reward for selfless ministry. Paul has invested in the pastor of the Philippians, Epaphroditus, and now they are investing in him by sending him to minister to Paul. Paul taught the Philippians well. He poured out his life out for the Philippians, like a "drink offering" (1:17). In return, they were pouring their lives out for him by sending him their pastor. He says,

> I have thought it necessary to send to you Epaphroditus my brother and fellow worker and fellow soldier, and your messenger and minister to my need. —*Philippians 2:25*

Paul as a selfless disciple produces a selfless church in Philippi.

### The Reward of Reproducing a Pastor

Epaphroditus seems to be the pastor at Philippi. Paul is reproducing here and in all the churches. Paul relied entirely on God to do the reproducing. He would say, "I have planted, Apollos watered; but God gave the increase" (1 Cor 3:6). As we are faithful to be selfless, God will indeed give the increase. And so it seems he did with Epaphroditus at Philippi. Later on, John Chrysostom (349-407) lists all the pastors of Philippi, and he names Epaphroditus as the pastor there at the time of the letter.[65] Epaphroditus is here called "your messenger" which could refer to him not only as Paul's emissary but the Philippians' pastor.

---

[65] Le Quien, *Oriens Christianus, II* (Paris: Ex Typographia Regia, 1740), 67.

He obviously has a very special relationship with the church as a whole since Epaphroditus is heartbroken that his church is worrying about him because he was near death in bringing a love offering and correspondence from the Philippian church to Paul. Paul says: "I am well supplied, having received from Epaphroditus the gifts you sent" (4:18).

### The Reward of Reproducing a Church

What a reward Paul had from this little church, that they would send their pastor to him. Philippi was no mega-church. The church at Philippi, though well-known and influential, would eventually grow to a modest size of at most 75 people amidst a town of 10,000.[66] Though modest in size they did big things for God and for the kingdom. They would grow somewhat rapidly. In the next century they would grow to be close to 1,000 people. The reward of discipleship is making disciples. The model is presented to us by Paul in Ephesians 4.

> And he gave the apostles, the prophets, the evangelists, the shepherds and teachers, [12] to equip the saints for the work of ministry, for building up the body of Christ, [13] until we all attain to the unity of the faith and of the knowledge of the Son of God, to mature manhood, to the measure of the stature of the fullness of Christ.
> —*Ephesians 4:11-13*

## TIMOTHY: A MODEL OF SERVICE (2:19-24)

Timothy is mentioned twenty-four times in Paul's letters and is identified with Paul in the writing of five letters.[67] Timothy was one of the better known of Paul's companions. His mother (Lois) and grandmother (Eunice) are both model Jewish women and are named in 2 Timothy 1:5. His father was Greek (Acts 16:1) but since he likely died when Timothy was quite young, the boy was raised by his godly mother and grandmother, who gave him a good working knowledge of the Old Testament Scriptures (2 Tim 3:15).[68] Timothy was Paul's son in the

---

[66] Eduard Verhoef. "The Church of Philippi in the First Six Centuries of Our Era" (Maartensdijk, the Netherlands: University of Pretoria, 2005), *HTS Theological Studies* 61, no. 1 & 2: 565-92.

[67] D. Jeremiah. *Count It All Joy.* 131-132.

[68] J. Phillips, *Exploring Philippians*, Php 2:19.

faith and seems to have been converted at the time of Paul's first missionary visit to Lystra and Iconium. Paul may have recovered from his stoning at Lystra in the house of Timothy's mother.

When Paul chose Timothy to be one of his companions on his second missionary journey, the apostle had Timothy circumcised to make him more acceptable to the Jews (Acts 16:1–4). Remember, Timothy is half-Jewish. He wanted to reach his own people. Paul always approached the synagogue congregation first when he entered a new town.[69]

Timothy is willing to do anything for Christ. He's willing to be sent. He's a minister to Paul in Rome where the apostle is under house arrest. Yet he's genuinely concerned for the welfare of the Philippian church. Paul writes about his son in the faith here in Philippians 2:19-24.

> **Philippians 2:19-24** | I hope in the Lord Jesus to send Timothy to you soon, so that I too may be cheered by news of you. [20] For I have no one like him, who will be genuinely concerned for your welfare. [21] For they all seek their own interests, not those of Jesus Christ. [22] But you know Timothy's proven worth, how as a son with a father he has served with me in the gospel. [23] I hope therefore to send him just as soon as I see how it will go with me, [24] and I trust in the Lord that shortly I myself will come also.

## Big Vision Service

Timothy had a big vision view of ministry. We read Paul's words and think nothing of the journey Timothy has to embark.

> **Philippians 2:19** | I hope in the Lord Jesus to send Timothy to you soon, so that I too may be cheered by news of you.

This is an 800-mile journey on foot. He couldn't look up Air BnB to find a place to stay. There were no Ubers or Internet. He had to figure this out. But Timothy was willing to travel and to pay a price for his service to Christ because he had a big vision of a big God. Timothy likely got to know Paul as Paul was nursed back to health after being stoned to death in Lystra. It was probably in Timothy's home, where his mother Lois and grandmother Eunice took care of the apostle. Timothy heard the stories for the gospel going forward.

---

[69] Ibid.

Timothy put himself last. It was a great joy for Timothy to serve the Lord. He was glad to be submissive in his service to the apostle Paul. Timothy was willing to be sent all around the Roman Empire on behalf of Paul. He was submissive to Paul, "as a son with a father" serving with the great apostle (2:22). Timothy served the Lord wherever Paul directed. And it really was the Lord directing them. It was often scary to go to the difficult situations. Paul was constantly encouraging Timothy. ("God's not given you a spirit of fear...").

Discipleship and growth are not at all possible without a big vision. To be a disciple is to be a learner. You need to see how others serve. Timothy was willing to submit and learn how to serve from the tutelage of Paul. Who are your teachers at Living Hope? Normally, it's pretty hard to program something like this. It has to happen naturally. But once you've found someone to help disciple you, you can get some accountability.

*Excuses for Small Vision*

No one has pursued me for discipleship. Who pursued Paul? He met with the Lord for three years before anything happened. That should not be the norm. But then he met Barnabas and received direction from Aquilla and Pricilla.

Greener grass syndrome. "I'll find a better discipleship situation elsewhere." That mentality always hurts yourself and Christ's church. If you want greener grass, water your own grass. Find ways to do discipleship. Persevere. Don't ever, ever, ever give up.

I can't disciple someone because I still have faith struggles. This one's a classic. We think we must operate at some higher level of spirituality to make disciples. Listen, we are not perfect saints; we are forgiven sinners. What matters is who we follow together—he's got enough perfection for all of us. Don't let this excuse keep you from obedience.

I don't know enough. While teaching and learning are central to discipleship, we don't need to know everything. Invite people into places where you are learning and praying and serving. And as you do that, your own learning will accelerate quickly.

I don't know what to do. Discipleship is not complicated; it's not about a technique or methodology. Wondering what to do? Here's my thing: *just start*. Invite a friend to discuss spiritual things. Take someone to church with you. Pray for a friend. Learn along the way. It's not nearly as complicated as you think. It's simply helping someone take the next step after Jesus.

That's the pastor's job. I love this one. As a pastor, I want to laugh out loud, mostly because it's so absurd. All disciples must make disciples. Pastors help us become better disciple-makers, so we can all do our one job.

I don't want to be presumptuous. Actually, it's not called presumption to help someone follow Jesus—it's called loving obedience. Remember: any trace of presumption or hierarchy is evidence that you've forgotten what's going on: we are not making people our disciples but disciples of Jesus.

I'm not an academic. You don't need to be. In some circle's discipleship has, unfortunately, become a kind of rigorous academic program—read these 40 books, pray 2 hours a day, etc. Discipleship is not primarily academic, though it includes loving God with our whole mind, as well as heart, soul, and strength. In the end, we are not becoming religious eggheads who know stuff but passionate followers of Jesus who serve him in the world. Be who you are.

I tried that once and it didn't go well. Yep. Sometimes things don't go well. That's just true. And we learn through it. But stopping because it didn't work out well? I don't think Jesus left us that option.

I don't have time. Then your priorities are wrong. At any job, how long would we last if we kept ignoring the one thing we had been tasked to do, claiming we don't have the time for it?

I don't feel I have much to give. This one really shuts people down, and often includes a combination of excuses. Here's the fact: none of us have that much to give, but by the Holy Spirit can give through us. Keep your relationship with Jesus in focus, and simply share where you are growing. Let Jesus be the giver.

I don't want to. This final one isn't an excuse—it's flat out disobedience. If we are honest, there are times when we hear Jesus' commission to us and we reject it. We don't want to. What do we do with that? We need to repent, reconnect with Jesus' heart for people, and get on with the task at hand. Because in the end, we only have one job. Are we getting it done?

## Big Hearted Service (2:20-21)

Timothy cared about the church! There was no one like him, who is genuinely concerned for the Philippians' welfare (2:20). Timothy was not the pastor at Philippi, but he loved that small church with a big heart. Listen to Paul's evaluation of Timothy's big heart.

> **Philippians 2:19-24** | For I have no one like him, who will be genuinely concerned for your welfare. [21] For they all seek their own interests, not those of Jesus Christ.

When we serve the Lord, it takes thick skin and a big heart. Timothy wouldn't stop loving the saints at Philippi. Dietrich Bonhoeffer famously said, "When Christ calls a man, he bids him come and die." Timothy was willing and able to die without becoming bitter or jaded by ministry. How is that possible? How do you remain "genuinely concerned" for the church when you are constantly suffering?

### *Timothy's Imprisonment*

Timothy is willing to care for the Philippians welfare no matter what the risk. The author of Hebrews records that he had been imprisoned and will be released. Who knows what all he's gone through for the saints?

> You should know that our brother Timothy has been released, with whom I shall see you if he comes soon. —*Hebrews 13:23*

### *How to Maintain a Big Heart (And Avoid Burnout)*

Keep your eyes on Jesus! Sinners sin. People will always fail themselves, the Lord, and you. Jesus will never fail you.

Stay humble. Most of the time when we are angry or dejected it is because of self-worship / idolatry. Humility and the fear of the Lord are necessary to keep perspective when people fail you.

Rejoice in God's love. Remember at the end of the day you are loved. He's not willing that any should perish, and that means he's not willing you should perish.

Remember you are not the Savior. You can't do it all. Delegate. Say no to things. Get proper rest. You are only human.

Take risks and see God break through. We have a big God who does big things in people's lives if you ask him. You need to take some risks. Have people over. Hand out a gospel tract. Introduce yourself to someone new at church. Sit in a different section of the church. Pray specifically and see God answer prayer.

## Big Dividend Service

If you will invest in others, God will give you dividends! Paul invested in Timothy, and it really paid off. Timothy cared about discipleship. He learned from Paul to do whatever it takes to disciple others. Paul says I have no one like him.

> **Philippians 2:22-24** | But you know Timothy's proven worth, how as a son with a father he has served with me in the gospel.[23] I hope therefore to send him just as soon as I see how it will go with me, [24] and I trust in the Lord that shortly I myself will come also.

Timothy is joyfully serving Paul and the church, and most of all the Lord, and his service is valuable. Timothy became a disciple of proven worth. Paul was eager to have him minister to the Philippians, and then Paul was looking forward, if it was the Lord's will, to join reunite with Timothy in Philippi. What great dividends Paul had with investing in Timothy. If you invest in others, God will give you dividends!

We have to be willing to put ourselves out there in service. And without real big vision, big hearted service, there will not be big dividends. What is your proven worth to God's kingdom? When you are spoken about by other members of this church or any church you are in, do they say: I know this man or this lady's proven worth! They are profitable.

## EPAPHRODITUS: A MODEL OF SACRIFICE (2:25-30)

Epaphroditus had been sent to Rome to minister to Paul, but shortly after arriving the the Philippian pastor becomes terribly ill. Ultimately, he recovered, but not before a long struggle where he lingered at death's door. News of his illness might have traveled back to Philippi, and the man was concerned that his friends back home would be worried about him. Furthermore, when he returned earlier than expected, some might think he returned as a quitter, so Paul was careful to write strong words in his defense.

### The Example of Sacrifice

> **Philippians 2:25-27** | I have thought it necessary to send to you Epaphroditus my brother and fellow worker and fellow soldier, and your messenger and minister to my need, [26] for he has been longing for you all and has been distressed because you heard that he was

ill. ²⁷ Indeed he was ill, near to death. But God had mercy on him, and not only on him but on me also, lest I should have sorrow upon sorrow.

I love how Paul describes Epaphroditus: "my brother and fellow worker and fellow soldier, and your messenger..." (2:25). The church of Philippi was the first church that Paul founded in Macedonia and likely in Europe (*cf* Phil 4:15; 1 Thess 2:2; Acts 16:11-12). This was a very new church, and they wanted to send their pastor to Paul. One the way he almost died: he was ill, near to death (2:27, 30).

In those days when people visited prisoners who were held captive under Roman authority, they were often prejudged as criminal types as well. Therefore, a visitor exposed himself to danger just by being near those who were considered dangerous. Paul says:

...he [Epaphroditus] nearly died for the work of Christ, risking his life to complete what was lacking in your service to me (2:30).

The Greek term Paul uses here for "risking"—*paraboleuomai*—is one that meant "to hazard with one's life . . . to gamble." Epaphroditus did just that.

*Riskers for Christ: Parabolani!*

In the early church there were societies of men and women who called themselves the *parabolani for Christ*, that is, the "riskers for Christ." They ministered to the sick and imprisoned, and they saw to it that, if at all possible, martyrs and sometimes even enemies would receive an honorable burial. For example, in the city of Carthage during the great plague of A.D. 252, Cyprian, the pastor of Carthage, showed remarkable courage. In self-sacrificing love for his flock and the world, he took upon himself the care of those sick with the plague and encouraged his congregation nurse them and bury the dead. What a contrast with the practice of the heathen who were throwing the corpses out of the plague-stricken city and were running away in terror![70]

As Christians, we are the *Parabolani* for Christ. We are the Riskers for Jesus! We've got to be there sacrificing our lives like Epaphroditus. Yes, it's inconvenient and even dangerous, but that's the true display of love for one another.

---

[70] William Hendriksen, "Philippians," *New Testament Commentary* (Grand Rapids, Mich.: Baker Book House, 1962), 144–45.

> By this all people will know that you are my disciples, if you have love for one another. —John 13:35

Epaphroditus wasn't extraordinary among Christians. We shouldn't look at him as a rare case. This is the commitment we are all called to. He was a pastor who became a messenger for Paul. Before email, cell phones and text messaging, people had to deliver messages by hand.

You don't have to be a hero to be part of the *Parabolani* for Christ! Moms, you are a risker for Christ every time you share the gospel with your little ones. You are a risker when you carefully nurture them in the Scriptures. You are standing against the cosmic powers of darkness. You are a hero! Dads, you are a risker for Christ as you stand against this emasculated age and lead your wife and children. Singles, you are a risker for Christ as you remain pure in this lascivious age of filth. As you make wise media choices. All of us are riskers for Christ when we pick up the phone and call each other outside of Sundays and shepherd each other.

This reminds me of the six-year-old girl who became deathly ill with a dread disease. To survive, she needed a blood transfusion from someone who had previously conquered the same illness. The situation was complicated by her rare blood type. Her nine-year-old brother qualified as a donor, but everyone was hesitant to ask him since he was just a lad. Finally, they agreed to have the doctor pose the question. The attending physician tactfully asked the boy if he was willing to be brave and donate blood for his sister. Though he didn't understand much about such things, the boy agreed without hesitation: "Sure, I'll give my blood for my sister." He lay down beside his sister and smiled at her as they pricked his arm with the needle. Then he closed his eyes and lay silently on the bed as the pint of blood was taken. Soon thereafter the physician came in to thank the little fellow. The boy, with quivering lips and tears running down his cheeks, asked, "Doctor, when do I die?" At that moment the doctor realized that the naive little boy thought that by giving his blood, he was giving up his life. Quickly he reassured the lad that he was not going to die, but amazed at his courage, the doctor asked, "Why were you willing to risk your life for her?" "Because she is my sister ... and I love her," was the boy's simple but significant reply.

So it was between Epaphroditus and his brother Paul in Rome, and so it is to this day. Danger and risk don't threaten true friendship; they strengthen it. Such friends are modern-day members of the *parabolani*, that reckless band of friends—riskers and gamblers, all—who love their brothers and sisters to the uttermost. Each one deserves our respect. When we need them, they are there. I have a few in that category. Hopefully, you do too.[71]

## The Honor of Sacrifice

> **Philippians 2:28-30** | I am the more eager to send him, therefore, that you may rejoice at seeing him again, and that I may be less anxious. [29] So receive him in the Lord with all joy, and honor such men, [30] for he nearly died for the work of Christ, risking his life to complete what was lacking in your service to me.

Paul says we should honor men like Epaphroditus, not because he is a pastor but because of their sacrifice. In this world, those who are honored are those who seem to take, take, take. The richest and the most glamorous are always honored in a pagan culture. But not in the church. Paul said, Epaphroditus was a man to be honored because of his sacrifice.

We believe Christians should live by a code of honor. Hopefully you honor those in authority over you whether you agree with them or not. We need to have a code like Daniel who served pagan kings. We should have a spirit of honor and gratitude that marks our lives. We say thank you to any elected officials. We say thank you to those who protect us day in and day out: police, fire fighters, our military.

Paul's argument is that this honor should extend to the church of Jesus Christ as well. We should show honor one to another. Epaphroditus was willing to give his life. Paul says let's honor him. Paul was willing to give his life. Let's honor him. Let's all give our lives for each other. Let's honor each other. This is sacred ground. Let's work out our salvation with fear and trembling because Christ gave his life for us. Above all, let's honor Christ! How about you? Do you honor those who are investing in your lives? Do you honor each other?

### Conclusion

Here are three great men of joy in ministry. How they loved serving the Lord. We are also called to serve the Lord with gladness. Let's close with a powerful and important Psalm.

---

[71] Swindoll. *Laugh Again Hope Again,* Kindle Edition.

Make a joyful noise to the Lord, all the earth! ² Serve the Lord with gladness! Come into his presence with singing! ³ Know that the Lord, he is God! It is he who made us, and we are his; we are his people, and the sheep of his pasture. ⁴ Enter his gates with thanksgiving, and his courts with praise! Give thanks to him; bless his name! ⁵ For the Lord is good; his steadfast love endures forever, and his faithfulness to all generations.   —*Psalm 100:1-5*

**By God's grace saints, let us serve the Lord with gladness!**

# 12 | PHILIPPIANS 3:1-3
## INCREASE YOUR JOY

*Finally, my brothers, rejoice in the Lord. To write the same things to you is no trouble to me and is safe for you.*
PHILIPPIANS 3:1

Do you ever feel like you are losing your joy? Joy is the birthmark of the birthright of the child of God. And if you're not living a life of joy you're living beneath your privileges as a Christian.

When I was a kid, my family visited Graceland in Memphis, Tennessee. It's amazing how people go crazy over this person, Elvis Presley, who is dead. People go crazy over the silliest things. In Philippians 3 Paul has crazy love for Jesus, who is alive. This is the love we need also. This passage is extremely important because it tells us what it means to know Jesus, what it means to find eternal salvation and ultimate satisfaction in life.

What do you treasure? Is there anything of surpassing value? Is there anything that deserves our life-long, passionate pursuit? The answer is yes. Paul describes it later in this chapter: "More than that, I also consider everything to be a loss in view of the surpassing value of knowing Christ Jesus my Lord" (3:8). Paul reminds us that nothing on earth compares to the *joy* knowing Jesus Christ as Lord and Savior. You will never regret pursuing Christ.

## 12 | Philippians 3:1-3
### Increase Your Joy

Did you know the most attractive quality of our life in order to bring people to Jesus Christ is the joy that we have? The people that you work with, if they can see that joy in you, the people that you go to school with, the people that you worship with. That's the reason I want our services to be services that are marked by joy, enthusiasm, and happiness. I'm not talking about cheerleader enthusiasm. The real meaning of the word enthusiasm is in God, *in Theos*.

We ought to worship the Lord with gladness. It's all right for a mortician to be a mortician there, but we haven't come to mourn a corpse today. We've come to hail a risen conqueror. His name is Jesus, and he is alive this morning in each one of us who knows him.

The Bible is the sufficient word of God, but I think many Christians don't know how to utilize it. So many Christians lack joy. What do you do when you are down and despairing? You're depressed. Maybe you say, "That's never happened to me, Pastor." Well, just hang on. Give it time. It happens to all of us.

How do you get up when you've fallen and think you cannot get up? I'm not talking about having fallen physically, but emotionally, spiritually, when you're down and don't seem to be able to recover. Now I'm not just talking about feeling bad about certain things.

Somebody asked a lady, "What do you do when you get, down?" She said, "When I get down, I get a new pair of shoes." Her husband said, "I wondered where you'd gotten that amazing collection."

Whether we actually live with joy or allow something to take it from us is a choice each of us makes every day. Living with joy is a decision we make again and again as we're continually faced with joy stealers such as worry, bitterness, guilt, negativity, and busyness. The Psalms are filled with joyful passages to encourage us. But you know Philippians is a book of joy. Let's look at three ways in Philippians 3:1-3 how you can increase your joy.

> **Philippians 3:1-3** | Finally, my brothers, rejoice in the Lord. To write the same things to you is no trouble to me and is safe for you. ² Look out for the dogs, look out for the evildoers, look out for those who mutilate the flesh. ³ For we are the circumcision, who worship by the Spirit of God and glory in Christ Jesus and put no confidence in the flesh.

## INCREASE YOUR WELLSPRING OF JOY (3:1)

What is the wellspring of joy? It's a relationship with Christ. We are united with Christ, but we need to practice the presence of God in a practical way. We need to rejoice in every circumstance, however difficult, that Christ is with us and guiding us through it.

> **Philippians 3:1** | Finally, my brothers, rejoice in the Lord. To write the same things to you is no trouble to me and is safe for you.

"Finally" does not mean to indicate that Paul has come to the end of this letter. This is only the halfway mark in the book of Philippians! There will be another "finally" to come (4:8). This word "finally" could be translated "moreover," "furthermore," "so then," or "now then." He's reviewing the main theme here. I'm going to say it and say it again and again and again and again. This is so important: Finally, most importantly, rejoice in the Lord!

A Christian possesses joy that the world never knows. Many assume that the opposite is true. They think the Christian life is one of drudgery. They presume we live an antiquated life in which we deny ourselves every pleasure. But nothing could be further from the truth. The Christian life is filled with unspeakable joy that far surpasses anything that anyone in this world could ever know. In fact, knowing Jesus Christ is the only source of true and lasting joy that there is.

### The Reason to Rejoice

We have a reason to rejoice: the Lord (3:1). The sphere in which joy is found is in a relationship with the Lord Jesus Christ. True joy is a gift from God that only he can give. The psalmist declared, "You have put gladness in my heart" (Psa 4:7). And, "In your presence is fullness of joy" (Psa 16:11). This joy is produced by the Holy Spirit in the believer. Paul writes, "The kingdom of God is ... joy in the Holy Spirit" (Rom 14:17). Again, "The fruit of the Spirit is ... joy" (Gal 5:22). There is not one drop of real joy to be experienced apart from him. All joy is in the Lord.

"The joy of which Paul writes is not the same as happiness (a word related to the term 'happenstance'), the feeling of exhilaration associated with favorable events. In fact, joy persists in the face of weakness, pain, suffering, even death."[72] We are called as Christians to focus on a sovereign, loving God who is superintending every detail of your life. There is a joy, a happiness in Christ that cannot come from the world. Your circumstances, your emotions, your money: nothing can take away the sense of contentment in Christ. Joy is a matter of focus. Consider Paul's plea to the Colossians.

> If then you have been raised with Christ, seek the things that are above, where Christ is, seated at the right hand of God. ² Set your minds on things that are above, not on things that are on earth. ³ For you have died, and your life is hidden with Christ in God. ⁴ When Christ who is your life appears, then you also will appear with him in glory. —*Colossians 3:1-4*

True joy is not dependent upon circumstances. Neither does it come from the things of this world. Authentic joy comes from having a personal relationship with God through Jesus Christ. Real joy comes from knowing the Lord. This source of joy rises above our circumstances and cannot be drained by the surrounding situation. It is available in good times and difficult times, in prosperity and poverty. No matter what transpires in someone's life, they can know joy.[73]

## The Command to Rejoice

*It is a duty for us to cultivate this joy.* We must daily put a stop to any tendency to murmur and complain about life. Instead we should praise! We must resist the temptation to depression and melancholy as we would to any form of sin.[74] We are commanded to rejoice. Paul says it in Philippians 4:4, "Rejoice in the Lord, always, and again I say, Rejoice."

The grammar here is interesting. "Rejoice" (3:1) is in the continual *present tense*. The means that the Philippian Christians, and we, are always to be rejoicing in the Lord. We are to rejoice not only on Sunday morning in their church gathering, but throughout the week in our homes and workplaces. We are to be always rejoicing in every circumstance of life. We should rejoice in good times, as well as bad times. We should be glad not only in prosperity, but in poverty and hard times. Rejoicing is to be our habitual emotion as Christians. What about when

---

[72] MacArthur. *Philippians*, 216.
[73] Lawson. *Philippians*, 136.
[74] Guzik, *Philippians*, Php 3:1–2.

I'm sad? Can I rejoice in Jesus when I'm sad? Jesus commands us to do so.

> Seeing the crowds, he went up on the mountain, and when he sat down, his disciples came to him. ²And he opened his mouth and taught them, saying: ³"Blessed are the poor in spirit, for theirs is the kingdom of heaven. ⁴Blessed are those who mourn, for they shall be comforted." —*Matthew 5:1-4*

In addition, "rejoice" is in the imperative mood. That means "rejoice" is a command to be obeyed. It is an act of the will in choosing to obey God. To rejoice in the Lord is the responsibility of every Christian to choose to obey. Paul is commanding his readers to rejoice. They may not have felt like rejoicing, but that did not give them an excuse to mope around. That would be living in disobedience to this command. Believers are always to rejoice in the Lord. There are reasons why we become discouraged, some of them significant. But there are always greater reasons to rejoice. God does not command what he does not make possible.[75] Rejoicing for a Christian is God's will.

> Rejoice always, ¹⁷pray without ceasing,¹⁸ give thanks in all circumstances; for this is the will of God in Christ Jesus for you.
> —*1 Thessalonians 5:16-18*

## The Choice to Rejoice

The truth is when we understand Romans 8:28-30, that God is using every circumstance to make us like Jesus, then we can make a choice to rejoice. This verb "rejoice" is in the active voice. This means Christians must take action to rejoice. We are to take charge in this matter. We have this obligation to direct our minds and hearts to rejoice in the Lord. We are the only ones who can fulfill this. God will not do this independently of our making this choice to rejoice in the Lord. When Paul states this in the active voice, this could be translated, "I command you to be always making every effort to be rejoicing in the Lord." We are to make every effort to choose joy in Christ.

## The Safety of Rejoicing

Paul says, it is safe to rejoice. He says, "I keep writing to you the same thing: rejoice, rejoice, rejoice." It's no trouble for me, but for you it is safe. Why would he say that? A joyful focus on Jesus keeps you

---

[75] Lawson. *Philippians*, 138-139.

moving in the right direction. All sin (complaining, anger, anxiety, despair) gives a place for the devil to counsel our hearts (Eph 4:26-27). You can just imagine, here is Paul, he's chained to a soldier. He's saying these words, and Epaphroditus (the pastor of Philippi) is writing them down. It's almost as if he can see the Philippians' eyes rolling as he brings up joy again.

> **Philippians 3:1** | Finally, my brothers, rejoice in the Lord. To write the same things to you is no trouble to me and is safe for you.

This is not tedious. I'm not a broken record. It's not like I've run out of stuff to say. Actually, it is safe. Why is it safe? You can't apply what you don't remember. The Bible teaches us many of the same things over and over again. Why? Because we are forgetful creatures. If we don't constantly shore up spiritual truth that we've heard before that we will forget it. If you don't hang on, and anchor down, and remind yourself of the things you learn they'll slip away. They say we only remember a small percentage of what we hear. The statistics are actually a bit depressing for a public speaker. Twenty-five percent (25%). You retain 25% of what you hear if you hear it twice. So Paul is constantly repeating it: Rejoice, rejoice, rejoice, rejoice! He does it because we are so prone to forget. When we forget to rejoice we get into a lot of trouble. How do we stay safe in joy? One way is by saturating our mind with the promises of God.

> Having therefore these promises, dearly beloved, let us cleanse ourselves from all filthiness of the flesh and spirit, perfecting holiness in the fear of God. —*2 Corinthians 7:1*

Joy keeps us protected from so many sins of our own fallen spirits. "The joy of the Lord is my strength" (Neh 8:10). What are some sins that take away our joy? Sinful anger (Eph 4:26-27, "Be angry and do not sin; do not let the sun go down on your anger, 27 and give no opportunity to the devil"), self-pity, bitterness, worldly curiosity, constant amusement, laziness, lust, fear, overly downcast spirit. You can think of many more! Joy protects us from falling into all of these and more.

Spurgeon said, "Glory be to God for the furnace, the hammer and the file. Heaven shall be all the fuller of bliss because we have been filled with anguish here below; and earth shall be better tilled because of our training in the school of adversity."[76]

## INCREASE YOUR WATCHFULNESS OF JOY (3:2)

Paul says, we need to watch out for those things and people that can steal our joy. Paul's main concern is the false teachers who threaten to steal the joy of the Philippians. They are the Jewish teachers who are saying you need to keep the law to be saved.

### A Description of Joy Stealers

**Philippians 3:2** | Look out for the dogs, look out for the evildoers, look out for those who mutilate the flesh.

"Look out!" Be on guard! False teachers are coming. Now, what Paul was telling us is this: that some of the meanest people in the world are in the world of religion. And, Paul says, "Beware." Don't you think just because a person is religious, he's nice. You will find more meanness in the world of religion than perhaps anywhere else. It was a religious crowd that crucified Jesus. And so, the Apostle Paul says, "Beware of dogs."

I heard about a missionary one time that was accosted by a lion. And, the missionary was afraid the lion would devour him, and he was hoping for some kind of mercy when he saw the lion fold his big, massive paws in front of him, bow his head reverently, and start to move his lips as though he was praying. The missionary said, "Can it be—a Christian lion?" But then, the lion noticed that the missionary was looking somewhat relieved, and the lion said, "Don't get your hopes up, I'm just asking the blessing before the meal."[77] Now, there are some people who may act very religious, but they're very cruel and very ferocious.

#### Dogs

These false teachers are first referred to as "dogs." This reference is not to a domesticated house pet, but to wild scavengers. These false teachers are like vicious, wild dogs that roam the streets in packs from one garbage dump to the next, devouring what has been thrown away.

---

[76] Charles Spurgeon, "The Minister's Fainting Fits," in *Lectures to My Students* (Edinburgh: Banner of Truth, 2008), 191.

[77] Adrian Rogers. Sermon, "The Things that Really Count" (Memphis, TN: The Adrian Rogers Legacy Collection, 2005), Philippians 3:1-9.

In this hunt, they attack innocent people and spread disease. These corrupters of truth feed on the trash of false doctrine. They spread the deadly disease of doctrinal error and moral decadence. They were marked by the uncleanness of their own immorality. They are vicious in character and attack the sheep. They are vile in their motives and filthy in their conduct.[78]

This description says it all. These are wild animals seeking only for themselves. The people Paul was referring to were very smooth Bible teachers. They were gentle on the outside, but when you got too close to them, they took advantage of you like a wild dog. These "dogs" do not give you hope in Christ but wound you.

### Evil Doers

Paul further refers to the false teachers as "evil workers." This speaks of their evil character, as well as their endless industry in spreading more bad character which ends in bad morals.[79] Bad doctrine always leads to bad living.

### False Teachers

These false teachers are also the "false circumcision" (NASB), which explains what they teach and impose upon others. The religious rite of male circumcision was taught in the Old Testament as a sign of God's covenant with the nation of Israel (Gen 17). The death of Christ fulfilled the meaning of circumcision (Col 2:10-14). But these Judaizers were attempting to keep people under the old covenant by requiring their followers to be circumcised. Thus, Paul refers to them as the false circumcision.[80] The point is: false teachers steal your joy. They're going to take the spotlight off of Christ and onto themselves. Be careful, because many will use even good doctrine to

## Watch Out for Joy Stealers

What are some things that steal our joy? There are so many temptations. The key to joy is a radical focus on Christ; it's what the Old Testament prophets called "the fear of the Lord." We are to practice the presence of God. So really the question is, what gets our focus off of

---

[78] Lawson, *Philippians*, 142-143.
[79] Ibid.
[80] Ibid.

Christ? Because that is what steals our joy. Let's look at a few possibilities.

Bad teaching about God. For example, the false idea that God is mad at his children. No, there is no condemnation (Rom 8:1). God doesn't punish his children. He disciplines them so that he might lavish his love on them. Get your view of God right. Exodus 20:3, "You shall have no other gods before me." You don't get to decide what God is like. He is a loving God and the shepherd of all his children.

Lack of daily worship/prayerlessness. You are a pillar of fire, child of God. When you leave your worship behind, you are like a dry, empty temple. "One thing have I asked of the Lord, that will I seek after: that I may dwell in the house of the Lord all the days of my life, to gaze upon the beauty of the Lord and to inquire in his temple" (Psa 27:4).

Passive men (and women). If you know the right thing to do and you don't do it, it's sin (Jas 4:17).

Grudge holding (Eph 4:26-31). Be the first to say, "Forgive me." Defuse anger quickly so you can be a blessing in the relationship.

Gossip. Manufacturing gossip or words that tear down the reputation of others will never add any joy to your life. On the other hand, when you use your words to build into the lives of others you bring joy to you and them as well. Psalm 40:3, "He put a new song in my mouth, a song of praise to our God. Many will see and fear, and put their trust in the Lord." Gossip tears down. Praise and encouragement builds up.

Approval seeking. Being liked by everyone is so overrated. It's much better to have God's approval and love others from a genuine place, instead of neediness.

Negative self-talk. We often let lies from Satan or others sneak in and destroy us. Instead, preach the word to yourself! Let God's word pour in and over and through your life.

Living in the past. You are a new creation (2 Cor 5:17). We are to forget that which is behind and reach forth to the high calling of God, which is to know Christ (Phil 3:13-14).

Fear of the future. Whatever your future holds, it means conformity to Jesus! (Rom 8:28-30).

## INCREASE YOUR WORSHIP THROUGH JOY (3:3)

Paul says, true Judaism, the true Israel or circumcision are those "who worship by the Spirit of God." Paul gives us the key to worship.

The first is circumcision of the heart. We have to have a sensitive, heart, cut by the word.

## A Sensitive Heart

> **Philippians 3:3** | For we are the circumcision, who worship by the Spirit of God and glory in Christ Jesus and put no confidence in the flesh.

What is Paul talking about? What is circumcision? Circumcision in the Old Testament was the cutting of the male foreskin as an outward sign of being set apart from the sinful world, in the service of the living God. It was a ritual that indicated what must happen to the heart. In itself, circumcision brought no redeeming value. It did not save, nor did it sanctify. It was a picture of what must take place in the heart. Circumcision stressed that there must be a cutting of the sinful heart that is hardened by sin. Getting close to God requires the cutting of the heart. Isn't that what you want? Our hearts need circumcision. Theologically this refers to the life-giving power of the Spirit in the heart to make you alive to God. But we need a constant cutting of the word and the Spirit. The word is the sword of the Spirit, and it is "sharper than any two-edged sword." Is your heart getting cut by the word? A baby doesn't circumcise himself. That's why we need each other.

The Bible is life-giving, called the "word of life" (Phil 2:16). The disciple (learner, follower) of Christ has an unbreakable connection with God through his word. The word is a living, active double-edged sword that pierces "to the division of soul and of spirit, of joints and of marrow, and discerning the thoughts and intentions of the heart" (Heb 4:12-13). The word is "like a fire" (Jer 23:29a). The Bible is a mirror that reveals (Jas 1:23). God's word is milk that nourishes us (1 Pet 2:2, "...like newborn babies, long for the pure milk of the word, so that by it you may grow in respect to salvation"). The Bible "is a lamp to my feet, and a light to my path"). We have been "born again... through the living and abiding word of God" (1 Pet 1:23). God's word is a weapons chest that keeps us from sin (Psa 119:11). God's word is an offensive spiritual weapon called the "sword of the Spirit" (Eph 6:17). You are blessed only as you "meditate on God's law day and night" (Psa 1:2).

We need discipleship groups. What do I mean? This is outside the small group ministry where you are staying accountable with two or three other brothers or sisters throughout the week. Paul says, "*We* are the circumcision, who worship..." You can't do this alone. We must worship together. We must allow God to cut into our hearts. Paul said to Timothy: "...what you have heard from me in the presence of many witnesses entrust to faithful men, who will be able to teach others also" (2 Tim 2:2). There are four levels of discipleship going on. Paul, Timothy, faithful men, others. That's how our D-groups ought to function.

## A Spirit-Filled Heart

**Philippians 3:3a** | For we are the circumcision, who worship by the Spirit of God and glory in Christ Jesus.

Circumcision refers to the sensitivity of the heart. It has the idea that your heart is cut and sensitive. Are you often wounded and healed by the word of God? How do you know you are living with a heart unhardened by the world? If the word of God doesn't lead you to worship, something is wrong. You see we all have a worship disorder. We want to worship the creation above our Creator. Our fallen natures want to worship comfort over our Creator. We would rather have self-worship over Christ our Savior.

Do you worship by the Spirit of God and glory in Christ? Are you Spirit-filled? What are some indications in Scripture that you are Spirit-filled? Ephesians 5:18 commands us to "be filled with the Spirit" and the following evidences are named: speaking Scripture (Psalms, hymns...) to each other (Eph 5:19a), singing in your heart to Jesus (Eph 5:19b), giving thanks (Eph 5:20), a spirit of humility and submission (Eph 5:21), the fruit of the Spirit (Gal 5:22-23), boldness (Acts 4:31, "...they were all filled with the Holy Spirit and continued to speak the word of God with boldness"), joy (Acts 13:52, "And the disciples were filled with joy and with the Holy Spirit"), conviction of sin (Jn 16:8, "And when he comes, he will convict the world concerning sin and righteousness and judgment), supernatural comfort, reminding you of God's promises (Jn 14:26, "the Comforter, which is the Holy Ghost, whom the Father will send in my name, he shall teach you all things, and bring all things to your remembrance, whatsoever I have said unto you"), prayer (Jude 1:20, "Pray in the power of the Holy Spirit"), and a peaceful heart. If a person is filled with the Holy Spirit he will not necessarily be noisy, highly excited or full of physical strength. The Spirit-filled life is a life of calm poise and quiet confidence (Isa 30:15, "...in quietness and in trust shall be your strength"). Remember the Holy

Spirit manifests his form as a dove at the baptism of Jesus. Consider that "the wisdom from above is first pure, then peaceable, gentle, open to reason, full of mercy and good fruits, impartial and sincere" (Jas 3:17). Are you worshipping in the Spirit throughout the day?

## A Crucified Heart

**Philippians 3:3c** | Put no confidence in the flesh.

The idea of no confidence is elsewhere illustrated as crucified. Galatians 2:20, "I am crucified with Christ…" We have to cut ourselves off from the unholy things of the world. The Lord says, "Be holy as I the Lord am holy." What does it mean to be holy? It means to be set apart for God's glory. Everything you do as a Christian should be holy and honoring to God. 1 Corinthians 10:31 says even our eating and drinking should bring glory to God. Your attitude to your wife and to your church family ought to be a holy cheerfulness. There is no excuse. We must "put no confidence in the flesh." Growth in grace is not going to happen by your own efforts. Effort must be supernaturally empowered by the Spirit of God. You can only go forward on your knees as it were with a spirit of worship. Don't trust yourself. Get into a life-on-life discipleship environment.

### Conclusion

Here are three pathways to joy. The joy of the Lord is our strength! Let me tell you the story of a recent wrestling match with my son William. I was a bit proud and wanted to show him that I still had it. My son is only 15 years old, but he towers over me at 6 foot 4 inches. He is strong, but I knew I could still take him down. Boy was I wrong. I had my daughter Kristen film it, and she is of course forbidden from sharing it with anyone. But what occurred surprised me. In less than a minute my powerful son very gently grabbed me and carefully laid my shoulders on the ground, like a gentle giant. He didn't want to hurt me. What happened? How did he get so strong? He grew!

We also need to grow in the joy of the Lord. This is how we know we are maturing in Christ. Our maturity is seen by our level of joy in the Spirit. No matter what the circumstances, a Christian has the supernatural ability to rejoice.

# 13 | PHILIPPIANS 3:4-11
## THE GREAT CHANGE

*Indeed, I count everything as loss because of the surpassing worth of knowing Christ Jesus my Lord. For his sake I have suffered the loss of all things and count them as rubbish, in order that I may gain Christ*
PHILIPPIANS 3:8

Every believer has a testimony of how they came to faith in Jesus Christ. In these verses, Paul presents his to us. Any testimony of true faith in Christ has three parts: my life before Christ, how I came to know Christ, and my life after knowing Christ. In a testimony, we always have an B.C. and an A.D. part of our lives. BC: "Before Christ" and A.D., "After Deliverance." Do you have that kind of testimony of your conversion?

**Philippians 3:4-9** | Though I myself have reason for confidence in the flesh also. If anyone else thinks he has reason for confidence in the flesh, I have more: ⁵ circumcised on the eighth day, of the people of Israel, of the tribe of Benjamin, a Hebrew of Hebrews; as to the law, a Pharisee;⁶ as to zeal, a persecutor of the church; as to righteousness under the law, blameless. ⁷ But whatever gain I had, I counted as loss for the sake of Christ. ⁸ Indeed, I count everything as loss because of the surpassing worth of knowing Christ Jesus my Lord. For his sake I have suffered the loss of all things and count them as rubbish, in order that I may gain Christ ⁹ and be found in him, not having a righteousness of my own that comes from the law, but that which comes through faith in Christ, the righteousness from God that depends on faith.

## LIFE BEFORE CHRIST (3:4-6)

Paul explains his life before his conversion in verses 4-6. Here Paul describes his old existence before he met Jesus Christ.

**Philippians 3:4** | Though I myself have reason for confidence in the flesh also. If anyone else thinks he has reason for confidence in the flesh, I have more:

What Paul means is, If mere religious efforts could gain anyone acceptance with God, then I am at the head of that list. Put another way, If anyone could find salvation through his self-righteousness, that was me. He lists all the things in which he once put his confidence. Yet Paul was completely wrong about trusting in all his good works. Isaiah says anything we do to gain or merit God's love and acceptance are nothing but filthy rags. Remember the words of Isaiah, "But we are all as an unclean *thing*, and all our righteousnesses *are* as filthy rags" (Isa 64:6a, KJV). In verses 5 and 6, Paul notes seven different facts in which he once trusted, none of which could commend him before God.[81]

**Philippians 3:5** | Circumcised on the eighth day, of the people of Israel, of the tribe of Benjamin, a Hebrew of Hebrews; as to the law, a Pharisee.

### Impressive Beginning

First, Paul explains that he had the right beginning. He was "circumcised the eighth day" (3:5). No Jew could have a more proper beginning than this. The Mosaic Law required that on the eighth day, a baby boy would be circumcised, which was the cutting of the male foreskin and the sign of the covenant. This ritual signified that there must come a time in which the heart of the individual must be circumcised as well. There must come the reality when that child is set apart by the Holy Spirit unto God. Circumcision was a religious ritual practiced by Israel with the significance that the heart must be cut by the word of God. Paul had the sign of the covenant. What a great beginning. Paul's

---

[81] This section is adapted from Lawson. *Philippians*, 152-153.

parents loved him. But no parent's love is great enough to save that child. We must each personally know the love of Christ. Though Paul had a great beginning, he is lost, lost, lost. Being born in the right home, with a Christian family cannot save anyone.

Perhaps you also had the right beginning. Maybe you were brought to church from the time you were born. Maybe you were sprinkled as an infant. Maybe you were dedicated to the Lord in a special church service. Whatever might have happened to you in your childhood, none of these things can give you a right standing before God.

## Impressive Nationality

Second, Paul had the right nationality. He was born "of the nation of Israel" (3:5). Sure, he was born in Tarsus, a Roman city, to Jewish parents who possessed Roman citizenship, but he also had citizenship in the nation of Israel, as a true Hebrew. Israel was God's chosen nation. God made his covenant with Israel through Abraham and promised that Christ would come through his family. To be a member of Israel was to inherit a great privilege (*cf* Rom 9:4-5). God placed his own presence among them and visited them in a fiery pillar of glory, day and night in the Tabernacle and Temple.

The people of Israel were privileged to receive the Scriptures for the whole world. No other nation had such an advantage through access to the word of God. God gave his law, he sent his prophets, and he gave his commandments, all to the chosen nation of Israel. Paul was born in the nation that was chosen to guard and keep the word of God. But that's not enough.

Our country has so many Bibles. No one in the history of the world has had access to such knowledge of God. But knowledge alone can't save anyone. It takes a trust, a full surrender to Christ. Paul had not surrendered. He was lost, though he had a fantastic homeland of Israel.

## Impressive Lineage

Third, Paul testifies that he had the right lineage: he was "of the tribe of Benjamin" (3:5). This was an impressive tribe to be from for a number of reasons. Benjamin was the favorite son of Jacob and Rachel after Joseph was taken to Egypt. Benjamin was also the tribe of the first king, King Saul, after whom Paul was named after. His Jewish name is Saul, and his Hellenistic or Greek name is Paul. So Paul is named after the first king of Israel. Then, of the twelve tribes of Israel, Benjamin was one of the two elite tribes that mostly stayed faithful to the Lord. They were one of the two tribes that remained loyal to King David's descendants when the kingdom divided; together, they formed the southern kingdom of Judah.

In the land assigned to Benjamin the capital city, Jerusalem, was situated. So, it was in the land assigned to Benjamin that the Temple was built, and the sacrifices were made. Paul was not only an Israelite; he was from an impressive tribe. Many today presume that the spiritual lineage of their family tree will give them a right standing with God.

## Impressive Upbringing

Fourth, Paul adds that he was "a Hebrew of Hebrews" (3:5). Though Saul born in Tarsus as a Hebrew, but he was raised in the capital city of Israel, in Jerusalem. Paul was not just as a Hebrew, but "a Hebrew of Hebrews" – everyday worshipping at the Temple in Jerusalem. Every day he wasn't just at a synagogue, he was at the Temple.

To be "a Hebrew of Hebrews" means Paul was raised according to strictest Hebrew tradition. He was reared in a Hebrew home and learned the Hebrew language. According to his own testimony (Acts 22:3), Paul would have begun his studies of the Hebrew Scriptures (likely around age 15) in the city of Jerusalem under the greatest Hebrew scholar of his time, the renowned Rabbi Gamaliel.

We find his own testimony in Acts 22:6, "I am a Jew, born in Tarsus in Cilicia, but brought up in this city, educated at the feet of Gamaliel according to the strict manner of the law of our fathers, being zealous for God as all of you are this day." Gamaliel was like the Yoda of rabbis! And Paul was training to be the next great rabbi of national renown. This was a true Hebrew of Hebrews.

Saul was also a member of the elitist of the elite of Hebrews, the Council of the Sanhedrin (See Acts 6:12; *cf* 6:15; 7:58). The Sanhedrin was *the governing body of 70 elders who ruled the Jews*. When Stephen the first Christian martyr was stoned, they brought him before the Sanhedrin, who charged him guilty, and to be put to death by stoning. Paul was so much "in" in the Sanhedrin, that he was the chief witness who actually held the coats of those who stoned Stephen.

You couldn't get any more Hebrew than Paul was. He was a diehard Hebrew. He was as religiously a Hebrew as anyone could possibly be. Maybe you can relate to this. Maybe you also had the right upbringing. Perhaps you were raised in a Christian home and attended a Christian school, and maybe you even learned the truths of the Bible as a young person. While these are all good things, none of them are able to save you. They are worthless if they don't point you to Christ.

## Impressive Standard

Fifth, Paul had an impressive standard by which he lived. "As to the Law [he was] a Pharisee" (3:5). According to the Jewish historian Josephus, there were about 6,000 Pharisees during the time of Jesus. The term Pharisee meant "separated one". These were the most elite religious Jews. These were the rock stars of the religious world. Paul was one of them.

What does this say about Paul? As a Pharisee he was an expert in the Old Testament Scriptures. Pharisees took the Bible literally. They believed it. They read it. They studied it for hours every day. They taught it. They preached it. They applied it. They enforced it. They were fiercely devoted to upholding the word of God. Moreover, Pharisees sought to live the Bible with all their might. So it was with Paul before his conversion; he was a walking, talking storehouse of Bible knowledge. Paul knew the Scriptures inside out. Maybe you are committed to the teaching of the Bible. Perhaps you know it well. Perhaps you teach it to others or preach to your church. But even this, while noble and commendable, cannot save you.

## Impressive Sincerity

Sixth, Paul had a powerful passion and sincerity. He adds that he was, "as to zeal, a persecutor of the church" (3:6). Zeal was considered the highest virtue of the Jewish faith. It meant simultaneous love and hate. It meant that you loved God so much that you hated whatever threatened that love. This is a wonderful virtue, but because Paul is a human, his zeal went wrong. Shockingly, all this amazing religion put a twist on the Scriptures that blinded him to the true Savior. Before Christ, Saul loved his Jewish faith so much that he hated the very Jewish Messiah Jesus! How much zeal did Paul have? He tried to kill Christians and succeeded. He admits to it in Acts 22.

> In one synagogue after another I imprisoned and beat those who believed in [Christ]. [20] And when the blood of Stephen [God's] witness was being shed, I myself was standing by and approving and watching over the garments of those who killed him. —*Acts 22:19-20*

Paul had authority to put people to death because he was an officer of the Sanhedrin, the most powerful governing body of the Jews. He was there as the primary witness at Stephen's death. Paul was not lukewarm about anything he did, and certainly not about religion. Paul was not apathetic, nor was he a "half in, half out" type of person. He was full of zeal and passion for holy things. He was filled with sincerity, so much so that not only did he love what he believed to be right, but he hated what he was convinced was wrong. From this character came his violent persecution against the church of the Lord Jesus Christ.

## Impressive Morality

Seventh, Paul had a high standard of morality. "...as to righteousness under the law, [I was] blameless" (3:6). He wasn't just concerned about the ten commandments; he was diligent about keeping all 613 laws prescribed in the Levitical law code. He was like the rich young ruler who said, "All these I have kept from my youth up" (Lk 18:21). These laws all pointed to the beauty of Jesus Christ, but Paul was so focused on the law that *he missed Christ*.

Had we been there, we would have stood back and looked at the life of before-conversion Paul and concluded that here was a straight arrow if there ever was one. He sought to live by the standard of God's law. He was outwardly moral. He was extremely upright. He was serious as one can be about God's law. But he was lost. So lost. He was dead in his sins. He "had a form of godliness, but denied it's power" (2 Tim 3:5).

Perhaps you are like this, too. You are well known as a good man or woman. You take following the Bible's commands very seriously. But this too will not save you. Paul had all this morality, but Christ got a hold of Paul, he called himself the "chief of sinners" (1 Tim 1:15). Compared to Christ Paul's righteousness (and our own righteousness) is filthy rags (Isa 64:5).

### *Paul Had Everything But Jesus*

Paul appeared to have everything going for him before conversion. If anyone could have ever earned their way to heaven by their own religiosity, Saul of Tarsus would have been exhibit number one, and at the head of the line. This man who would become the apostle of Christ had an impressive beginning, nationality, lineage, upbringing, standard, sincerity, and morality. But before his conversion he hated Christ, and he killed Christians.

*Everything Minus Jesus Equals Nothing*

You see, Paul had everything except for one thing. He had everything... except Jesus Christ. Here is the ultimate math equation for your life: everything minus Jesus equals nothing. If a person does not have Christ, they have nothing. Paul had everything except everything that he needed. Everything minus Jesus equals nothing.

How does this first part of Paul's testimony compare to the first part of your testimony? Could it be that you once were lost in religion? Perhaps you were sincere about spiritual things, but sincerely wrong. Could it be that this describes where your life is at this moment? Maybe you are reading this and coming to the realization that you are a religious person but have never been personally converted to Jesus Christ. If so, it is important for you to know where you stand. A right diagnosis, it is said, is half the cure. But it is only half. You need to experience what now follows.

## COMING TO KNOW CHRIST (3:7-9; ACTS 9:1-5)

Next Paul describes what happened to him at conversion, when he came to know Christ.

> **Philippians 3:7-8** | But whatever gain I had, I counted as loss for the sake of Christ. ⁸ Indeed, I count everything as loss because of the surpassing worth of knowing Christ Jesus my Lord. For his sake I have suffered the loss of all things and count them as rubbish, in order that I may gain Christ.

In one second, Saul of Tarsus was changed. One glimpse of Jesus made him see that everything he used to love and live for was human excrement and worthless compared to the surpassing worth of knowing Christ. Once he met Christ, Paul was never the same again. So before we begin looking at the next verses, we need to see how Paul was introduced to the worth of knowing Christ, so that he was willing to forsake everything for Christ. In coming to know Christ, we know the reach of Christ, the riches of Christ, and the righteousness of Christ.

### We Know the Reach of Christ

Consider the long reach of Christ to bring sinners to himself. Wherever you are, he will find you. The reach of Christ is beyond what we can imagine. He leaves the ninety and nine to find the one lost wandering sheep. Do you remember when he found you? He calls to you: "Come to me, all who labor and are heavy laden, and I will give you rest" (Mt 11:28). He's calling you right now. His says to his servants and ambassadors, "Go out to the highways and hedges and compel people to come in, that my house may be filled" (Lk 14:23). The Bible says God's reach is so long! "God demonstrates his own love toward us, in that while we were yet sinners, Christ died for us" (Rom 5:9). He is "not willing that any should perish but that all should come to repentance" (2 Pet 3:9).

Wherever you are, God's reaching for you. He reaches out to rebellious Israel: "I will not execute my burning anger; I will not again destroy Ephraim [Israel]; for I am God and not a man, the Holy One in your midst, and I will not come in wrath" (Hos 11:9). "Come, let us return to the Lord; for he has torn us, that he may heal us; he has struck us down, and he will bind us up" (Hos 6:1). God's reach is so far, he can reach every person. Jesus was "crowned with glory and honor because of the suffering of death, so that by the grace of God he might taste death for everyone" (Heb 2:9). Wouldn't you agree that God has a far reach?

God's reach is so far that he grabbed the worst self-righteous legalist who was later nicknamed, "the chief of sinners." God has a longest arm in the universe. He'll find you wherever you are. He's after you with his unrelenting love. Our Lord has a far reach. He's got a long arm. "Is there anything too hard for the Lord?" (Jer 32:27). "Is the arm of the Lord too short that it cannot save?" (Num 11:23).

God's long arm of love for Saul of Tarsus is on full display in Acts 9. Here is probably the greatest conversion ever recorded. We see the unrelenting love of God coming after Paul. Look at this. Paul is killing Christians, and the Lord tracks him down, not to destroy him, but to save him. Look at our loving God!

> But Saul, still breathing threats and murder against the disciples of the Lord, went to the high priest [2] and asked him for letters to the synagogues at Damascus, so that if he found any belonging to the Way, men or women, he might bring them bound to Jerusalem. [3] Now as he went on his way, he approached Damascus, and suddenly a light from heaven shone around him. [4] And falling to the ground, he heard a voice saying to him, "Saul, Saul, why are you persecuting me?" [5] And

he said, "Who are you, Lord?" And he said, "I am Jesus, whom you are persecuting." —*Acts 9:1-5*

### *A Surprising Love*

What a surprising day it was that Saul of Tarsus was saved. God is going to show his love to a man that hates his dearly beloved Son Jesus Christ. We read in Acts 9:1, "But Saul, still breathing threats and murder against the disciples of the Lord ..." Here we see his zeal as a persecutor of the church. Paul was adamantly opposed to anything that did not adhere to his religious traditions in Judaism. He "went to the high priest [2] and asked him for letters to the synagogues at Damascus, so that if he found any belonging to the Way, men or women, he might bring them bound to Jerusalem" (Acts 9:1-2). The early Christians were referred to as those belonging to the Way, because they walked the narrow path headed to life. They lived according to the word of God in a dark and devilish generation—like stars shining in the dark. But Saul was in the darkness at this point—and so if he found any belonging to the Way, he was determined to "bring them bound to Jerusalem." He wanted to drag them back and have them stand trial, with the hope of putting them to death. The first Christian martyr, Stephen, had recently been stoned to death, with Saul standing by approvingly (Acts 7–8). Who was to know what Christian would be next? Who could know that Paul would one day become a martyr for Jesus Christ himself?

"Now as he went on his way, he approached Damascus" (Acts 9:3), about 150 miles north of Jerusalem, when "suddenly a light from heaven shone [flashed] around him." This light was the Shekinah glory of God—the very presence of the living God—shining brighter than the sun in the sky. Saul woke up that day wanting to persecute the church, and by midday, he was part of that church of Jesus. He woke up a persecutor and went to sleep a precious, adopted child of God!

Every conversion occurs suddenly. Every new birth occurs suddenly. It is not a process over a long period of time. There may be a process that leads up to conversion, but there is a moment, there is a time, when we cross the line; we step out of the world and step into the kingdom of heaven. This event, which we read of in Acts 9, is when Paul entered through the narrow gate leading to life.

This was not only a surprising day, it was a day when Saul met the Savior. Saul fell to the ground and heard a voice saying to him, "Saul, Saul." It was repeated with intensity: "Why are you persecuting me?"

(Acts 9:4). The glory of God shines, and we find out who Saul is persecuting: Jesus of Nazareth. To persecute the church is to persecute the Head of the church, the Lord Jesus Christ. Jesus lives in the church as he indwells the true believers of the church. To come against the church of the Lord Jesus Christ is to come against Christ himself.

## A Saving Love

God's reach is so far for this self-righteous Pharisee, that in a moment, Saul of Tarsus is converted. This was the day of salvation for Paul. We know because of what Saul called Jesus. He cried out, "Who are you, Lord?" (Acts 9:5). Paul's resistance against Jesus Christ was over. The Lord answered: "I am Jesus, whom you are persecuting." Jesus personally introduced himself to Saul of Tarsus. God appears to a man named Ananias (*different from the other Ananias from Acts 5*) in a vision and says that Saul of Tarsus "is a chosen instrument of mine to carry my name before the Gentiles and kings and the children of Israel" (Acts 9:15).

God's love transforms us at a point in time. In that moment when he met Jesus, Saul didn't know his great future. He simply understood that he was face to face with the King of heaven, the Lord Jesus Christ. Instantly, he saw that he had been wrong all of his life. In that moment, Saul was apprehended by God, and he yielded. Immediately, he confessed the lordship of Jesus Christ. He knew he was Lord! Who are you? he asked. But he called him Lord. He knew he was Lord. In that split second, he became a believer in Christ. He laid down his life at the feet of the Lord Jesus Christ. You may not know the very moment you were saved, but there is a line of demarcation in the Christian life. There is a moment when "you turned away from idols to serve the living and true God" (1 Thess 1:9, NLT). "He... delivered us from the domain of darkness and transferred us to the kingdom of his beloved Son" (Col 1:13). Saul of Tarsus stepped across the line by faith and became a true follower and disciple. In that instant, Saul was converted by the grace of God.

## A Love Embraced through Faith

Saul came "by grace, through faith" (Eph 2:8-9). He saw that he was wrong. He realized he was hateful. And this hateful man embraced the love of God, by grace through faith. Works couldn't get him anything but filthy rags.

What is faith? I'll tell you it's not complicated. Jesus said, it's so simple, that if you come to him, you have to have the faith of a little child. Let me tell you what faith is in a simple way. Faith is a surrender to the love of God in Christ. It's a trust and a surrender to the fact that Jesus, in his death, gave himself up willingly for you. "God so loved [put your name] that he gave his one and only Son, that whoever believes in him shall not perish but have everlasting life" (Jn 3:16). That's faith. Surrender to God's love. Stop trusting in your own ability to make God love you. You don't have to fix yourself up first. God already loves you. Surrender to that love, and *he'll* fix you up.

## We Know the Riches of Christ

In coming to know Christ, we know the reach of Christ, but we also know the riches of Christ. Let's go back to Philippians 3, and realize that something beautiful happened that day. Paul's day of conversion was also a day of accounting. Paul calculated the worth of knowing Christ. He says, nothing can compare to the worth of knowing Jesus!

The forceful phrase *indeed* (3:8) is an untranslatable string of five Greek particles (lit. "but indeed therefore at least even"). It strongly emphasizes the contrast between the worthless efforts we make to clean ourselves up that do not impress God, compared to the incalculable worth of knowing Christ.[82] Paul is saying, *this equation is important! Paul* begins,

> **Philippians 3:7-8** | But whatever gain I had, I counted as loss for the sake of Christ. ⁸ Indeed, I count everything as loss because of the surpassing worth of knowing Christ Jesus my Lord. For his sake I have suffered the loss of all things and count them as rubbish, in order that I may gain Christ.

Religiously, Paul looked rich, but he was spiritually bankrupt. Knowing Christ is worth losing everything! That's Paul's conclusion. Let's consider the comparison: In Christ, I have.... *everything*: total righteousness, a perfect record, adoption into God's family, abundant life now, and eternal life at death. Without Christ, I have... *excrement*. "All of the cherished treasures in his gain column suddenly became deficits."[83] Paul must have been thinking about what Isaiah said: "But we

---

[82] MacArthur, *Philippians*, 234.
[83] Ibid., 234.

are all as an unclean *thing*, and all our righteousnesses *are* as filthy rags" (Isa 64:6a). Paul says, "I count everything as loss because of the surpassing worth of knowing Christ Jesus my Lord" (Phil 3:8).

All of those things Paul listed before—self-effort and religion, upbringing and nationality—he used to think they would gain him entrance to heaven. But they were not gain in the eyes of the Almighty. And so, having encountered Jesus, he said, "those things I have counted as loss" (3:7b). They are loss, literally worthless. He says they are rubbish. Literally he calls them human excrement.

## We Know the Righteousness of Christ

In coming to know Christ, we know the righteousness of Christ. Paul mountain top of joy is found in verse 9: to be found in Christ! And to be found in Christ is to have his perfect righteousness applied to you.

> **Philippians 3:9** | And be found in him, not having a righteousness of my own that comes from the law, but that which comes through faith in Christ, the righteousness from God that depends on faith.

What an exchange! My rags for his robe of righteousness! How does this happen? It's something that I need to rest in. It's something Christ has already done. It's a righteousness that comes from Christ. It's just like Paul says in 2 Corinthians 5. "God made him who had no sin to be sin for us, so that in him we might become the righteousness of God" (2 Cor 5:21).

We are righteous in Christ! It reminds me of the little girl who was allergic to bees. One sting of a bee would take her life in less than an hour. One day she was riding in the car along the highway with her daddy. In the car flew an angry bee with a big stinger. The little girl began to panic. She began to wail. Daddy! A bee! Daddy, I could die. Daddy, is that bee going to sting me? Oh Daddy, I'm so afraid! She cried and she wailed. The bee buzzed around the car,

The angry bee harassed the father, and as soon as he could cupped that bee in his hand. He could feel the angry hornet hitting the inside of his hand. He would not stop. And then.... "Ouch!" yelled the father. He felt that stinger in his hand and let the bee go.

The bee flew erratically by that little girl again. She was terrified! The bees gonna get me Daddy!

The father showed black stinger in his hand to his daughter. Sweetheart, that bee cannot hurt you. Soon he'll die. I took the stinger for you.

That's what Christ has done. He's taken the sting of death for you. Paul quotes Hosea 13:14, "O death, where is your victory? O death, where is your sting?" (1 Cor 15:55). The sting of death is defeated! Jesus has taken on our filthy rags and given us his robe of righteousness!

## GROWING IN CHRIST (3:10-11)

We will look at this more in depth in our next study, but what Paul says: knowing Christ is the abundant life! This is the way to live! We were never truly alive until we experienced the resurrection of Christ.

> **Philippians 3:10-11** | That I may know him and the power of his resurrection, and may share his sufferings, becoming like him in his death, [11] that by any means possible I may attain the resurrection from the dead.

This is our life after coming to know Christ. It is growing in our relationship with the Lord. We are going to have an entire message on this next week, but for now, understand that conversion is just the beginning. We are to be like Paul in 2 Corinthians 3.

> And we all, with unveiled face, beholding the glory of the Lord, are being transformed into the same image from one degree of glory to another. For this comes from the Lord who is the Spirit.
> —*2 Corinthians 3:18*

How do we get there? I want to know Christ better! I want to grow in knowing Christ. We long to know Jesus better. Paul says, "that I may know him and the power of his resurrection, and may share his sufferings, becoming like him in his death..." (Phil 3:10). God says, "Draw near to me and I will draw near to you" (Jas 4:8). How can we draw near to our precious Lord? Here are ten practical ways to know Christ better.

Come with total surrender to Christ's love. This is another way of expressing true faith in Christ. Faith is a radical surrender of all you are and all you have to the love of Christ. This is the first baby step. Faith is not a work. You simply give your life unconditionally to God to love you. Do that now.

Come to God's word hungry. God is ready to satisfy you and renew your mind. Psalm 1:2-3 says growth comes through the slow meditation and consideration of God's word. The Bible is a book of God's love on every page (that's why it's called 'good news'). Experiencing God's love is the key to joy and growth. Take it slowly. You are probably more wounded than you care to admit. You can't feed a steak to a person in the ICU. Let God heal you through knowing Christ.

Come to Jesus needy. Remember intimacy is more than knowledge. There are many who "worship what they do not know" (Jn 4:22). Never in the history of the Christian church has so much theological knowledge been available to so many people as it is today. You can have an encyclopedic knowledge of Scripture and miss Jesus (Jn 5:39–40). Biblical knowledge that actually *drives us to trust* in Christ is better than the finest gold (Ps 19:10). Knowing Christ better means being vulnerable, humble and honest when we come to the word. Assume you are not righteous in yourself. Come in need of the Physician to heal you.

Find his wholeness in your brokenness. Every kind of brokenness you experience can lead to a corresponding blessing if you're willing to die to your own: will, goals, dreams, desires, expectations, plans, rights, and reputation. If you choose to die to yourself, God will pour out blessings like a character that reflects His own, a witness that leads to other people's lives being transformed, and rewards from God himself.

Find his nearness in your loneliness. No one understands your struggles more than Jesus. He "tasted death for every man" (Heb 2:9). This is the ultimate expression of love. Jesus gave all that he had (which is everything) to know you intimately.

Come ready for radical sacrifice. Knowing such a loving Savior demands sacrifice. All should know his love. All should be sacrificed so that the whole world may know. Sacrifice all for knowing him and sharing him with others.

Come ready for joyful holiness. Knowing Christ means union with him in death and resurrection. You have to die to anything that is unholy. God's glory is pure, sincere, good, and holy. It is love and kindness. It is totally selfless. Holiness is doing everything for the glory of God. You are chosen, separated and called for the God's glory. Cut off all that does not honor him.

Stand for Christ, and stand alone if you must. Be willing to stand out and speak up for Jesus in all areas of your life, and with whoever you meet. Take a strong public stand for the uniqueness of who Jesus is; for the truth of the entire Bible; and for the necessity of living a life of integrity, purity, and humility in order to please God.

Seek him, find him, and praise him for answered prayer (Mt 7:7). We serve a God who moves mountains. Our great God woke up balancing the 200 billion galaxies that contain 200 million stars each. That's just an estimate. He did that before you ate breakfast. Praise him! Watch him work. He has unlimited resources.

Live moment by moment, looking to Jesus. Bring Jesus home. Don't just be a Sunday Christian. Don't just be a Christian when you are in public or in church. Live honorably and walk humbly at home. Lay your life down for those closest to you at home first. Live a life of integrity in your private life. Let Jesus by his Spirit fill you in your free hours.

Jesus stands ready to help you come closer. He says, "Come to me, all who labor and are heavy laden, and I will give you rest. 29 Take my yoke upon you, and learn from me, for I am gentle and lowly in heart, and you will find rest for your souls. 30 For my yoke is easy, and my burden is light" (Mt 11:28-30).

## Conclusion

In Christ alone we stand. Not in any righteousness of our own. Christ is so merciful to reach us. What a testimony you have if you know Christ! The more you draw near to Christ, the more you are going to want to tell others. I hope God is forming your Discipleship Groups of 2 or 3 others that you can shine your light with. I pray as you draw near to Christ, both individually and together, that the light of Christ will shine and you will "make disciples of all nations" teaching all people about the love of God seen in Jesus Christ. Isn't he wonderful?

When I was a kid, I worked as a cook at Ponderosa Steakhouse. I hardly knew the Bible because I was a brand-new Christian. One thing I did know was the Roman's Road: a list of verses through Romans that clearly explained the gospel. Though I knew very little, every time I was on break, I shared what little I knew. I would sit down at the break table and open my Bible. Almost every single time, I had someone sit down across from me and ask me, "What are you reading?" I didn't know much, but I shared with them what I knew. I knew how someone could come to Christ. I pointed every single worker and manager to Jesus Christ in that restaurant, though I knew very little. If you know the gospel (*Jesus died for my sins*), then you know enough to tell someone. "Go into all the world and preach the gospel to every creature" (Mk 16:15, KJV).

# 14 | PHILIPPIANS 3:10-16
## PRESSING ON TO THE PRIZE

*But one thing I do: forgetting what lies behind and straining forward to what lies ahead, I press on toward the goal for the prize of the upward call of God in Christ Jesus.*
PHILIPPIANS 3:13-14

How do we run the race of life with joy? Paul equates the Christian life to a race, and he says, don't look back but look ahead to the goal of knowing Christ more and more. One of the problems that most people have on this earth is that they are running the wrong race. They are not even in the "knowing Christ" race. They want a house, a wife, kids, the job, the vacations. There is nothing wrong with living life, but these things in life are gifts, not gods. Our driving focus in life cannot be founded on any of God's gifts to us. God is the foundation. If you build a house and make the wall materials the foundation, your house is going to sink. You need something strong: something concrete. The concrete we build on in this life is knowing Christ.

You've got to get into the race by believing the good news. If Jesus' death for your sins and resurrection for you is good news, then you are believing. You entrust your life to him. Being born again means that you entrust Christ to live in you by his Holy Spirit by believing the good news that Jesus died for you. Paul explains all this in Philippians 3:1-9. It's our filthy rags for his robe of righteousness. Paul says in Philippians

3:10-11, knowing Christ is my greatest ambition. He knows him, but he wants to know him better.

One of our greatest enemies in life is complacency. *What is complacency?* Complacency is defined by the dictionary as a "smug satisfaction." It's to look at your life. Saying "I've achieved enough. I'm doing ok. I'm doing enough." Paul's going to give us the remedy. Paul is sitting in a rented home under house arrest, chained to one of Caesar's elite guards. He's there 24/7 stuck in Rome. He can't go anywhere. But he says, I'm running a race. I'm not satisfied. I'm not complacent. I want more. Now remember, Paul is in shackles under house arrest in Rome. His friend, the pastor of the church at Philippi, Epaphroditus is with Paul as he's writing this letter. He's going to bring the letter of Philippians back to Philippi. And Paul gives us some amazing verses about running the race and gaining the prize.

Maybe someone should remind Paul that he's in prison. Paul says: we need to run the race! We need to endure! We need to press on to the prize. Listen to this man who hated complacency. Paul might have been shackled, but he knew the gospel is unshackled.

> **Philippians 3:10-16** | That I may know him and the power of his resurrection, and may share his sufferings, becoming like him in his death, [11] that by any means possible I may attain the resurrection from the dead. [12] Not that I have already obtained this or am already perfect, but I press on to make it my own, because Christ Jesus has made me his own. [13] Brothers, I do not consider that I have made it my own. But one thing I do: forgetting what lies behind and straining forward to what lies ahead, [14] I press on toward the goal for the prize of the upward call of God in Christ Jesus. [15] Let those of us who are mature think this way, and if in anything you think otherwise, God will reveal that also to you. [16] Only let us hold true to what we have attained.

How do we press on? Persevere? We are told that "for the righteous falls seven times and rises again" (Pro 24:16). No matter how many times we fall and fail, there is a holy ambition to know Christ in the heart of every Christian. Paul's desire was to persevere to know Christ and to be like him. No matter what held him up or made him stumble, he was always getting up again for that prize. How can I run my race with great joy? We run with ambition, endurance, and grace we strive for the prize of knowing Christ better.

# RUN WITH AMBITION (3:10-11)

**Philippians 3:10-11** | That I may know him and the power of his resurrection, and may share his sufferings, becoming like him in his death, [11] that by any means possible I may attain the resurrection from the dead.

In the church of Philippi, as well as many of the other churches scattered throughout the Roman Empire, the churches were connected to believing Jews because that's how Paul would start his church planting endeavors. He would begin in the synagogue. Sadly, there were some of the Jews that didn't think it was enough to know Christ alone. They wanted to add to what Christ did. Paul talks about these kinds of false teachers and compares them to wild "dogs" who had selfish motives and lives that were evil and not holy (3:2). Our joy is not to increase in religious knowledge, but to know Christ. That's what Paul says was his personal ambition.

## A Personal Ambition

**Philippians 3:10a** | That I may know him.

What a wonderful ambition: to know Christ! We cannot know God the Father except through Christ (Jn 14:6).

### *Knowing Christ Personally is Objective*

And Paul had an objective faith in a righteousness outside of himself. That's where we must be unshakable in our assurance. It is by grace we are saved through faith in Christ: his righteousness, his substitutionary atonement on the cross. He bore the full wrath of God for us. Hallelujah! Therefore, to know Christ, we must come to him by an objective faith. We must surrender to who he is and what he has done: his person and work. Everything else, compared to knowing Christ is merely dung (*cf* 3:8-9).

> I count everything as loss because of the surpassing worth of knowing Christ Jesus my Lord. For his sake I have suffered the loss of all things and count them as rubbish, in order that I may gain Christ [9] and be found in him, not having a righteousness of my own that comes from the law, but that which comes through faith in Christ, the righteousness from God that depends on faith" (3:8-9).

We come through his righteousness, and not our own. We come as sinners to a righteous God who is willing to make us righteous through the blood of Christ. Do you know him? Have you come to this wonderful realization that you come to a holy and perfectly righteous God in all the rags of your sins? Are you trusting and fully abiding in him? Are you righteous today in with an alien righteousness? Do you stand before God in the righteousness of Christ? You come by faith.

### Knowing Christ Personally is Subjective

Possessing Christ's righteousness by faith was not an end but in fact for Paul was the starting point. Indeed, how could anyone ever get satiated with our infinite Redeemer? Never. Paul's emphasis here is on gaining a deeper knowledge and intimacy with Christ. Having been converted, Paul suddenly had a new hunger and ambition in life. He wasn't studying books about doctrine or systematic theology because there was none. Upon conversion, he wanted not just to know his faith rested objectively in the death of Christ, but subjectively in a relationship with Christ. He knows him, but he wants to know him better!

To understand the difference between an objective and subjective faith, consider your parents. Objectively you know that they will always be your parents. There is a biological tie to them. Now subjectively, you may do something to hurt their hearts. They may need to correct you. They may need to discipline you. But you are still their child. So it is with our relationship with Christ. Through objective faith, you are born again into God's family. No one and nothing can change that. "There is no condemnation for those who are in Christ Jesus" (Rom 8:1). Nothing can separate you from the love of God in Christ. Our faith is in Christ alone and we are assured of his righteousness and perfection. That can never change. But our relationship with God, on a practical level, changes all the time. There is a subjectivity to our intimacy with Christ. Sin can get in the way of our communion and intimacy with God. Objectively our standing is absolutely perfect for those whose faith is in Christ. But subjectively, our progress at times will be interrupted. We will progress. Of course, he promises to keep us from falling away (Jude 1:24-25). But there are times we may need correction. Like a good Father, God will guide his children home. He may need to correct us, but he will never stop being our good, good Father. There's an intimacy, a revelation of Christ to every child of God that needs to grow and grow and grow. Paul says to the Galatians:

I would have you know, brothers, that the gospel that was preached by me is not man's gospel. ¹² For I did not receive it from any man, nor was I taught it, but I received it through a revelation of Jesus Christ.
—*Galatians 1:11-12*

### Knowing Christ Personally is Progressive

The word "to know" is not merely intellectual, but to know intimately, to know the finest details, to feel or touch, to appropriate and understand the weight of knowing that person.[84] The ideas is "that I may progressively become more deeply and intimately acquainted with Christ, perceiving and recognizing and understanding the wonders of his Person more strongly and more clearly" (Amplified Bible). Spurgeon writes...

> Paul means, "That I may know him more than I now do;" for he knew him ...but he felt as if he had not begun really to know Christ. He was like a child at school, who has learnt to read and to write, and knows so much that he begins to want to know more.

From the moment of his conversion on, the purpose of Paul's life was "that I may know him" (3:10). If he already knows Christ, why does he want to know him who he already knows? The answer is that he wants to know Christ more deeply and have a more intimate relationship with him. He wants to learn more of his teaching and draw closer to his heart. He wants to enter into a closer, experiential fellowship, a more intimate communion.

We have the same desire of Enoch of old in the Bible. "Enoch walked with God, and he was not, for God took him" (Gen 5:24). Enoch had such a close walk with God, that God translated him directly to heaven without dying. Wouldn't that be amazing. We want to be transformed into his likeness. I wish it could happen like Enoch, but Paul tells us how transformation comes in 2 Corinthians 3. Walking with Christ transforms us. Paul compares Moses knowledge of God with the New Testament Christian, and says we have the great Moses beat! "And we all, with unveiled face, beholding the glory of the Lord, are being transformed into the same image *from one degree of glory to another.* For this comes from the Lord who is the Spirit (2 Cor 3:18).

---

[84] Joseph Barber Lightfoot, ed., *Saint Paul's Epistle to the Philippians*, Classic Commentaries on the Greek New Testament (London: Macmillan and Co., ltd, 1913), 150.

The more we know Christ, the more we are transformed into his likeness (2 Cor 3:18; Rom 8:29-30). We are called to grow in knowing Christ. Paul, though he was a mature man of God, was like a schoolboy when it came to knowing Christ. He felt like he was just getting started.

We must be like the woman with the issue of blood who touched the hem of Jesus garment. She wasn't content to be like the throngs around him but pushed through the crowd to touch his garment. And power went out of him. That's what we need. Push through child of God. Whatever trial; whatever difficulty. Don't let it stop you from knowing Christ deeper. Don't let the world stop you from touching him. You need to feel his virtue healing you. The personal ambition of every Christian is to know Christ. We know him objectively, but we want to know him personally and subjectively, applied to our own lives.

### *Knowing Christ Personally is Substantive*

Knowing Christ is not superficial, but extensive and deep and satisfying. It's like the difference between seeing a photograph and knowing the real person. You can possibly see a ton of video and photos of my wife and see and know more about her scientifically and aesthetically. You can study what she's done or written or said. But no one can know here like I know her as my wife. No one is a friend to her like I am. No one can know her in marriage like I know her. We have a one flesh union. We know the highs and lows the failures and victories.

You can say you know Christ and have scientific knowledge, but do you know him intimately? Are you walking with him? Now intimate knowledge must come first from objective knowledge. You cannot know him intimately until you first know him objectively, that is you know who he is, his person, and what he has done, his work. But now knowing him, I want to know him better. That's my highest personal ambition.

## A Powerful Ambition

Paul says, my personal ambition is: *I want to know him*. How Paul? In what way? "I want to know him and…

**Philippians 3:10b** | …the power of his resurrection.

This ambition of knowing Christ is not only personal, but it's powerful. Our faith in Christ is lived out in supernatural power. Dear ones, the same Holy Spirit that raised Christ from the dead lives in us. Paul talks about this resurrection power for every Christian in Ephesians as "the immeasurable greatness of his power toward us who believe, according to the working of his great might that he worked in Christ when he raised him from the dead" (Eph 1:19-20).

I don't have to think anything is separating me from knowing Christ: I can't say that sin on Satan or my family or my own weakness is keeping me from knowing him fully. In Christ, I have the power of the resurrection. In that power there is no weakness. I can live the victorious Christian life in the power of the resurrection of Christ. The only thing separating me from a consistent Christian life is a daily surrender to that power found in Christ by faith.

Dear saint: you are guaranteed victory in this life. There is no sin Christ did not die to conquer in you.

## A Passionate Ambition

> **Philippians 3:10c** | And may share his sufferings, becoming like him in his death.

This ambition has one passion: die to this world and live to God. Now, what does that mean—how do I become "like him in his death"? It doesn't mean that you could die for sinners. He died alone; nobody could do that for him. But what it means is that, when he died for me, I died with him. His death had my name on it. And, if I want to know him, I have to say no to me and yes to him. I have to die to myself. I have to die with Christ. I have to be buried with Christ, that I might be raised with Christ. I want to know him personally. I want to say yes to Christ and no to me. Someone said it this way: "When self is on the throne, Christ is on the cross. When self is on the cross, Christ is on the throne."[85]

## A Prayerful Ambition

> **Philippians 3:11** | ...that by any means possible I may attain the resurrection from the dead.

Until the resurrection from the dead, we are called to "walk in newness of life" (Rom 6:4). It's a prayer. I want to walk like I'm going to rise!

---

[85] Adrian Rogers, "The Crucifixion of King Self," in *Adrian Rogers Sermon Archive* (Signal Hill, CA: Rogers Family Trust, 2017), Php 2:1–11.

### What is Certain

Paul's prayer is that he might be ready at the second coming of Jesus, when God raises all his people from the dead. Paul was awaiting that moment when:

> In a moment, in the twinkling of an eye, at the last trumpet. For the trumpet will sound, and the dead will be raised imperishable, and we shall be changed... [54] ... then shall come to pass the saying that is written: "Death is swallowed up in victory. —*1 Corinthians 15:52, 54*

Paul knows what is certain: the resurrection of the dead. The dead in Christ shall rise! What is uncertain is the pathway there. Our resurrection from the dead is certain at Jesus' second coming. We know that for certain. Paul knew that for certain. Jesus taught this truth: "I am the resurrection and the life; he who believes in me will live even if he dies" (Jn 11:25). Christ promised his disciples, "Because I live, you will live also" (Jn 14:19). It is the resurrection of Jesus that gives us such a glorious prospect beyond the grave.

### What is Not Certain

What is not certain is the means by which he brings us. It's like Job said: "...he knows the way that I take; when he has tried me, I shall come out as gold" (Job 23:10). We don't know the way and the means he takes us, but he know! Until the resurrection from the dead, we are called to "walk in newness of life" (Rom 6:4). It's a prayer. I want to walk like I'm going to rise! I'm not certain of all the trials and tribulations I have in front of me, but I know who is with me, and *I want to walk today like I'm going to rise when Jesus comes.*

### Christianity is a Lens, Not a List

So Paul says, I want to know Christ in power, being alive to God, and in Christ's suffering and death, being dead to the world. In everything that happens, I see Christ! "By whatever means possible, I am looking forward to the resurrection when Jesus comes again." For Paul Christianity is a lens, not a list.

We come to our lives and whether we are caring for the children until they fall asleep in our arms, or we go to our job and work hard we seek to know Christ and his glory in everything. It's not like I have God at the top of my list and then I'm done. God is on every part of my list, so that by whatever means possible, I am looking to that trumpet sound when I see Jesus. C.S. Lewis said it this way: "I believe in Christianity as I believe that the sun has risen: not only because I see it, but because by it I see everything else."[86] I see all things through the lens of knowing Christ. If I'm changing a diaper or rocking a child to sleep, driving to work, or figuring out a job for my boss, I see all things by the light of knowing Christ. I want to know him. I'm alive to God and dead to this world.

## RUN WITH ENDURANCE (3:12-14)

> **Philippians 3:12-14** | Not that I have already obtained this or am already perfect, but I press on to make it my own, because Christ Jesus has made me his own. ¹³ Brothers, I do not consider that I have made it my own. But one thing I do: forgetting what lies behind and straining forward to what lies ahead, ¹⁴ I press on toward the goal for the prize of the upward call of God in Christ Jesus.

Paul is not complacent when it comes to his Christian life. Remember, he's under house arrest in Rome. He's got shackles on. But he compares his life to running a race. Maybe someone should tell Paul he's in prison. He should be more realistic. But Paul won't have any of it. He says I press on toward the goal for the prize of Jesus. I want to know Jesus and do his will. The Christian life is so difficult. How can I run so as to win the race? I can never do it in my own strength. How can I run with endurance?

### Enduring with A Proper View of the Present

Paul has a powerful way of getting rid of complacency in his life. He knows he's perfect in Christ, but he's not yet perfect in this life. He's perfect in Christ, but he knows he falls far short of that perfection in this life. Paul says in verse 9: I'm perfect in Christ. But here in verse 12, he says: I'm not perfect. Which is it Paul?

*Paul is Humble*

> **Philippians 3:12a** | Not that I have already obtained this or am already perfect...

---

[86] C.S. Lewis, *Weight of Glory: And Other Addresses* (San Francisco: HarperOne, 1976), 140.

Paul has been made perfect in the righteousness of Christ (3:9), right? Why does he say I'm not already perfect? Paul I'm confused. Paul is positionally righteous in Christ, just like you are, amen. That means all your sin is forgiven: past, present, and future. That's good news isn't it! That's the gospel: Jesus died for my sins. "There's now therefore no condemnation for those in Christ Jesus" (Rom 8:1). For God's children, the good news really is good news. It's the best news ever. The rest of the world yawns at the gospel, but God's children shout and dance. We rejoice at the good news.

So why does Paul say, "I'm not already perfect"? It's because while he's positionally perfect and righteous in Christ (justification), he's in a process of being made practically righteous in this life. Each day we are being conformed more and more to look like Jesus in our hearts and lives. That's sanctification. When it comes to his sanctification: Paul is not satisfied. He's not complacent. We must never think we are anywhere near where God wants us to be in the Christian life. Despite having seen Christ in visions, been taught direct revelation from him, and walked closely with him in suffering, Paul says, It's "not that I have already obtained this or am already perfect..." (3:12a). Paul says: *I want perfection, but I'm still so far from it. I have not already obtained perfect knowledge of Christ.* Paul says this in other places, that in this life we "we see in a mirror dimly," but one day we will see Christ "face to face" (1 Cor 13:12).

We must always have a humble view of where we are. I think of the great evangelist George Whitefield. Around his 54th birthday, after making it through a dangerous storm on a ship, George Whitefield wrote in his diary, "Oh, to begin to be a Christian."[87] That's his goal. He had been preaching for over 30 years and was greatly used of God. But at 54 years, he says, "I want to begin to be a Christian."

### *Paul is Hungry*

**Philippians 3:12b** | But I press on to make it my own, because Christ Jesus has made me his own.

At present Paul says, "I press on..." Like an athlete wanting to win a championship, Paul is never satisfied with where he is. "I press on!"

---

[87] John Gillies, *Memoirs of the Life of the Reverend George Whitefield* (Ann Arbor, MI: Text Creation Partnership, 2009), 246.

He's hungry! I press on to "make it my own" or "to seize the perfection of knowing Christ". *I want to seize the one who seized me. I reach after Christ who has reached me!*

Paul says, "I press on to make it my own..." Make what his own? The perfection of knowing Christ. Paul wants to seize the knowledge and relationship he will have with Christ in the resurrection right now. On the day of Christ's second coming, we will know Christ perfectly. We should reach after Christ now in that way!

The verb translated press on (*diōkō*) is the same one Paul used in 3:6 to recall that he persecuted the church in his pre-conversion days. He persecuted or literally "pressed on" the church. With the same tenacity, Paul now "presses on" to know Christ. The same kind of commitment that once drove Paul on to stamp out Christianity now drove him on to proclaim it everywhere. [88] So Paul says: *I want to seize Christ the way he seized me!* Paul had one consuming passion: *I want to take hold of Christ the way he took hold of me.* I want to embrace the one who embraced me! He's made me his own, and I want to live like Christ is my own. Paul is hungry: I want to seize him who seized me!

In the present life, we are pressing on, driven to know Christ and seize him who seized us. That's our goal. Do you remember the way Christ took hold of you? He wants you to take hold of him. That's what we are to do now in the present. But what about the past? Sometimes the past can slow us down.

## Enduring with A Proper View of the Past

> **Philippians 3:13** | Brothers, I do not consider that I have made it my own. But one thing I do: forgetting what lies behind and straining forward to what lies ahead.

While I'm looking to seize Christ, Paul says, "Brothers, I do not consider that I have fully made Christ my own." He's made me his own! Glory to God! But I've not yet fully made him my own. I want that more than anything, but I'm not there yet. I haven't fully seized Christ. I'm not there yet. So what should I do? Should I bemoan this fact? Should I be in despair?

No! This one thing I do: I forget the past. I have to forget what lies behind. While the verb rendered forgetting (*epilanthanomai*) can refer

---

[88] J. Phillips, *Exploring Philippians*, Php 3:12b.

to having no memory of something, here the verb has the softer sense of pay no attention to.[89] After all, Paul has just finished listing his past accomplishments (3:5–6). These past accomplishments are among what lies behind.[90] His persecution of the church and great failures of Christ are also what lies behind.

Jesus said, "No one, having put his hand to the plow, and looking back, is fit for the kingdom of God" (Lk 9:62). The runner in a race cannot afford to look back. He will lose his speed, lose his direction, and, if he is not careful, lose the race. This is not an easy assignment for any of us. It is the result of a decision we make. We simply decide that we will not be controlled by our past.[91] What was done was done! Both the heartache of the former life and nostalgia of the "good ole days" of his Christian life would paralyze him in terms of what God wanted in the future. Every day was a new adventure.[92]

How do we apply this? Race cars have no backup camera. Don't get stuck in your failures. Don't rest on your victories. First of all, we must forget our *failures*. If we look at our past failures as opportunities to learn and grow, then it is all right to remember them. If we allow them to fill us with despair and defeat, we must forget them. In other words, we may allow our failures to teach us but not to terrorize us. But then, don't rest in your *victories*. Yesterday's power is not sufficient for this hour. When David was supposed to be out winning more victories he was at home, and his pride led him to great failure. Don't rest in your victories. Surge ahead to higher ground!

## Enduring with A Proper View of the Future

> **Philippians 3:13b-14** | Straining forward to what lies ahead, [14] I press on toward the goal for the prize of the upward call of God in Christ Jesus.

Not only to I forget the past, but I strain with all my might to the future. I strain forward to what lies ahead.... I exert myself to the uttermost. Paul strains forward to the prize! This word "strain forward" is

---

[89] Harmon, *Philippians*, 356.
[90] Ibid.
[91] D. Jeremiah. *Count It All Joy*, 172-173.
[92] Richard R. Melick, *Philippians, Colossians, Philemon*, vol. 32, The New American Commentary (Nashville: Broadman & Holman Publishers, 1991), 139.

particularly graphic, bringing to mind the straining muscles, clear focus, and complete dedication of the runner in his race to the prize. Both mental and physical discipline were necessary.[93]

What's the "prize" that lies ahead in the future? What goal is Paul pursuing? Based on the previous passage, it's a fuller knowledge of Christ. It involves gaining Christ. That's what Paul wants—to know Christ more and more; and in knowing him more, he will become more like him. This pursuit is a lifetime adventure. To illustrate this pursuit, Paul uses athletic imagery to convey his passion for the Savior. Be careful that you don't adopt a passive attitude about the Christian life. Growth in Christlikeness isn't an impassive stroll. The New Testament uses disciplined athletic imagery elsewhere to describe the effort involved in growing in Christ. Consider just two of them:

> Do you not know that in a race all the runners run, but only one receives the prize? So run that you may obtain it. [25] Every athlete exercises self-control in all things. They do it to receive a perishable wreath, but we an imperishable. [26] So I do not run aimlessly; I do not box as one beating the air. [27] But I discipline my body and keep it under control, lest after preaching to others I myself should be disqualified. —*1 Corinthians 9:24-27*

> Therefore, since we are surrounded by so great a cloud of witnesses, let us also lay aside every weight, and sin which clings so closely, and let us run with endurance the race that is set before us, [2] looking to Jesus, the founder and perfecter of our faith, who for the joy that was set before him endured the cross, despising the shame, and is seated at the right hand of the throne of God. —*Hebrews 12:1-2*

Now that's passion! Running, exercising self-control, not running aimlessly, not boxing the air, disciplining one's body—all of this displays the apostle's passion.

## RUN WITH GRACE (3:15-16)

We are called to run this race not only with patient endurance and ambition, but with grace. There are false teachers among them who want to legalize everything. We can't do that. Look how gentle Paul is with his fellow runners.

---

[93] Ibid., 139.

## Grace to Engage

**Philippians 3:15** | Let those of us who are mature think [*attitude*] this way, and if in anything you think otherwise, God will reveal that also to you.

He was always thinking about others in the race. In Paul's last words on the earth (book of 2 Timothy), Paul is thinking about all his brothers and sisters.

> I have fought a good fight, I have finished my course, I have kept the faith: [8] Henceforth there is laid up for me a crown of righteousness, which the Lord, the righteous judge, shall give me at that day: and not to me only, but unto all them also that love his appearing.
> —*2 Timothy 4:7-8*

Paul knew he was not running alone. Paul challenged the Philippians to come down from the grandstand and get in the race. Some of them, of course, were already in it and were doing well; he described them as "perfect"—that is, mature or initiated. Paul encouraged these faithful brethren to be of the same mind as himself: to forget what had already been attained, to set new goals, to run to achieve them, and to keep their eyes fixed on Christ.[94] Those who are truly mature will have this humble mindset. We've not yet attained, but we are hungry to get there.

Paul says to those who are "think otherwise" than running the race to get involved. Paul was so gracious in how he challenged them to get off the grandstands and get involved. Are you maturing in Christ? Keep going! If not, get involved. Paul did not lay down any laws. He called those who are truly saved to run toward maturity, and he trusted God to reveal his will to every child of God. The Spirit of God is working in us to know him and the power of his resurrection. Are you stuck in your spiritual life? Get involved. Let the Spirit lead you to an encourager. Let someone know you are struggling.

## Grace to Persevere

Are you running faithfully? Don't be discouraged.

**Philippians 3:16** | Only let us hold true to what we have attained.

---

[94] J. Phillips, *Exploring Philippians*, Php 3:15–16.

Keep going. Life is short. We will be home soon, so so soon! Christ is worthy! "Don't be weary in well doing" (Gal 6:9). By God's grace we will, as Paul urged us, persevere. We will to hold true to what we have attained. "Hold true" (*stoicheo*) means "to walk in line with." It is a military term that pictures soldiers marching in a row. The idea is to keep in step with what is required. The Philippian believers must march in formation with the word of God. They must stay in step with the same truths which Paul had earlier taught them.[95]

Let's live what we say we believe. Christ has attained true and perfect righteousness for us and he possibility of a higher and holier walk with him. I'm not giving up. I want to seize him who seized me. My eye is no the prize!

## Conclusion

In the 1986 New York City Marathon, almost 20,000 runners entered the race. What is memorable is not who won, but who finished last. His name was Bob Wieland. He finished 19,413th—dead last. Bob completed the New York marathon in 4 days, 2 hours, 47 minutes, and 17 seconds. It was unquestionably the slowest marathon in history—ever. So, what is it that made Bob Wieland's marathon so special? Bob ran with his arms. 17 years earlier while in Vietnam, Bob's legs were blown off in battle. He sits on a 15-pound saddle and covers his fists with pads. He uses his arms to catapult himself forward one arm-length at a time. At his swiftest, Bob can run about a mile an hour, using his muscular arms to catapult his torso forward. He advances one "step" at a time. Bob Wieland finished four *days* after the start. What did it matter? Why bother to finish? There is a victory to experience in just finishing the course.[96]

The Christian life is much like this. the Bible says, "Many who are first will be last; and the last, first" (Mt 19:30). It will take another world to determine who the real winners are. One thing Bob Wieland was not: complacent. He would not take not make excuses. He saw the goal before him, and one arm length at a time, he completed the race in four days. We don't know how long our race is dear saint, but of anyone in the world, we have no excuse for complacency. Look at the prize we have: knowing Christ. Is there any greater goal?

---

[95] Lawson, *Philippians*, 171.

[96] Steven J. Lawson, *In it to Win It: Pursuing Victory in the One Race that Really Counts* (Eugene, OR: Harvest House Publishers, 2013), 174.

# 15 | PHILIPPIANS 3:17-21
## CITIZENS OF HEAVEN

*Our citizenship is in heaven, and from it we await a Savior, the Lord Jesus Christ, who will transform our lowly body to be like his glorious body, by the power that enables him even to subject all things to himself.*
PHILIPPIANS 3:20-21

Have you ever been home sick? I used to serve at a Christian camp in Pennsylvania. We had an Indian theme, so I was Chief Matt at Mountainview Bible Camp in Scranton, Pennsylvania. This was part of my time at Child Evangelism Fellowship, and we would go street to street in Philadelphia and all around the state pointing kids to Christ. Then for two weeks, these kids got to go away from the city streets to a Christian camp. It was so amazing since some of them had never seen so many trees and wilderness before. But you know as fantastic as this was for them, many of them would get homesick after a few days. They'd have to go see Nurse Ginny. Nurse Ginny would play ball with them or get their minds off of their homesickness.

As Christians we are homesick for heaven, aren't we? If you are a person who has entrusted your life to Jesus, this world is not your home. Anytime you travel overseas, a passport is required. Your passport is a document of citizenship, denoting your country of origin and permanent residence. Your name is written on that document along with your place and date of birth. Jesus said that our "names are written in heaven" (*cf* Phil 4:3; Lk 10:20) because we have been born again. That makes us tourists and foreigners here on earth. This world is not my home, I'm just passing through. I want to encourage you as citizens of heaven in how though we are homesick for heaven, we can bring the culture of heaven to earth through the gospel.

> **Philippians 3:17-21** | Brothers, join in imitating me, and keep your eyes on those who walk according to the example you have in us. [18] For many, of whom I have often told you and now tell you even with tears, walk as enemies of the cross of Christ. [19] Their end is destruction, their god is their belly, and they glory in their shame, with minds set on earthly things. [20] But our citizenship is in heaven, and from it we await a Savior, the Lord Jesus Christ, [21] who will transform our lowly body to be like his glorious body, by the power that enables him even to subject all things to himself.

Why did Jesus leave us behind? Why couldn't we go to heaven immediately after we were saved? Why do we have to wait? Because we are called to "make disciples of all nations" (Mt 28:18-20). This is logical in the passage. Paul has just said, we have a high calling of knowing Christ better (3:10-16). Now we need to do the work of discipleship. Listen to Paul.

## CITIZENS ARE DISCIPLES (3:17)

Listen to Paul talk about discipleship.

> **Philippians 3:17** | Brothers, join in imitating me, and keep your eyes on those who walk according to the example you have in us.

We are no longer of this world. We are to be looking to another world. We are to keep your eyes on those who are looking to another world. As citizens of heaven, we are from another world. Because of that we are called to bring the kingdom culture of heave to earth. We are called to pray and live God's will: "Your will be done on earth as it is in heaven" (Lord's Prayer, Mt 6:10). Since coming to Christ, we are no longer of this world. We no longer have the world's culture. The Holy Spirit has moved in to our hearts. Jesus says we are no longer "of this world."

> They are not of the world, just as I am not of the world. ¹⁵ I do not ask that you take them out of the world, but that you keep them from the evil one. ¹⁶ They are not of the world, just as I am not of the world.
> —John 17:14-16

We are to be importing the culture of heaven to earth. The citizens of Philippi knew how to import culture. They would bring the culture of Rome to the Greek people. The Philippians had the great honor of holding Roman citizenship. This was not just a perk, but they imported the culture of Rome. They brought in the language of Rome which was Latin instead of Greek. They imported the values of Rome to Philippi. They lived as citizens of the city of Rome among the Greek people of Philippi.

Paul says something that the Philippians could relate to: I'm looking to Christ for my culture. I'm importing the kingdom culture of heaven to earth. He says: "Join in imitating me!" I'm a kingdom citizen. I'm a citizen where Jesus Christ is absolute King and Sovereign. He's the ruler of my life. He is Lord and Christ. Those were two titles used for Caesar. That's what Caesar Augustus began. He said he was a god and should be worshiped. He's Lord and Christ. What blasphemy. Only Jesus is Lord and Christ! We need to bring that kingdom culture here to earth.

Paul had seen the risen Christ. The risen Christ lives in all of us. "Keep your eyes on those who walk according" to another kingdom (3:17). Walk with all those who have Christ ruling as Lord in their hearts. That's our culture.

What is culture? Merriam Webster defines it: "the set of shared attitudes, values, goals, and practices that characterizes any given group of people." Here's another: "enlightenment and excellence of taste acquired by intellectual and aesthetic training." Have your eyes and tastes been enlightened and trained by heaven? Paul says: the culture and atmosphere and values I'm importing are from heaven. Follow those who follow Christ. This is the principle of discipleship. Jesus said, "It is enough for the disciple that he become like his teacher" (Mt 10:25). As the twelve were to follow the teaching and example of Christ, so the Philippians were to follow the same in Paul. During his first trip to Philippi, Paul became their teacher, and they his disciples.

## A Disciple is Counter Cultural

Let me add as kingdom citizens, we are to be counter cultural! The world worships itself. We reject self-worship. We are counter cultural. The world is all about conforming us to its culture, but Christ dwells in us to be counter cultural. Isn't that what the Spirit tells us in Romans 12?

> Do not be conformed to this world, but be transformed by the renewal of your mind, that by testing you may discern what is the will of God, what is good and acceptable and perfect. —Romans 12:2

As disciple makers, we are culture makers. We are not just importing a set of values, but we are offering a Person to people. When the Person of the Holy Spirit reveals the love of the Father to you, you can cry out: Abba!

The world is constantly trying to conform us to the culture of hell. It's very deceptive. Most of the entertainment of the world, television, YouTube, and social media is trying to conform you to a system that is in rebellion against the living God. We stand against this world, and daily we have to renew our minds, renew our friends and influences. We need to examine who's influencing our thoughts. We need to get the culture of heaven in your heart. Don't miss what Paul is saying here.

> **Philippians 3:17** | Brothers, join in imitating me, and keep your eyes on those who walk according to the example you have in us.

To be a disciple of Christ, we have to be disciple makers. This was Jesus' last command, his marching orders: "Go make disciples of all nations..." (Mt 28:18ff). The Christian life was not just theory and doctrine to Paul. He and all faithful Christians are the living example of the spiritual instruction we bring to the world.[97]

## A Disciple is a Prototype

> **Philippians 3:17** | Brothers, join in imitating me, and keep your eyes on those who walk according to the example you have in us.

Paul has just said he's not perfect, and he's not already attained, but he does say that Christians should be prototypes. The Greek word Paul uses for "example" is *tupos*. It means a prototype or a mold that

---

[97] Lawson, *Philippians*, 172-173.

imprints something, leaving a pattern or print on the object. How has Christ left a pattern and print on your life? Are you courageous and bold enough to live in such a way that leaves Christ's imprint on others? How should you and I leave a pattern or print on the lives of people we influence?

At the end of college I worked as an iron worker on the south side of Chicago. National Bullet Proof. When we were building Sox park, the cell, or whatever it's called now, we put in bullet resistant ticket booths. Every deal tray had the stamp of our company on it. I had a prototype with our name: National Bullet Proof. Hey, we are all prototypes. We are to have the imprint of Christ on our lives. And we are to be intersecting and impacting the lives of those around us.

## A Disciple is a Partner

> **Philippians 3:17** | Brothers, join in imitating me, and keep your eyes on those who walk according to the example you have in us.

Can I just say, you can't do this alone. You need brothers if you are a man and sisters if you are a woman to hold you accountable to that imprint of Christ. Join! Keep your eyes on those who walk according to the example you have. Like Paul, we are foreigners on a pilgrimage toward paradise, and we have a passport of citizenship. As Christians, we should have a certain walk (lifestyle) that characterizes our citizenship. As citizens, we need partners in our walk, those who motivate and encourage us and keep us accountable. We can't grow well without other Christians investing in us. And to really grow, you need to be helping others grow. In other words, who is discipling you? Who are you discipling? Back to the race analogy, we need to show others in the Body how to train and how to run the Christian race. We are all trainers.

> What you have heard from me in the presence of many witnesses entrust to faithful men, who will be able to teach others also. [3] Share in suffering as a good soldier of Christ Jesus. [4] No soldier gets entangled in civilian pursuits, since his aim is to please the one who enlisted him. [5] An athlete is not crowned unless he competes according to the rules. [6] It is the hard-working farmer who ought to have the first share of the crops. [7] Think over what I say, for the Lord will give you understanding in everything. —*2 Timothy 2:2-7*

Two things stand out in these examples: Discipline and Integrity. This is the key to discipleship. To be a disciple is to be a learner. A soldier, an athlete and a farmer have one thing in common! Discipline! That's part of the word "disciple." Discipline is to be faithful to a task. Does that describe you? Are you helping others to be faithful? Are you disciplined and predictable and faithful? What makes us faithful? It's the power of the Holy Spirit that works within us. Without that power we cannot run the race. Are you helping others to serve faithfully?

Are you disciplined in your life? Do you have the spiritual disciplines in your life. Are you regularly eating the word of God to such an extent that it makes you want to read more. If there's no hunger for the word and for fellowship with the Lord or fellowship with godly guys or godly girls.

Soldiers, athletes, and farmers have integrity. Why? Because they put in the work. If a soldier doesn't train he dies. If athletes don't train, they lose. If farmers don't plant, they have no crop. We have a lot of work. When you are at home married men, you need to love your wives. You need to be praying with your wife. You are warriors. You are God's men. You need to be a good soldier of Christ, a good athlete, a good farmer of Christ! Ladies, invest in your husbands. You can start with being content in Christ. Don't look for your contentment in your spouse.

## CITIZENS ARE DISCERNING (3:18-19)

In contrast to those who are running the race with patience, being transformed into Christ's image through resurrection power and suffering with Christ in this life, there are those who live as enemies of the cross.

> **Philippians 3:18** | For many, of whom I have often told you and now tell you even with tears, walk as enemies of the cross of Christ.

There are those who Paul calls enemies of the cross. He has tears. What's causing his sorrow? It seems there were men and women who once fellowshipped with the saints there in Philippi, but they fell away. They were not "all in." They were what Jesus called "stony ground hearers." They were not "all in". That's something to cry about. They didn't think about their legacy, and they fell away. They just added Jesus to their lives. Listen, Christians are folk who are all in. That doesn't mean we are perfect, but we believe Jesus is a perfect Savior! The only fear ordained by God is the fear of God, and when you fear God, you don't fear anybody else.

## Discerning But Compassionate

Paul seems to be referring to people had at one time attended at the church of Philippi, but who have fallen away. They are bothering the faithful race of the Christians there.

> **Philippians 3:18** | For many, of whom I have often told you and now tell you even with tears, walk as enemies of the cross of Christ.

C.T. Studd said, "Some want to live within the sound of church or chapel bell; I want to run a rescue shop, within a yard of hell."[98] The fact that there are eternal residents of hell dwelling on earth with us right now ought to cause us great concern.

Paul's heart was that of a soul winner. His heart broke for the enemies of the cross among his own people. "I am speaking the truth in Christ—I am not lying; my conscience bears me witness in the Holy Spirit— 2 that I have great sorrow and unceasing anguish in my heart. 3 For I could wish that I myself were accursed and cut off from Christ for the sake of my brothers, my kinsmen according to the flesh" (Rom 9:1-3).

## Discerning In Enemy Territory

Often when we come to Christ, there is this unrealistic expectation that things are going to be easier than they are. Can you relate? But the Spirit tells us through Paul we are in enemy territory.

> **Philippians 3:18** | For many, of whom I have often told you and now tell you even with tears, walk as enemies of the cross of Christ.

Paul says, one of the hardest things about discipleship is that you have to stay faithful in enemy territory. That means you need to expect war in a warzone. Who were these enemies of the cross Paul was speaking of? Most believe these were either legalistic Jewish false teachers or loose antinomian Gentiles who had fallen away. Paul had warned the believers of Galatia that there were some Jews who wanted to avoid being persecuted for the cross and that they hoped to "boast in your

---

[98] Charles Thomas Studd in Janet & Geoff Benge, *C.T. Studd: No Retreat* (Seattle, WA: YWAM Publishing, 2005), 150.

flesh" (Gal 6:12–13). So it is conceivable to apply the marks that Paul lists in Philippians 3:18–19 to Judaizers.[99] They wanted religion in order to promote themselves. They thought they were very special and did not want to suffer.

Probably these were Gentiles who had professed faith in Christ. They had made a big splash in the church. Maybe became members. But Paul says with tears: they have fallen away and become enemies of Christ. Wow. How can someone who professes Christ just fall away? How hard is it to do discipleship when Satan is busy trying to thwart our purposes? There are those among them that once walked among those in the church but are now "enemies of the cross of Christ."

Think of Demas. He was a companion of the apostle Paul, but Paul says, "Demas, in love with this present world, has deserted me" (2 Tim 4:10). Are there some who sometimes we allow into the church because they seem to have a solid testimony, but then they fall away. Sadly yes. And we should have great tears for them. Even Jesus had one of his disciples, Judas Iscariot, who fell away. Judas was from such a prominent family and was the only one of the twelve who was from the Jerusalem area. The rest were from Galilee.

Philippi was a small place. Likely these men had regular contact with most of the congregation. The intensity of Paul's tearful grief indicates that their apostasy had been a very personal loss to Paul. Literally Paul says, "I speak weeping." There were tears as this letter was written. Evidence that these former converts had become "enemies of the cross of Christ" is indicated by the way they now walked.[100] John Calvin said, "They pretended to be friends; they were, nevertheless, the worst enemies of the gospel."[101]

Just saying you are a Christian doesn't make you one. A person who truly believes in the death and resurrection of Christ and trusts in him with saving faith walks a certain way. Paul says: there are many whom I weep over, because the are no longer following Jesus. In fact, they walk as enemies of the cross of Christ.

Old Testament people of faith "walked with God" (Gen 5:22; 6:9; Mic 6:8). They were instructed to walk in the ways of the Lord (Deut.

---

[99] D. Johnson, *Philippians*, 231–232.
[100] Hughes, *Philippians*, 157.
[101] John Calvin, *The Epistles of Paul to the Galatians, Ephesians, Philippians and Colossians* (Grand Rapids: Wm. B. Eerdmans Publishing Company, 1996), 107.

8:6; 10:12; 30:16; 1 Kgs 2:3; etc.), and not to walk "in the way of sinners" (Psa 1:1). In other letters, Paul's shift from expounding God's saving work to enjoining our fitting response was marked by his summons to a new way of "walking": "As you received Christ Jesus the Lord, so *walk* in him" (Col 2:6); "*Walk* in a manner worthy of the calling to which you have been called" (Eph 4:1). Those saved by grace through faith are God's workmanship, created in Christ Jesus to *walk* in good works (Eph 2:8–10). We are no longer to "*walk* as the Gentiles do" in mental darkness, calloused consciences, and insatiable sensual appetite (4:17–19).[102]

## Discerning Idols of the Heart

You don't want to become the wrong prototype. Everyone on earth is being imprinted and impacted by something. Paul uses the "enemies of the cross" as bad examples, or a bad prototype. They are bad because of what they worship.

### The Destiny of Idolatry

**3:19a** | Their end is destruction.

Ultimately, spiritually deaf and blind people end up destroyed in hell. Whatever is Lord of your life determines your destiny. There is only one Lord that leads us to eternal life. If you serve idols, they will send you to hell. We are doing discipleship and ministry on the edge of hell. Everyone who does not have Jesus as Lord is from hell and are living their hellish life before us.

### The Demand of Idolatry

**3:19b** | Their god is their belly.

Idolatry is a slave master. Jesus said that There are only two prototypes: those conformed to the world (worshiping idols), and those conformed to Jesus Christ (worshiping God). Again, remember Romans 12:2, "Do not be conformed to this world, but be transformed by the renewal of your mind." The human heart can never be fully satisfied by anything in this world. Human appetites become slavery for the unbeliever.

---

[102] D. Johnson, *Philippians*, 230.

> The idols of the nations are silver and gold, the work of human hands. ¹⁶ They have mouths, but do not speak; they have eyes, but do not see; ¹⁷ they have ears, but do not hear, nor is there any breath in their mouths. ¹⁸ Those who make them become like them, so do all who trust in them. —*Psalm 135:15-18*

Bottom line: When you trust in yourself, worship your own understanding, or worship things that should be gifts from God and you turn them into your little god and savior, then you become like those idols. Your eyes become blind to God's beauty. Your ears become deaf to God's word. You speak but you have no life in your heart. You feel dead.

Sin is a worship disorder. What is it that leads people to hell? "Their god is their belly" (3:19b). That's self-worship. We can't be ruled by our own appetites or our own way of thinking. We are those who have denied ourselves and followed Christ. We are those who lean not to our own understanding. We have put off the old life and put on the new life, renewed in Christ. We have turned from idols to worship the true and living God.

Self-worship is the root of all idolatry. Ezekiel 14:3, "Son of man, these men have taken their idols into their hearts, and set the stumbling block of their iniquity before their faces." Idolatry blocks your view of God. Idols are those things we turn to instead of God. If you are looking to others for your contentment, or if you are looking to this world for satisfaction and contentment, you are worshipping self.

### The Depravity of Idolatry

**Philippians 3:19c** | And they glory in their shame.

Instead of blushing, they now glory in moral wickedness. I have seen this with my own two eyes. They may not have had good answers in the church. Maybe they got hurt in life. But now, life hurts so much that they turn to shameful things to take away the pain. The more pain comes, the more they turn to immorality. They shame pushes them to more and more desperate measures. They keep turning their conscience off further and further.

### The Desire of Idolatry

**Philippians 3:19d** | With minds set on earthly things.

Virtually everything draws the lost person toward possessions: things that have price tags, things that are tangible, things that can be owned and must be maintained. In the words of Paul, they "set their minds on earthly things."[103]

We must be discerning. There are enemies of the cross of Christ all around us. We must be influencing them, not them influencing us. We must warn them of their fate. Their idolatry leads them to destruction. As citizens of heaven, instead of being discouraged or dragged into the world by them, let us "shine our lights" that they might come to know Christ and glorify our Father in heaven!

## CITIZENS ARE DEVOTED (3:20-21)

We look to the day when Jesus comes and changes our culture permanently.

**Philippians 3:20-21** | But our citizenship is in heaven, and from it we await a Savior, the Lord Jesus Christ, [21] who will transform our lowly body to be like his glorious body, by the power that enables him even to subject all things to himself.

He's going to wipe out the culture of rebellion on this earth and bring his kingdom here. Every knee shall bow, and every tongue will confess that Jesus Christ is Lord!

### Devoted to our Homeland

**Philippians 3:20a** | But our citizenship is in heaven.

We can't wait for this day when Jesus comes again! But until then, our devotion is to our homeland. Our citizenship is in heaven! Paul directs our eyes to the prize of the upward call: here is the finish line! Paul says earlier that we should do the best we can to be a prototype of a Christian so that others can follow us as they follow Christ.

The city of Philippi was named after King Philip II of Macedon, father of Alexander the Great. It was a prosperous Roman colony, which meant that the citizens of Philippi were also citizens of the city of Rome itself. They prided themselves on being Romans (cf Acts 16:21), dressed like Romans and often spoke Latin. No doubt this was the background for Paul's reference to the believer's heavenly citizenship (3:20-21).

Since our citizenship is in heaven, we ought to be importing the culture of heaven to earth. We do that by walking with the risen Christ.

---

[103] Swindoll, *Laugh Again,* 166.

It's not just behavior, but he wants our hearts. The best way to walk with Christ is a life of constant communion and prayer. Read his love letter to you every day. He loves you. Bring him your struggles.

Then it is our responsibility to bring others into Christ's kingdom. Thankfully, the Holy Spirit indwells all who come into the kingdom. That's where the real kingdom change comes in the hearts of people. It's through the indwelling Holy Spirit. He gives witness to our spirit that we are children of God.

## Devoted to our King

**Philippians 3:20b |** And from it we await a Savior, the Lord Jesus Christ.

We are patriots of our earthly homeland. We want our country to thrive. But above all, we are patriots of heaven, with our ultimate allegiance given to Jesus Christ. We are awaiting our Savior, the Lord Jesus Christ. While we are waiting, we are supposed to be doing the work of verse 17. We are to be discipling other around us. We are to be growing and walking in the Spirit. Waiting for our Savior is hard. It's hard to be away from home. It's hard to be homesick. It's tough to undergo culture shock. We are to be importing the culture of heaven to earth. God is growing us as citizens of heaven. But while we are waiting God is doing a great thing. Some of you are struggling. You are tired. You are exhausted. You are hurting. You want Christ to come again, but you just don't know what

We are like those little baby eagles in the nest. We love the comfort. That's how it is when first get saved. We feel so loved. It's so amazing. But then the mama eagle pushes the little eaglet out of the next. Is that a sign of rejection? No! It's how we learn to fly! Some of you are falling from the nest. And for us as Christians, falling from the nest is not a one-time experience. Over and over and over we experience. Using the nest illustration, let me say that Jesus is coming again to bring us back to the nest.

## Devoted to Our Future

**Philippians 3:21 |** Who will transform our lowly body to be like his glorious body, by the power that enables him even to subject all things to himself.

This world is not all there is. There is so, so much more. There is coming a day when Christ will come with power and glory to rescue us from this mess. While they are still living in Philippi, Paul therefore reminds them that they must eagerly wait with great expectation for Jesus Christ to return from heaven. In that moment, he will appear and take them to their eternal home. When that happens, all will be changed. When Jesus comes, we are glorified. That means that we are going to have a new body that does not sin. We are going to have the perfect strength the Lord without any sin, distraction, or limitation. God has the power to do this, because all things are subject to him! He upholds everything by his power. He loves you and has the power to sanctify you and glorify you.

## Conclusion

Are you homesick for heaven? Import heaven's culture into your own life. We get all four seasons in Chicagoland, don't we? We had winter in the early morning. By the time we get out of church it'll be spring with 50-degree weather. This afternoon we'll have summer. And this evening we will have Fall. The seasons change, don't they? But Jesus never changes! He is King of kings and Lord of lords. Let's bring his kingdom culture to this earth and make disciples of all nations!

# 16 | PHILIPPIANS 4:1-5
## DISARMING DISHARMONY

*Therefore, my brothers, whom I love and long for, my joy and crown, stand firm thus in the Lord, my beloved. I entreat Euodia and I entreat Syntyche to agree in the Lord.*
PHILIPPIANS 4:1-2

How about you? Do you know the Christian life is a life of sacrifice? Jesus is worthy of your sacrifices.

In a parable she entitles "A Brawling Bride," Karen Mains paints a vivid scene, describing a suspenseful moment in a wedding ceremony. Down front stands the groom in a spotless tuxedo—handsome, smiling, full of anticipation, shoes shined, every hair in place, anxiously awaiting the presence of his bride. All attendants are in place, looking joyful and attractive. The magical moment finally arrives as the pipe organ reaches full crescendo and the stately wedding march begins. Everyone rises and looks toward the door for their first glimpse of the bride.

Suddenly there is a horrified gasp. The wedding party is shocked. The groom stares in embarrassed disbelief. Instead of a lovely woman dressed in elegant white, smiling behind a lacey veil, the bride is limping down the aisle. Her dress is soiled and torn. Her leg seems twisted. Ugly cuts and bruises cover her bare arms. Her nose is bleeding, one eye is purple and swollen, and her hair is disheveled. "Does not this handsome groom deserve better than this?" asks the author. And then the clincher: "Alas, his bride, *the church*, has been fighting again!"[104] Calling them (and us, the church) Christ's bride, the apostle Paul writes to the Ephesians:

> Husbands, love your wives, as Christ loved the church and gave himself up for her, [26] that he might sanctify her, having cleansed her by the washing of water with the word, [27] so that he might present the church to himself in splendor, without spot or wrinkle or any such thing, that she might be holy and without blemish.
>
> *—Ephesians 5:25-27*

What a wonderful plan but hardly a realistic portrayal. I mean, can you imagine what the wedding pictures would look like if Christ claimed his bride, the church, today? Try to picture him standing next to his brawling bride. It is one thing for us to survive the blows of a world that is hostile to the things of Christ, but to be in disharmony with one another, fighting and arguing among ourselves. It's just unthinkable.[105] Unthinkable and unnatural though it may seem, the bride has been brawling for centuries. We get along for a little while and then we are back at each other's' throats. After a bit we make up, walk in wonderful harmony for a few days, then we turn on one another. We can switch from friend to fiend in a matter of moments. It's not what God planned. He has something better for us. But we have to realize what love is. Love means we're family. It means we're committed to each other. Sometimes a children's comic strip can bring it down to earth so we can understand.

In a "Peanuts" cartoon, Lucy says to Snoopy: "There are times when you really bug me, but I must admit there are also times when I feel like giving you a big hug." Snoopy replies: "That's the way I am… huggable and buggable."[106]

> **Philippians 4:1-5** | Therefore, my brothers, whom I love and long for, my joy and crown, stand firm thus in the Lord, my beloved. **[2]** I entreat Euodia and I entreat Syntyche to agree in the Lord. **[3]** Yes, I ask you also, true companion, help these women, who have labored side by side with me in the gospel together with Clement

---

[104] Karen Mains. *The Key to a Loving Heart* (Elgin, IL: David C. Cook, 1979), 143–44.

[105] Swindoll, *Laugh Again,* 175.

[106] Ibid., 176.

and the rest of my fellow workers, whose names are in the book of life. **⁴** Rejoice in the Lord always; again I will say, rejoice. **⁵** Let your reasonableness be known to everyone. The Lord is at hand.

How can you disarm the disunity and division that so easily disrupts us in our homes, in our church, and in our community? What are the tools that protect us from getting distracted from the wrong fight? We need a big heart (4:1), a warm embrace (4:2-3), and a lasting joy (4:4-5).

God wants to carry us forward in this community. He wants to fill this place with people who love him. He wants to bear fruit through us. Now we can say: it's not about numbers. And you are right. But it is about people: people with souls. They are dying and going to hell. The Father in heaven has sent his Spirit into our hearts to pour out his love to this lost and dying world. Do you want a church that moves when God moves? Then we can't be blocked from blessing by interpersonal conflict. We need to learn to fight for God and not with each other. In Philippi, you have two women who were once warriors for Christ who are now warring with each other. And the first thing Paul says is: you have to have a big heart.

## A BIG HEART (4:1)

Listen to Paul talk about how he personally thinks about the church at Philippi. Paul's a man who's been hurt a lot. He's been stoned. He's been falsely accused by churches. He's been hurt in so many ways by the churches. But he's a man with a gigantic heart. This is a major mark of how the world knows that we belong to Jesus. "By this all people will know that you are my disciples, if you have love for one another" (Jn 13:35). Paul loves his fellow believers in Philippi. Listen to him.

### A Big Heart Because of Our Family

**Philippians 4:1a** | Therefore, my brothers, whom I love and long for.

The love is genuine because this is Paul's forever family. Part of our justification is not only that we've been counted as righteous in God's law court. It's more than that. The result of justification is an adoption proceeding. We have been adopted in to God's forever family. That'll make your heart grow big!

He calls them family: my brothers (and sisters). Is there a more intimate term than calling each other family. Ten billion years from now, we will be family. Let's treat each other as family. Family means vulnerability. I usually lock my front door. Actually, we have several locks, how about you? But you: my beloved brothers and sisters in Christ, you are welcome into my house. No locks for you. You are my family. I love you. I esteem you.

God has adopted us into his family. He has given us a love far greater than anything in this selfish world. I not only love you my brothers and sisters, I long for you. Your fellowship enriches me and builds my faith up. I grow closer to Christ when I am with you. I learn more about his beauty and riches in your fellowship. We are family: forever and ever we will always be God's children. That makes my heart grow big for you.

Now if we really are brothers and sisters, you can't close your heart to me. I cannot close my heart to you, amen? Jesus said, "Truly, I say to you, as you did it to one of the least of these my brothers, you did it to me" (Mt 25:40). Instead of gossip or hurt or simply ignoring one another, we are called to fellowship and work together. Let's bring heaven down to earth. We can't live according to earth's rules. When disharmony comes, let's be bold and forgive. Let's be strong and move on. Let's be family and build each other up. We can't just pick and choose which part of the body of Christ we will fellowship with. Think through the congregation here at Living Hope. Who are you not treating as a brother or a sister? Is your heart growing smaller and smaller when it comes to one person or another?

I challenge you, if the Holy Spirit truly lives in you, stop resisting his conviction. Stop resisting his movement on your heart to love that person who hurt you in this church. They hurt your feelings. They gossiped about you. They have ignored you. In the name of Jesus forgive them. By the power of the resurrection, go to them today. Love on them today with Calvary love. You may need to tell them: "I forgive you." You may have some reconciliation that needs to happen. Do it.

As you do it to them, Jesus says, "You do it unto me." Are you ignoring Jesus? Are you putting off Jesus? If that person who hurt your feelings is family with Jesus, then they are family with you. Stop living in disharmony. Stop living with a small heart. Get it right, child of God. Stop cherishing that sin of bitterness.

Husbands and wives, are you living in harmony at home? Stop cherishing hurt. If Jesus loves your spouse, you should too. If Jesus laid down his life for your spouse, you should do the same. If Jesus has tender emotions toward your spouse, you should also ask God to make your heart tender. You can't just ignore a brother or sister in Christ. You are commanded to love them and long for them.

## A Big Heart Because of Our Future

**Philippians 4:1b |** Therefore, my brothers, whom I love and long for, my joy and crown.

When he calls them his "joy and crown", he's thinking of the tribunal of Christ, when we all see Jesus. Paul had planted and watered, but God gave the increase (1 Cor 3:6). Paul will receive a crown just for planting and watering, like all of us. Here the "crown" is the *stephanos*, the wreath awarded to the victor in the games (not the *diadēma*, the symbol of sovereignty).[107] As we invest our lives in those around us and we see God work, we will receive a reward.

*Don't miss this*: the reward is not something that will pass away. Paul is saying that the Philippians themselves are his reward. On the day Jesus returns, their lives will be totally healed and restored. That will be reward enough for Paul. And that is our reward together: to see each one of us perfect in his sight when he comes again! If that doesn't grow your heart to be so big, I don't know what will. That means your neighbor sitting next to you is your crown and your reward. Turn to your neighbor and say: *you are my crown*.

## A Big Heart Because of Our Focus

Our focus is standing firm in Christ so that he can carry us forward. Standing firm never means standing still. As Christians, we don't want to be stagnant. God is never stagnant. He carries us forward when we focus on him. He wants us to find healing and power in our focus on him.

**Philippians 4:1c |** Therefore, my brothers, whom I love and long for, my joy and crown, stand firm thus in the Lord, my beloved.

---

[107] F. F. Bruce, *Philippians*, Understanding the Bible Commentary Series (Peabody, MA: Baker Books, 2011), 137.

What does it mean to "stand firm...in the Lord"? In one sense it means it's in the power of the Lord, not in myself. This is very similar language to Ephesians 6. We are to put on the whole armor of God. Ephesians 6:13-14, "Therefore take up the whole armor of God, that you may be able to withstand in the evil day, and having done all, to stand firm. 14 Stand therefore..." and put on the belt of truth, the breastplate of righteousness, the gospel shoes (boots), the shield of faith, the helmet of salvation, and the sword of the Spirit (word of God).

The imagery of standing firm is gaining ground in victory. We stand firm in the Lord who gives us the victory. He's already won! Many Christians don't realize everything we need for victory in this life is something you already possess in Christ, you just need to learn how to use it.

It's like the sweet spot for the clutch of a manual transmission for a car. It's hard at first. But you need to get habituated to it. It's hard to go from neutral to first gear. And then learn all the gears. But once you do, you get used to it. Christians love holiness like race car drivers love speed! God is on the move. He wants you to be happy in him. He never changes. If you want to be happy, you have to submit and stand firm in the sovereign Savior who loves you and gave his life for you. Surrender to wherever he is taking you. He's working it all out for your good and his glory.

We can never compromise with the enemy. He wants to get you off that "sweet sopt" of holiness. He want to strip you of your Holy Spirit power. We can't use his tools of bitterness and hate and grudge holding. Our enemy is the world, the flesh and the devil. This is war. The enemy doesn't want to play nice. He wants to destroy you. You cannot negotiate with a terrorist because he wants to devote you to destruction. We must devote our enemies to destruction. So Paul says in Ephesians – "Stand Firm". We might say today: "Don't retreat!" We Christians are like soldiers who refuse to turn back. We cannot retreat. We have an enemy that God wants to win over to himself. We can't have friendly fire if we are going to convert the enemy. The Spirit says: stand firm.

I want you to understand that standing firm does not mean standing still. We need to stand firm in the Lord because indeed, he is carrying us forward. A focus on the Lord gives us spiritual stability.

Are you stuck in your walk with God? Some people are stuck because they are lost and dead in their sins. They have no real walk with

God because they have never been born again. The Spirit says, "stand firm in the Lord." You can't stand firm unless you are first in Christ. Remember this: there's no meaningful change without Christ in your life. So you know Christ. What are somethings that slow you down spiritually? You may be stuck or spiritually unstable for a number of reasons. You know Christ but you have a sin in your life that is holding you hostage. You've tried everything but you don't know what to do. There's an important relationship in your life that brings you constant hurt. Perhaps you have isolated yourself from others, and you have little to no fellowship. Maybe you have distorted thinking like a bad record that plays over and over again. Perhaps you have impaired hearing, and the word no longer has its impact because you are overwhelmed with the background noise of fear, or anger. You've lost your focus.

Whatever the reason your stuck, right now is your moment to get unstuck. You don't have to be stuck anymore. Whatever your problem, Jesus is the answer. "Stand firm in the Lord!" Stop trying to change yourself. You say: *that's too simple*. Nope. It's not. That's your problem. You think you need to jump through hoops. "Seek first the kingdom of God and his righteousness, and all these things will be added to you" (Mt 6:33).

Seek Christ through all the means of grace. If it's isolation: experience Christ in Christian fellowship. If it's a sin in your life: experience Christ in heartfelt repentance in prayer. Christ has set you free. Experience Christ as the good Shepherd in Christian counsel and accountability. If it's a hurtful relationship, bring Christ there. You may need a counselor or a pastor. Get Christ in that relationship. That's actually what Paul is about to say. Paul brings up two women in the church who can't seem to get along: Euodia and Sytyche, otherwise affectionately known as: "You Odious" and "Soon Touchy." These are actually two very honored, very godly women in the congregation, but they've gotten their eyes off of Christ.

That brings us to a second mark of spiritual stability: not only do we need a big heart, we need a warm embrace.

## A WARM EMBRACE (4:2-3)

Most of the time, spiritual instability comes because of the inability to get along with other saints. We need to learn to fight for God and not with each other. We need to have thick skin and a very big heart. With that big heart, we need to embrace each other as family, and in union with Jesus Christ.

In verse 1, we noticed it was love by which the world would know we are Jesus' disciples. But now he gives another mark of a healthy vibrant church that reaches the world: unity. At the bare minimum, it means that when the general calls us to fight for him, we will miss the call if we are fighting against ourselves.

> **Philippians 4:2-3** | I entreat Euodia and I entreat Syntyche to agree in the Lord. ³ Yes, I ask you also, true companion, help these women, who have labored side by side with me in the gospel together with Clement and the rest of my fellow workers, whose names are in the book of life.

## Embrace in the Lord

> **Philippians 4:2** | I entreat Euodia and I entreat Syntyche to agree in the Lord.

Unity in the church comes because of our union with Jesus Christ. One of the main themes of the New Testament is that we are in union with Christ. We are in Christ. That happens because God the Father and God the Holy Spirit are dwelling in me. We are indwelt by the Triune God. Jesus said, it is not only our love that will show his glory to the world, but also our unity will show the glory of God to the world. Jesus said, "...that they may all be one, just as you, Father, are in me, and I in you, that they also may be in us, so that the world may believe that you have sent me" (Jn 17:21). You can have love without unity, but you cannot have real unity without love. I loved my friends when I was a kid, but there were times we did not get along with each other.

When I was a kid, my friends and I would go to the wrestling mats at the Oak Forest Park District and fight it out. When I moved down south, it seemed like we boys fought for the fun of it. We'd hit each other and wrestle, and then we'd be best of friends. That's kinda how boys are. But you know, we fight in the church sometimes. This little church in Philippi was graced by two magnificent women, Euodia and Syntyche, whom Paul memorably described here as having "labored side by side with me in the gospel together with Clement and the rest of my fellow workers, whose names are in the book of life" (3:3). These two were no weak sisters by any means because Paul's description employed a gladiatorial term, better rendered as "fought side by side with me."[108] These women had been in the same conflict with Paul against the evil one, and now they were fighting with one another, so much so they need an apostolic rebuke.

Their fighting was holding back the forward progress of the gospel. These women have done fantastic work with Paul and Clement, but they seem to be willing to halt the work of the Lord by their disunity. They're thinking of themselves. Look at the history of Euodia and Syntyche, they worked together in spreading the gospel. Most of all their "names are written in the book of life." Yet conflict is now defining the relationship.

Sometimes our conflicts can be mountains that get in the way of what God wants to do in our lives. When I was in Spain we would have to drive through the Pyrenees Mountains on the border of Spain and France. Anytime there was an accident, traffic came to a standstill. This happened quite often. Finally, they built a superhighway above the mountains, and this never happened again. God says there is a way to drive on the superhighway. I love the verse in Matthew 17, "If you have faith like a grain of mustard seed, you will say to this mountain, 'Move from here to there,' and it will move, and nothing will be impossible for you" (Mt 17:20). Can I ask you a serious question? What disagreement is holding you back from god's kingdom purposes? Are you willing to walk by faith to remove those mountains of strife and disunity in your life? Do you just say you believe the Bible or do you really live by it? Well here are a few steps of obedience when there is spiritual instability in your life between you and another brother or sister in the Body. How do we remove these mountains of disunity?

*1. Go straight to Jesus.*

When we are offended, the first thing we need to do is to go straight to the Lord. "Be angry and do not sin; do not let the sun go down on your anger, 27 and give no opportunity to the devil" (Eph 4:26-27). "When my heart is overwhelmed: lead me to the rock that is higher than I" (Psa 61:2, KJV). You've got to get your heart right with the Lord or you are just going to pour gasoline on the fire. Let the Lord give you a love for the one who has offended you. At the very least, you are to love your enemies.

---

[108] Markus Bockmuehl. *The Epistle to the Philippians*, Black's New Testament Commentary (London: A & C Black Limited, 1998), 258.

### 2. Deal with your own heart: repent & forgive

And while you are with Jesus, get your heart right. Deal with your heart. There is probably a very big log in your eye. That's how Jesus describes it. "How can you say to your brother, 'Let me take the speck out of your eye,' when there is the log in your own eye? 5 You hypocrite, first take the log out of your own eye, and then you will see clearly to take the speck out of your brother's eye" (Mt 7:4-5). My own heart is the problem (Jer 17:9). I cannot lean to my own understanding (Pro 3:5-6). Where does conflict come from? James 4:1, "What causes quarrels and what causes fights among you? Is it not this, that your passions are at war within you?" You do what you do because you want what you want. "What comes out of the mouth proceeds from the heart, and this defiles a person. 19 For out of the heart come evil thoughts, murder, adultery, sexual immorality, theft, false witness, slander. 20 These are what defile a person..." (Mt 15:18-20). Sinful desires come from the heart. We do what we do because we want what we want. The only thing that can change our heart (and the desire therein) is the word of God. When you are offended, go to the Lord right away. Repent first of your own sin. "For if you forgive others their trespasses, your heavenly Father will also forgive you, 15 but if you do not forgive others their trespasses, neither will your Father forgive your trespasses" (Mt 6:14-15).

### 3. If you need to talk, have the right attitude.

Often we are willing to talk, but we end up making the matter worse. "A brother offended is harder to win than a strong city, and contentions are like the bars of a castle" (Pro 18:19, NKJV). "I therefore, a prisoner for the Lord, urge you to walk in a manner worthy of the calling to which you have been called, 2 with all humility and gentleness, with patience, bearing with one another in love, 3 eager to maintain the unity of the Spirit in the bond of peace" (Eph 4:1-3).

### 4. If you know someone is offended, fix it.

If you suspect you may have offended someone, it's a good idea to find out – and fix it! In fact, Jesus thinks you need to tend to that before you worship him. "If you are offering your gift at the altar and there remember that your brother has something against you, 24 leave your gift there before the altar and go. First be reconciled to your brother, and then come and offer your gift" (Mt 5:23-24).

### 5. If you need help, get it.

Get help when you need it. If you've tried to reconcile and it hasn't worked, don't give up. In fact we are commanded to bring another person into it if things aren't working. Look over at Matthew 18.

> If your brother sins against you, go and tell him his fault, between you and him alone. If he listens to you, you have gained your brother. [16] But if he does not listen, take one or two others along with you, that every charge may be established by the evidence of two or three witnesses. [17] If he refuses to listen to them, tell it to the church. And if he refuses to listen even to the church, let him be to you as a Gentile and a tax collector. —*Matthew 18:15-17*

You may have to get a leader, elder, or biblical counselor involved, but work at it until it is resolved. This is not just a suggestion but a command.

## Embrace Help

I want you to see that Paul specifically says we all need help. These godly women need help. As disciples of Christ we should embrace help. You can't live the Christian life alone. We all need help in the realm of conflict. He himself is helping them. Look how he helps them: he points their gaze to the cosmic realm: "they labored (literally fought) side by side with me in the gospel...whose names are written in the book of life."

> **Philippians 4:3** | Yes, I ask you also, true companion, help these women, who have labored side by side with me in the gospel together with Clement and the rest of my fellow workers, whose names are in the book of life.

They need to stop fighting on earth so they can fight for the cosmic, kingdom realm. These women need help. They need a reminder to set their minds on things above (Col 3:1). Paul is saying: There's a place. There's a Person in whose presence things don't just stay the same. There's a place where someone sits on a throne who says, "Behold I make all things new" (Rev 21:5). Do you know what that means? In the Lord's presence, things don't just stay the same. They get stronger.

They get newer. They get fresher. They get brighter every second. Forever. Triple every second, and on it goes.[109] We need to get into God's presence and see where he moves us. Let go of these "lesser things." Why are you so worried about these lesser things? Do you have hurt? Get into God's presence. Be renewed. Be strengthened.

That's actually how Paul closes this section in Philippians 4:4-5. He says whatever you do: rejoice in the Lord! I love that command. God wants your happiness.

## A LASTING JOY (4:4-5)

**Philippians 4:4-5** | Rejoice in the Lord always; again I will say, rejoice. ⁵ Let your reasonableness be known to everyone. The Lord is at hand.

Paul basically says in verse 4: stop your pity party. Get your eyes off yourself and get your eyes on Christ. It's a flesh defeating focus!

### Joy In Christ Enriches My Own Heart

Look at this command:

**Philippians 4:4** | Rejoice in the Lord always; again I will say, rejoice.

We've got to get our focus off of self and onto the Lord. Joy does not come by focusing on personal hurts. Bitterness never brought anyone closer to Jesus. I want a Psalm 115:1 kind of heart. It reads, "Not to us, O Lord, not to us but to *your* name be the glory, because of your love and faithfulness." You can be sure when ministry or anything becomes about our personal hurts, we are seeking our own glory when we need to be seeking God's greatness and power. When we start focusing on the Lord, something amazing begins to happen in our hearts: we begin to rejoice! Focus on his love for you. Isn't it amazing "there is now no condemnation in Christ Jesus" (Rom 8:1)?

I'm so glad he saved my soul. He's the Lord of creation, the God of beauty and majesty, the Savior of humanity. He is awesome in power and glory. He used all that power to pour out his love for me. I've got so much to rejoice about that I don't have time for pity parties.

---

[109] Timothy J. Keller, *The Timothy Keller Sermon Archive* (New York City: Redeemer Presbyterian Church, 2013).

## Joy In Christ Enriches the Hearts of Others

Paul then moves from our *walk with God* (rejoice) to *our walk with other people* where he says: "be reasonable." You can tell who is really rejoicing in the Lord by our personal relationships. That's what Paul says in verse 5. A person who really walks with the Lord has a reasonableness, a gentleness, a meek disposition that is unaffected by the drama and chaos of human interpersonal conflicts and offenses. There're too many people that don't know Jesus for me to take offense and have self-pity! Listen to Paul's next instruction:

**Philippians 4:5a** | Let your reasonableness be known to everyone.

Here he directs our attention from the Lord, the source of our joy, to other people, who are often the source of our stress. The key term, which the esv conveys as "reasonableness," which means: "clemency, graciousness, forbearance," or even "magnanimity."[110] The term refers to the calm and kind disposition that enables a person to offer a nonviolent, even generous, response to others' aggression. Aristotle explained this "gentle reasonableness" as *a willingness to forgo one's own rights according to the letter of the law*.[111]

Here Paul expands the circle of those to be treated "gently" beyond the borders of the church. We are to display such forbearing kindness to "everyone," including those who are making our lives miserable. As children of a Father who sends sunshine and rainfall on the just and the unjust (Mt 5:45), as brothers and sisters of the beloved Son who died for us while we were his enemies (Rom 5:10), believers should extend kindness rather than retaliation to those who harass and oppress them.[112]

## Joy In Christ Encourages Us That Time is Short

**Philippians 4:5b** | The Lord is at hand.

Paul concludes this section with the most hopeful words in the Bible: "the Lord is at hand" (4:5). There's coming a day when all conflict

---

[110] BAGD, s.v. epieikeia and epieikēs, 292.

[111] Aristotle, *Nichomachean Ethics*, 5.10.8, cited in G. Walter Hansen, *The Letter to the Philippians*, PNTC (Grand Rapids: Eerdmans, 2009), 288n40. See John Reumann, *Philippians: A New Translation with Introduction and Commentary*, AYB (New Haven, CT: Yale University Press, 2008), 611–12.

[112] D. Johnson, *Philippians*, 267–268.

is ended. Don't get hung up with conflict. Move on. Don't get weighed down with bitterness. Look up! Look up saint! Your redemption is nearer than ever. He's coming soon. Indeed, you can almost see him in the clouds: "The Lord is at hand!"

## Conclusion

What is it that is holding you back? We are called to be fighting for the Lord not fighting with each other. Our enemies are the world, the flesh, and the devil.

When I was a kid, my Uncle Lew had a big yacht that we would sail on Lake Michigan. He would take us to wonderful places on that yacht. We would see other boats. And sometimes we would go to another bay and stop and see the sights. There are so many things we saw. I could never have seen those marvelous places without Uncle Lew's yacht. One summer, we had to delay our sailing because there were some repairs to be made. The ship was leaking. My cousin Russ had to repair the ship. God wants us to set ourselves for sailing. He wants to use you in ways both big and small. Are you ready to set sail? You can't set sail if there's a hole in your ship. Get things right today. Get that heart of yours repaired. God wants to use you. Let's set sail!

# 17 | PHILIPPIANS 4:4-9
## WHEN PANIC ATTACKS

*Do not be anxious about anything, but in everything by prayer and supplication with thanksgiving let your requests be made known to God. And the peace of God, which surpasses all understanding, will guard your hearts and your minds in Christ Jesus.*
PHILIPPIANS 4:6-7

Anxiety is a serious problem in the world today. As a young person, my mother worked at a video store, and she would bring home worldly and wicked materials for me to watch when I was only 11 and 12 years of age. To make things worse, I dealt everyday with the personal plague of fatherlessness. There is no worse plague that is destroying our nation than fatherlessness. Beyond that because my mother fended for herself, we would move constantly. We moved to a new location and a new school about once a year.

All of this severe culture shock left me at age 12 in the seventh grade with what might be described as PTSD, or Post Traumatic Stress Disorder. For three years of my life, age 12 to 15, I was plagued with almost constant terror. What I want to consider tonight is that because of regeneration you can be free from crippling fear. It's what I call terror. There are times in life when we are controlled by crippling fear, anxiety and worry. I want to share an extreme example from my own life so that you can have hope and a strategy to be free from fear.

## *The Terror Defined*

What I went through was not your ordinary anxiety, I have come to understand that I have endured PTSD most of my life. PTSD is normally thought of as something soldiers have because they keep replaying the terrors of the battlefield. The truth is PTSD is not a disease, but simply a description of symptoms. I want to encourage us this morning that God's word is powerful enough to help us trust in God no matter what we feel like. Let me be clear, I am not saying that a person can always be free from the feelings of fear and anxiety. What I am saying is that no child of God ought to be controlled by them. Jesus said, we cannot have two masters. If Christ is our master, then fear cannot be our master.

Let me describe what I have gone through most of my life so that I can give you great hope in the gospel to transform you from a slave to fear to a slave of Jesus. I can remember the moment my fear began. It was the 1980s. It was September 1986. I was just beginning the seventh grade. In the 1980s there was all kinds of talk about HIV and AIDS. I watched TV incessantly. My parents would use the television to babysit me my whole life.

I was very self-conscious because all my friends had dads and guns. I am the youngest in my family. I have brothers that are over a decade older than me. For my 12th birthday they bought me a 22 semi-automatic rifle with a scope. I would go hunting with my friends, but I had an irrational fear that because I didn't have a father, I would somehow turn out wrong. I began to feel such terror. I thought I would become like the people in the pornographic videos I saw. I did not have thoughts of sensuality, but terror. I later came to find out that my mother showing me those porn videos was really a form of abuse. I was terrorized by this abuse and it led me to an even bigger problem. The fear would not go away. I was afraid of so many things.

## *The Terror Described Physiologically*

Where did the terror come from? Physiologically, this experience of terror is caused by a buildup of a stress hormone called cortisol. This is what causes the symptoms of PTSD. In combination with that, there is another stress hormone called adrenaline (also known as epinephrine). The cortisol produces a feeling of doom, and the adrenaline is a fight or fight hormone that causes a feeling of terror.

That's the pathology of fear, but I want to tell you from a firsthand basis what I experienced for three years as a child, and I have had to learn how to cope with these things from the word of God as a Christian.

### The Terror Described Personally

What began as a fear of being different, became all the more destructive as I became a slave to fear for three years. I would try to do anything to get rid of it. It led me from being an honor roll student to me failing my classes. It led me to fornication, alcohol, and drugs at a very young age. I wanted to do anything to get rid of the fear.

The fear was so powerful that I lost my appetite and at times vomited at the feeling of fear and terror. I often had thoughts of suicide. I was constantly tired. My body felt like I was beat up constantly, so I had a daily feeling of exhaustion, like someone constantly running in terror 24/7. The nights were the worst. For three years I was often so afraid that my clothes were soaked with sweat, and at the times of most intense terror, as a teenager I would curl up in the fetal position next to my mother.

As I said, I turned to the world for relief. I was afraid of pornography because they caused me terror, but I destroyed my life and the lives of girls through fornication. I would often become intoxicated as a junior higher with wine that was readily available where we lived in the Bayou of Louisiana near Lake Ponchatrain. That went on until September of 1989, when a group of evangelists from the Assemblies of God (The Power Team / Strike Force) preached the gospel to me at a large evangelistic event. At that moment the entire focus of my life was radically redirected. I was born again. For many years the terror and fear I experienced in such a defeated and devastating way was now left behind. I now had heavenly joy in Christ. My sins were forgiven. I was a new creation. I was born again!

So that means all my fear and terror went away, right? No. For over a decade I was free from crippling fear. From the moment I was born again at age 15 (September 1989) until I had been one year on the mission field of Spain as a missionary church planter in the Basque Region of Spain in September of 2002, I was completely free from crippling fear. One day while I was in Sunday School in Spain, enjoying the teaching, all the feelings of terror and crippling fear came back. There was no trigger, but there were physiological reasons it all returned. Physically, because of culture shock and the intense pressure of living in a new culture and learning a new language, the cortisol in my body built up to a crisis level which released a rush of adrenaline in me, that gave me a feeling of terror and put me in "fight or flight" mode.

Because of the adrenaline I could not sleep. I called my pastor in the United States. He told me to cling to Christ, which I tried to do. Days went by with very little sleep. I kept getting worse. My wife was getting very worried about me. Imagine being terrorized ... your life continually threatened ... your heart gripped with fear. Imagine every day ... waking to the thought: what if this fear never goes away? It's terrifying. That's what I was experiencing. Now maybe you can't relate to that, but I'm pretty sure you've suffered with anxiety and worry to some degree. What can we do when panic attacks? How can we find God's peace in the storm? What is the answer? We find it in Philippians 4:4-9.

> **Philippians 4:4-9** | Rejoice in the Lord always; again I will say, rejoice. **⁵** Let your reasonableness be known to everyone. The Lord is at hand; **⁶** do not be anxious about anything, but in everything by prayer and supplication with thanksgiving let your requests be made known to God. **⁷** And the peace of God, which surpasses all understanding, will guard your hearts and your minds in Christ Jesus. **⁸** Finally, brothers, whatever is true, whatever is honorable, whatever is just, whatever is pure, whatever is lovely, whatever is commendable, if there is any excellence, if there is anything worthy of praise, think about these things. **⁹** What you have learned and received and heard and seen in me—practice these things, and the God of peace will be with you.

How should we respond when anxiety harasses us? Often the panic attacks and lasting PTSD symptoms that come from stress (flooding the body with cortisol and epinephrine) are absolutely paralyzing. These "fight or flight" hormones are good to deal with emergencies, but if a person is not able to move on, they will weigh a person down and even paralyze a person emotionally. I read somewhere a good illustration: "Ducks walk out from a lake, flap their wings, and they fly off. When you face something stressful, you need to be able to shake it off and move on with life." Philippians 4 helps us "shake it off"!

They put on cigarette packages that, "Smoking may be hazardous to your health." And, I want to tell you, dear friend, that wrong thinking can also be hazardous to your health. And so, this morning, we're going to have "a check-up from the neck up." We're going to find out if you have healthy thinking. There are times when troublesome circumstances interrupt the normal flow of events. Paul gave three commands to help the readers solve these: rejoice (4:4-5), rest in God's peace (4:6-7), renew your mind (4:8-9). [113]

## REJOICE (4:4-5)

Now, the Bible says, "As a man thinks, so is he" (Pro 23:7). I just want to ask, is Jesus Lord of your heart? Then you should be rejoicing.

### Rejoice in the Lord

Paul tells us what to do when panic attacks. Have you ever had a panic attack? Listen to Paul.

**Philippians 4:4a** | Rejoice in the Lord.

If you've ever suffered from panic or worry or serious anxiety, when you hear Paul, you might not like his advice. It sounds simplistic and dismissive. Just trust God! Well, we already know that.

A popular song when I was growing up was: "Don't worry, be happy!" That was the that song. But for the person who struggles with worry, such counsel is sadly so simplistic, it's almost cruel.[114] Paul's advice seems trite when we hear it, but it's true. But let me say it a different way: Don't magnify your problem. Magnify the Lord. I love what the David says in Psalm 34:3, "O magnify the Lord with me, and let us exalt his name together." God is so big compared to your problem. When you put our awesome, amazing, infinite God next to your problem, the problem, no matter what it is, seems small.

---

[113] Outline from Melick, *Philippians*, 148.
[114] Robert D. Jones, "Getting to the Heart of Your Worry," ed. David A. Powlison, *The Journal of Biblical Counseling, Number 3, Spring 1999* 17 (1999): 21.

Isaiah tells us in Isaiah 40, who can we compare God too? There's no one like him. He "sits above the circle of the earth, and its inhabitants are like grasshoppers; who stretches out the heavens like a curtain, and spreads them like a tent to dwell in" (Isa 40:22).

When God humbled King Nebuchadnezzar of Babylon, the king praised God and said in Daniel 4:35, "All the inhabitants of the earth are accounted as nothing, and he does according to his will among the host of heaven and among the inhabitants of the earth; and none can restrain his hand...." Do you believe that God is absolutely sovereign? Isn't he a good Shepherd for all those who entrust their lives to him?

When panic attacks us, the first thing we need to do is rejoice. Do you know that God is in control no matter what is happening in your life? He's sovereign over your circumstances. Rejoice! God doesn't command us to rejoice in circumstances. Sometimes we weep over our circumstances. He does tell us to rejoice over our pain and our heartbreaks. What does he say: Rejoice in the Lord! Jesus is the Source of our joy! "The joy of the Lord is my strength" (Neh 8:10).

Do you feel weak, overwhelmed, discouraged? Joy never comes by looking at how good or bad our circumstances are. Circumstances change. Joy comes from one source: focusing on the sovereign Lord who never changes.

## Rejoice Always

**Philippians 4:4b** | Rejoice in the Lord always.

Paul now gives us the divine command: "Rejoice in the Lord always." This means we have a reason for joy always. Our joy doesn't depend on our circumstances. He loves you, with an unchanging love, therefore you can rejoice always. Our joy is to be in the Lord, and it is to be unchanging. The circumstances of Paul's life reminded him of the joy available in the Lord, and he wished that joy for them as well. Paul knew that no situation is beyond the Lord's help. Christians can always rejoice in that, if nothing else.

Rejoice: God's love for you is never changing. Rejoice: We love him because he first loved us. His love is unconditional. Romans 8 says there is nothing that can separate you from the love of God in Christ Jesus. Why should we rejoice? Because of his great love for us!

Romans 8:31-39, "What then shall we say to these things? If God is for us, who can be against us?³² He who did not spare his own Son but gave him up for us all, how will he not also with him graciously give us all things? ³³ Who shall bring any charge against God's elect? It is God who justifies. ³⁴ Who is to condemn? Christ Jesus is the one who died—more than that, who was raised—who is at the right hand of God, who indeed is interceding for us. ³⁵ Who shall separate us from the love of Christ? Shall tribulation, or distress, or persecution, or famine, or nakedness, or danger, or sword? ³⁶ As it is written, "For your sake we are being killed all the day long we are regarded as sheep to be slaughtered." ³⁷ No, in all these things we are more than conquerors through him who loved us.³⁸ For I am sure that neither death nor life, nor angels nor rulers, nor things present nor things to come, nor powers, ³⁹ nor height nor depth, nor anything else in all creation, will be able to separate us from the love of God in Christ Jesus our Lord."

## Rejoice Again and Again

Paul then repeats what he has just said.

**Philippians 4:4c** | Again I will say, rejoice.

Again, Paul says, rejoice. What's the point? We need to hear this reminder again and again and again. *Rejoice! Ah, I see you've forgotten, so I'll say it again: rejoice!* We are creatures that are prone to forget, so Paul knows, and we all know we need this constant reminder. When everything is hard and you are down, you need to remember to rejoice. There is not a moment in our lives as believers that we should not be rejoicing in Christ. This is particularly true when we are going through a trial. "Blessed are they that mourn," our Lord said (Mt 6:3). We are to rejoice even when we are mourning. Why? Because the Lord is in control, working all things all for our good and his glory.

## Rejoice Restfully

Rejoicing leads to a very peaceful, joyful soul. Look at what he says:

**Philippians 4:5** | Let your reasonableness be known to everyone. The Lord is at hand.

The Lord is near. His second coming could be today! He's returning for us out of this great big mess. That reality has a calming effect on us: it makes us reasonable. It literally means "having a gentle, considerate spirit." There is a peace that calms the noisy soul!

What is reasonableness? It's the opposite of this is a noisy soul. This reasonableness is a reflective, peaceful soul. Paul goes from rejoicing to reasonableness, or gentleness is another way it could be translated. There is a sense of calm and reason and gentleness is the idea. There is a meekness and quietness that comes over us when we are sweetly resting in Jesus. The opposite of the reasonableness is a chaotic noisy soul.

> For thus said the Lord God, the Holy One of Israel, "In returning and rest you shall be saved; in quietness and in trust shall be your strength." —*Isaiah 30:15*

Do you have a quiet soul that comes from rejoicing in the Lord? If not, I want to give you some instructions as to how to get God's peace and rest in it.

### Rejoice Expectantly

**Philippians 4:5b** | The Lord is at hand.

There ought to be no worries for the true believer in Christ. The Lord is at hand! Amen?! Whatever you are worried about, remember it may not happen for a number of reasons, chief of which is the second coming of Jesus! He's coming again saints. Every eye shall see him, even those who pierced him and put him on the cross. Every knee will bow. Every tongue will confess that he is Lord and God. Some will enter into the new creation with joy, while others will depart into everlasting fire. If you are in Christ today, rejoice! Your redemption draws near. Christ is coming victoriously, and we who know him will join him. Suddenly, in the blink of an eye, we will see him. The living and the dead will be brought before him. Those who know him will reign with him forever and ever. Amen! Rejoice!

## REST IN GOD'S PEACE (4:6-7)

Of all the blessing Jesus wants to give you, he says "Come unto me, and I will give you rest." He wants to give you rest. We can be very chaotic when we are worried, but God moves in the rhythm of grace. He says, "Be still and know that I am God." He says to the wind and waves: "Peace be still." God's best for us is unhindered communion and fellowship with him. Remember Adam and Eve walked with God in the garden of Eden in the cool of the day. That's God's best for us. Satan wants to take it away. Paul mercifully warns us: be anxious about nothing.

## God's Rest Should Be Universal

**Philippians 4:6a** | Do not be anxious about anything.

There is some worry, fear and anxiety that is *sinful*. But some fear is healthy. I have a healthy fear of lions. I like to obey that sign at the zoo: "Keep Your Hands Away From The Lions' Cages." I think it's good to have a healthy fear of heights, so you don't get near the edge of the Grand Canyon. That would be a stupid way to die, right? God gave us the capacity to fear for a good purpose: to keep us safe.

*There is a Healthy Fear*

God gave us every emotion for a proper use, to be helpful to us and honoring to him. Because of fear we are able to escape injury and dangers that otherwise would destroy most of us before we reached maturity. There is a good kind of care for responsibility and a good kind of fear that will keep us from getting torn to pieces. We are also called to have a healthy fear of God (Pro 1:7).

But what about fear and anxiety and worry that cripples us? There is a kind of fear that can lead us to despair, or anger, or depression. The key with sinful fear, is we need to know how to identify it. The question you must ask yourself if you are fearful or anxious in a way that goes beyond healthy concern is: what am I afraid of? Anxiety is sinful because it causes you to worship something other than God. Do you want comfort, people pleasing, a lack of someone's anger… what is the idol you are worshipping? Are you trying to get peace apart from God? Often you cannot shake them and sometimes you may find yourself doing all sorts of things that you do not want to do to try and keep the fear at bay. Indeed, fear may get such a tight grip upon you that at times it may seem to be some powerful force from the outside that takes you captive.

When Paul says never to be anxious, what is he getting at? Why can't we worry about everything? I mean, I think I'm pretty good at worry. When I was a kid, I was afraid of getting lost, so much so that my mom called me a "worry wart." I was afraid I would get lost, especially when we would visit my dad in downtown Chicago at the First National Bank. But I remember when my mom promised me that she would always find me if I got lost, I got over it. When we would go to

Venture, I remember I would even get lost on purpose just so I could hear my mom's name over the intercom: "Barbara Black, please come to the front desk and pick up your child. Barbara Black..."

## There is a Sinful Fear

Worry robs us of God's peace and rest. God wants us trusting him in his perfect peace at all times. When we are worrying, we are demonstrating our lack of trust in God. Why would worry and anxiety be so sinful? Because we become afraid when we magnify anything to be bigger than God. Anxiety, therefore, is idolatry. If you are worried, then you are making something bigger than God in your life. Nothing should control you outside of Jesus Christ.

Jesus is the Master of everything, right? Do you remember the story of Jesus and his disciples on the sea? He's the master of the sea. Remember they thought they were going to die? The storm was so high. They said, "Master, don't you care that we perish?" And remember what Jesus did? He commanded the wind and the waves: "Peace be still" and they obeyed his voice. Jesus is the only Master worth serving, amen? Jesus is bigger than your circumstance.

Jesus said we can only have one Master. If you try to have two masters (Mt 6:24), it will tear you in two directions. "A double minded person is unstable in all their ways" (Jas 1:8). When we are controlled by fear, anxiety or depression we will often let fear be our Master. I need to stay in bed. I can't get up to go to work because I'm so depressed. I can't produce at work like I used to. I'm just giving up on work. I can't wear that shirt because it reminds me of the trauma and fear. I can't go down that elevator, can't go that way to work, can't.... etc. I will do anything to get rid of this fear (drink, entertainment, lust, even anger, etc.). We as Christians cannot think this way. We have one Lord. We cannot be slaves to fear. We have to have the mentality: "I am going to serve Jesus however he leads me no matter what I feel like." I'm going to trust that Jesus is good! Jesus alone is my master. Fear is not my master. Choose to do what Christ commands you no matter what you feel like.

Worry is an idol, a Lord that wants to master you. The first commandment is that we cannot worship idols. Worry is putting the weight of the world on your own shoulders. Martin Luther said, "Pray and let God worry." There is only one God. He can rule the world all by himself. He doesn't need your help. How many things are we supposed to worry about? He says, "Don't worry about *anything*." God tells us 365 times in our Bible not to fear or worry. We forget don't we? Worry is a master that is defeated by submitting and swearing allegiance to another Master: Jesus. Jesus is the only one that can carry your burdens. That's why you are called to prayer and thankfulness.

## God's Rest is Possible

How do we find rest? Focus on God's care, his supply, and his plan.

> **Philippians 4:6** | Do not be anxious about anything, but in everything by prayer and supplication with thanksgiving let your requests be made known to God.

It is always great when someone in research science spends time and money to prove something that we knew all along. In a study done at the University of Exeter researchers have found that "the brain response to a perceived threat is stopped when we are reminded that we are loved and cared for!" Who knew? How do we find rest? We find shelter in the most high God. We find shelter in the in the Shadow of the Almighty.

### *Focus on God's Care*

*Prayer*: What is prayer, but communion with a God who loves you? The first way to rest in God is: worry about nothing; pray about everything. It's a moment by moment trusting in God. God says to us in Isaiah 26:3, "You keep him in perfect peace whose mind is stayed on you, because he trusts in you." Again in Isaiah 41:10, "Fear not, for I am with you; be not dismayed, for I am your God; I will strengthen you, I will help you, I will uphold you with my righteous right hand." Anxiety leaves when we realize we can take shelter in God by "prayer and supplication with thanksgiving." This is formal language, so let me say it plainly: God wants your heart. He wants to be God of your heart all by himself. He wants to rule your heart by his love.

### *Focus on God's Supply*

*Supplication* means that God will supply, no matter what you are going through. God will be there. He's bigger than your problem. He's going to give you grace sufficient for the trial. He will do it in his way and in his time.

Worry is a sin because it tries to find shelter in someone or something else than God. Paul here tells us not to be anxious and worried, trying to hurry God's plan. His timing for supplying your need is absolutely perfect. The goal is not to remove the problem, but to humble you. He wants you to know he cares so much that you will start rejoicing when you give your heart and your cares to him. "Humble yourselves...casting all your care on him for he cares for you." (1 Pet 5:6). Prayer is an act of humility. It's saying, I don't have the answers! God will supply the grace you need in this trial. Paul testifies about God's grace.

> To keep me from becoming conceited because of the surpassing greatness of the revelations, a thorn was given me in the flesh, a messenger of Satan to harass me, to keep me from becoming conceited. ⁸ Three times I pleaded with the Lord about this, that it should leave me. ⁹ But he said to me, "My grace is sufficient for you, for my power is made perfect in weakness." Therefore I will boast all the more gladly of my weaknesses, so that the power of Christ may rest upon me.
> —*2 Corinthians 12:7-9*

### *Focus on God's Final Plan*

*Thanksgiving* is the realization of joy when you realize God's never going to leave you! He's got plans for you. You are in those plans. His final plan is that all would work out for your good and his glory, conforming you to Jesus (Rom 8:28-29).

## God's Rest is Delightful

What happens when we let Jesus be Master over our lives? The peace of God protects you and guards you!

> **Philippians 4:7 |** And the peace of God, which surpasses all understanding, will guard your hearts and your minds in Christ Jesus.

Where does the peace of God come from? It comes from a God who guards us with his love.

> He who dwells in the shelter of the Most High will abide in the shadow of the Almighty. ²I will say to the Lord, "My refuge and my fortress, my God, in whom I trust. —*Psalm 91:1*

You and I serve a God that is so big, his protection of you passes understanding. In order to have that peace, you've got to magnify the Lord over your problems. You will not be disappointed if you let God guard your heart and mind. He'll give you a peace that passes understanding. The answer to anxiety is the peace of God.

Paul made three statements about this peace. First, it is divine peace. He did not envision a situation where circumstances changed, or external needs were met. This peace was a characteristic of God which invaded the Christian. Second, it "transcends all understanding." "Transcends" means "excellent."[115] Third, it guards and protects our hearts and minds from worry. Do you have the trust that God loves you? That perfect love of God casts out all human fear. It protects your heart from worry.

## RENEW YOUR MIND (4:8-9)

The key to having long term peace is mind renewal.

### The Practice of Mind Renewal

Look at how Paul says, we need to be done with lesser things. We need to think on things that are true and excellent.

> **Philippians 4:8** | Finally, brothers, whatever is true, whatever is honorable, whatever is just, whatever is pure, whatever is lovely, whatever is commendable, if there is any excellence, if there is anything worthy of praise, think about these things.

There are eight standards of mind renewal found in this verse (true, honorable, just, pure, lovely, commendable, excellent, and praiseworthy). You see the problem with anxiety and fear is that our mind is often defiled, and we need to renew our minds.

> Put off your old self, which belongs to your former manner of life and is corrupt through deceitful desires, [23] and to be renewed in the spirit of your minds, [24] and to put on the new self, created after the likeness of God in true righteousness and holiness. —*Ephesians 4:22-24*

*Truth*: God is sovereign and I'm in control of my own emotions. I am not a victim. God is using all things for good. So much of what causes us to worry is simply not true. 80 to 90% of what brings us into panic never happens. We need to think on what is true. *Honorable*: I know who I am in Christ. I am a saint. God has blessed me with all spiritual blessings. I am a child of God. I am honorable and will think

---

[115] Melick, *Philippians*, 149.

on honorable things. *Just*: God is just to forgive me. God is just to give me a harvest of righteousness if I obey him. *Pure*: We are to think on things that glorify the Lord. Is there anything you are ashamed to have in your thoughts? Get rid of it. *Lovely*: This is not just beautiful things, the most beautiful, but also dwelling on God's love. *Commendable*: This means we think the very best about people. We are not gossips but think things that are of good report. *Excellence*: This means virtuous, or the very best. Often, we use our eyes and ears for garbage cans, and we wonder why we don't have peace. *Praise-worthy*: This speaks to something that everyone would agree is good and godly. Put that in your mind. The Psalmist (likely David) described it in Psalm 1.

> Blessed is the man who walks not in the counsel of the wicked, nor stands in the way of sinners, nor sits in the seat of scoffers; ²but his delight is in the law of the Lord, and on his law he meditates day and night. ³He is like a tree planted by streams of water that yields its fruit in its season, and its leaf does not wither. In all that he does, he prospers. —*Psalm 1:1-3*

## The Power of Mind Renewal

Jesus said we can only have one Master. If you try to have two masters, it will tear you in two directions. A double minded person is unstable in all their ways.

> **Philippians 4:9** | What you have learned and received and heard and seen in me—practice these things, and the God of peace will be with you.

Look at Paul. Follow him as he follows Christ. Christ was in the midst of the storm and he was sleeping. The disciples had to wake him up. Yet he woke up and controlled the wind and the waves. Paul was in so many trials and tribulations. He says to rejoice! Rest in God's peace! Renew your mind. Let's make this our practice, and the "God of peace will be with you." Amen!

### Conclusion

When panic attacks, it's all about focus. Isaiah gives us a simply understanding of all that Paul said to the Philippians. Isaiah says, "You will keep him in perfect peace whose mind is fixed on you because he trusts in you" (Isa 26:3). Do this, according to Paul by learning to rejoice, rest in God's peace, and renew your mind. And God's peace will guard you!

# 18 | PHILIPPIANS 4:10-14
## HAPPY IN JESUS ALONE

*I have learned in whatever situation I am to be content. I know how to be brought low, and I know how to abound. In any and every circumstance, I have learned the secret of facing plenty and hunger, abundance and need. I can do all things through him who strengthens me.*
PHILIPPIANS 4:11-13

Everyone is seeking for happiness in the world today. I can remember a popular song when I was a child: *"Looking for love in all the wrong places."* I believe most people are looking for happiness and love in all the wrong places. The point of this morning's message is simple: Happiness, real joy is found in Jesus Christ alone. Everyone and everything else is offering a happiness or love that will quickly fade away. Looking for ultimate happiness anywhere else but in Christ is idolatry. But people are looking everywhere for happiness.

I read an article about Madonna, and her greatest shock when she reached stardom was that she was not much happier than when she was poor. She couldn't believe that you can have all this money and fame and success and be so miserable.

People play the lottery because they think money will bring them instant happiness. So many people who win say over and over that winning the lottery was the worst thing that happened to them. For example, Jack Whittaker won $314 million in 2002. Within 4 years, he had gambled it all away. Several stories I read about lottery winners say that some even committed suicide before they could spend all the money. Yet people think money and fame can make them happy. How many professional athletes made millions in the NFL or NBA or in boxing, and are today flat broke? What is the answer for happiness? What is the secret to infinite happiness no matter what is happening in our lives? We find it in Philippians 4.

> **Philippians 4:10-14** | I rejoiced in the Lord greatly that now at length you have revived your concern for me. You were indeed concerned for me, but you had no opportunity. [11] Not that I am speaking of being in need, for I have learned in whatever situation I am to be content. [12] I know how to be brought low, and I know how to abound. In any and every circumstance, I have learned the secret of facing plenty and hunger, abundance and need. [13] I can do all things through him who strengthens me. [14] Yet it was kind of you to share my trouble.

It is Christ alone that can make us happy. In fact, we can be happy in Christ alone with or without people (4:10-11), money (4:12-13), trials (4:14). We see the secret of contentment laid out over and over again in the book of Philippians. "For to me to live is Christ, and to die is gain" (1:21). He says, "I have suffered the loss of all things and count them as rubbish, in order that I may gain Christ" (3:8). "That I may know him and the power of his resurrection" (3:10). Paul says he's in a race to gain "the prize of the upward call of God in Christ Jesus" (3:14). You get the idea. Happiness is not in the pursuit of things on this earth. Lasting and meaningful happiness is found in Jesus. This is Paul's point here in Philippians 4.

## HAPPY IN CHRIST WITH OR WITHOUT PEOPLE (4:10-11)

People were very important to Paul. He laid down his life over and over again for people. Paul wrote 13 books in our New Testament. He has taught the Philippians about the importance of people and how we relate to each other in the Body (1 Cor 12; Rom 12). But you know as well as I that even the best of people on this planet let you down.

> **Philippians 4:10-11** | I rejoiced in the Lord greatly that now at length you have revived your concern for me. You were indeed concerned for me, but you had no opportunity. [11] Not that I am speaking of being in need, for I have learned in whatever situation I am to be content.

A decade has passed from the time Paul went to Philippi to plant the church and got thrown into Philippian jail and got beat up. At first, they were able to support Paul even when he left Philippi, went over to Thessalonica. They sent aid as he said a couple of different times. Supported him through that, but something happened. And we don't even know what it was that happened. They lost touch somehow. But Paul was not disillusioned. His trust wasn't in people. It was in his Savior and God. He will later say: "But my God will supply every need of yours according to his riches in glory in Christ Jesus" (4:19).

## The Principle of Happiness with People

People – friends and family – are wonderful, but can't do what Jesus can do. Jesus is "a friend who sticks closer than a brother" (Pro 18:24). He's the one that says, "I will never leave you or forsake you" (Heb 13:5). Listen, ultimate happiness doesn't come from your spouse, but from our ultimate Spouse and Bridegroom, Jesus Christ. Ultimate happiness doesn't come from your friends, but from the Friend of sinners, Jesus Christ.

Paul, as you know was in Rome under house arrest (Acts 28:17-31). He's in a situation where he is never alone. He's got a Roman soldier attached to him 24/7. Every four hours it's a new soldier. That's six different soldiers he's chained to every day. He's got people visiting him all the time. Some of you would love that. You love people. Some of you love privacy. Paul had no privacy. Even those who love people need privacy and alone time. Am I right? Paul learned whatever state he was in to be content. Whether he was with people or not with people. He didn't need people to be happy. Paul says was big on the fact that the Philippians sent their pastor, Epaphroditus, to see him. The Philippians loved Paul and sent their pastor, a letter, and a financial gift to him while he was under house arrest.

> **Philippians 4:10-11** | I rejoiced in the Lord greatly that now at length you have revived your concern for me. You were indeed concerned for me, but you had no opportunity.

They had been concerned but didn't have an opportunity to help him. Now Paul wasn't upset while he was waiting that first year in his "prison" in a house in Rome. He wasn't saying: "Those Philippians forgot about me. God must not love me. God's people must not love me." No, Paul's happiness was not dependent on people. Can we agree that people are important in our lives? We need people. You cannot be a lone ranger Christian and obey God. You need people. You need the local church. You know how it is. Maybe you've been providentially hindered from coming to church for a week or two. It has a major effect on your life. We can all agree that the we need God's people. It's sometimes hard to get to church, but we are always glad when we are here. But people are needy. People are sinners. People are not always safe. We are all sinners right? When you look in the mirror, you know that you are a lot of work. You sometimes are a big mess. Don't be surprised when people around you are a big mess as well.

## The Practice of Happiness with People

So what's the answer? Paul gives it to us right here.

> **Philippians 4:11** | Not that I am speaking of being in need, for I have learned in whatever situation I am to be content.

We shouldn't look to other people where we need them in some ultimate way. We need them generally speaking to help us grow and change in Christ. People can't give you ultimate happy. Don't look to people for happiness. Do you see this theme in Scripture? So many people get all messed up every two years when we have elections. Listen. God is in control, not man. Don't trust in mankind. They will let you down.

> Do not trust in princes, in mortal man, in whom there is no salvation.
> —*Psalm 146:3*

> Thus says the Lord: 'Cursed is the man who trusts in man and makes flesh his strength, whose heart turns away from the Lord... ⁷ Blessed is the man who trusts in the Lord, whose trust is the Lord. ⁸ He is like a tree planted by water, that sends out its roots by the stream.
> —*Jeremiah 17:5, 7-8*

You must not find your happiness in people. It's wonderful to be around people. It's wonderful to be alone and have your privacy. Don't find your happiness in either. You can't go to either extremes. Don't look for happiness in your spouse or in your friends, or in your church. The ultimate source of happiness is Christ. Don't think by being married you'll finally be happy. That's idolatry. Don't think, "If I could just be single and alone, I'd be happy." That's idolatry too. Being with people or alone does not get anyone ultimate happiness. Happiness comes from the Lord. Remember, "the joy of the Lord is my strength" (Neh 8:10).

## The Person that Gives True Happiness

People are a blessing. They are going to help you grow and hold you accountable. But they are also going to mess up and disappoint you. They will at times hurt you. The answer is not to get so upset that you cut yourself off from people or that you try to find your happiness in people by being with them all the time. Find your happiness in Jesus Christ alone. He alone can give us contentment.

> **Philippians 4:11** | Not that I am speaking of being in need, for I have learned in whatever situation I am to be content.

Paul has been in a lot of messed up situations. People have really hurt Paul. Demas forsook him, falling in love with the present world (2 Tim 4:10). Here is a list that still falls short of all he suffered from people. It comes from 2 Corinthians 11. Paul labored for people. He was beaten and given "stripes above measure." He was put in "prisons frequently." He faced death often at the hands of people. He "received forty stripes minus one" from the Jews on five different occasions. Three times he was "beaten with rods" by these people he was trying to reach. Once, he says, "I was stoned" to death by the people he was trying reach. Three times, he says "I was shipwrecked" trying to reach people for Christ. God raised Paul from the dead. And he goes on: "...a night and a day I have been in the deep, in journeys often, in perils of waters, in perils of robbers, in perils of my own countrymen, in perils of the Gentiles, in perils in the city, in perils in the wilderness, in perils in the sea, in perils among false brethren, in weariness and toil, in sleeplessness often, in hunger and thirst, in often fastings, in cold and nakedness" (2 Cor 11:23-33). All this for and because of people. Paul was even abandoned by most of his friends while imprisoned (2 Tim 1:15). Wouldn't you think Paul would give up on people? No! His happiness wasn't in people but in Christ. Do you see? You can't have your happiness in people or else you will be very disappointed.

## **HAPPY IN CHRIST WITH OR WITHOUT MONEY (4:12-13)**

Now, Paul wasn't trusting in money either. He was happy the Philippian church brought him a gift. It helped meet his needs. But Paul is not trusting in money. He is trusting in the Lord. He's learned the secret of contentment. It's that he's happy no matter how much or how little he has.

> **Philippians 4:12-13** | I know how to be brought low, and I know how to abound. In any and every circumstance, I have learned the secret of facing plenty and hunger, abundance and need. <sup>13</sup> I can do all things through him who strengthens me.

Paul has been brought low. He's been well taken care of at times. His happiness does not depend on his poverty or prosperity. His secret to happiness is found in verse 13, "I can do all things through Christ who strengthens me." It's hard to serve God without any money. It's also hard to serve God with a lot of money. Both are hard, but we have the power and strength of Christ whether you find yourself poor or rich.

Money and wealth and blessing is not where you find happiness. "No one can serve two masters, for either he will hate the one and love the other, or he will be devoted to the one and despise the other. You cannot serve God and money" (Mt 6:24). Your goal cannot be to gain money. That's idolatry. Your goal is to serve the Lord Jesus Christ. Money will not make you happy. The goal is to be content with what God has given you.

Would you agree that God is sovereign over your money? What does the Bible say is the best view to have of money? It's sovereignly given. Don't be anxious about money because God loves you and will provide for you. "Seek first the kingdom of God and his righteousness, and all these things will be added to you" (Mt 6:33). Or as Paul says to Timothy, "But godliness with contentment is great gain" (1 Tim 6:6).

I need to know that there is no more gracious, forgiving, merciful and kindhearted being in all the universe than God almighty. The tragedies of sin are unspeakable. But "where sin abounds, grace much more abounds" (Romans 5:20). Solomon, in the book of Ecclesiastes, is eminently qualified to tell me that life without my Creator, who I know from the New Testament is Christ—life without Christ is empty and futile - meaningless! What is Solomon saying? He's not a bitter old man just being pessimistic and grouchy. He's warning here. He's essentially saying that whatever is done selfishly and simply to enjoy as an end in and of itself always disappoints. In other words, the promises of money, sex, and power are all empty outside of God. The New Testament carries this theme in many places. One obvious one is – Mark 8:36, "For what shall it profit a man, if he shall gain the whole world, and lose his own soul?" What's the answer? Nothing. Me gaining the whole world will be vanity! It's all vanity without Jesus! Take the world but give me Jesus.

Paul tells us what he thinks of earthly riches compared to Christ back in Philippians 3:7-8, "Whatever gain I had, I counted as loss for the sake of Christ. 8 Indeed, I count everything as loss because of the surpassing worth of knowing Christ Jesus my Lord. For his sake I have suffered the loss of all things and count them as rubbish, in order that I may gain Christ." Christ's life, death and resurrection is so much better than money. Whatever money can buy, Christ's life and death bought you infinitely more.

## HAPPY IN CHRIST WITH OR WITHOUT TRIALS (4:14)

Paul is writing from a Roman jail cell in a rented house. One thing you don't hear is grumbling. Paul is not complaining about his circumstances. He trusted in a Sovereign God. Are you a grumbler? Remember Paul had said, "Do all things without grumbling or disputing" (2:14). Are you entitled? Paul was a grateful person.

### God is in Control of Trials

This life is filled with troubles and trials. Jesus said, "In the world you will have tribulation. But take heart; I have overcome the world" (Jn 16:33). Trials and difficulties will come. Those who put their happiness on having a trouble-free life will be terribly disappointed. Paul understood that his happiness was not based on trial-free living. He put his trust in a sovereign God who is working "all things together for good..." that we "might be conformed to the image of his dear Son" (Rom 8:28-29). Remember what James, the pastor at Jerusalem has told us. "Count it all joy, my brothers, when you meet trials of various kinds,3 for you know that the testing of your faith produces steadfastness.4 And let steadfastness have its full effect, that you may be perfect and complete, lacking in nothing" (Jas 1:2-4). The Philippians sent their dear pastor Epaphroditus to visit Paul, and it relieved him that this Philippian pastor would share in Paul's trouble. That sweet Philippian church sent their pastor and sent a gift as well. Paul says:

> **Philippians 4:14** | Yet it was kind of you to share my trouble.

> Here was Paul in Rome chained to a Roman soldier. He's giving thanks. He's thinking of others. He's basically writing a thank you note. He's not grumbling. He's not complaining. He's not doubting God's goodness. He's not leaving the faith.

## Trials are a Test for the False Convert

Remember the parable of the sower. Trials test whether your faith is genuine. Lots of people get excited about the cross but not all endure to the end. Why is that? In Matthew 13 you have a parable of the heart. It compares the heart to different soils. Many people are rocky ground hearers. They hear the word of God and rejoice, but then they fall away. Listen to Jesus in Matthew 13:

> What was sown on rocky ground, this is the one who hears the word and immediately receives it with joy, [21] yet he has no root in himself, but endures for a while, and when tribulation or persecution arises on account of the word, immediately he falls away.  —*Matthew 13:20-21*

There are some who are false converts in the church, and false converts are revealed through trials and tribulations because they fall away. If you read Matthew 7, Jesus tells us that some of these false converts are pastors and preachers. I've seen them myself. When things are good, they continue, but when things are hard, they fall away. Jesus will say to them, even though they've preached the word, "Depart from me, I never knew you" (Mt 7:21-23).

## Trials are a Gift for the Believer

For the believer, trials are a gift from God, given to us to draw near to him, to humble us and to pry the idols from our hearts. Trials put us in the fire and purify us. Job said, "But he knows the way that I take; when he has tried me, I shall come out as gold" (Job 23:10). The way that we all take is conformity to Christ. God is melting us and molding us through the tragedies and difficulties in our lives. I've seen some of you go through the most horrendous trials, and you have drawn near to God. It's amazing! You have the true mark of God dwelling in you. I will tell you this, for some of you, the world is not worthy of you, the way you have endured suffering (Heb 11:38).

## God's Plan for Your Trials

Paul knows that "all things work after the counsel of God's own will" (Eph 1:11). God is sovereign over my circumstances. We can face all these challenges and trials, successes, and failures with and because of Jesus. We need to be reoriented from circumstance-sufficient, self-sufficient, creation-sufficient to Christ-sufficient. We can be content in all circumstances when we are content in Christ because Christ is with us in all circumstances. He's got a plan to conform us to himself. That means God is bigger than your trials. Cling to him in your trials.

### Conclusion

The average American home is 1,000 square feet bigger than it used to be 40 years ago even though our families are smaller. The average American diet has 500 more calories per person than it was 40 years ago. I think that shows. The average American turned a wheel multiple times to call someone 40 years ago. Now we have smart phones that give us access to virtually any medical information or person in the world, and it fits into the palm of our hand. Life expectancy has gone up over a decade in the last 40 years. Emissions have plummeted in the last 40 years. Yet with all this more and better stuff, we are more unhappy than we've ever been. That's because stuff can't get you happiness. People can't give you lasting contentment. People will fail you. Money will fail you. Trials will come. But Jesus Christ will never fail you. He is the same yesterday, today and forever!

# 19 | PHILIPPIANS 4:15-23
## GROWING THROUGH GENEROSITY

*My God will supply every need of yours according to his riches in glory in Christ Jesus.*
PHILIPPIANS 4:19

Often, we don't think of the subject of joy when it comes to our finances. Honestly there are great worries and concerns, especially if you have children in your care. We worry about medical bills, paying off college debt. We hope we can keep a job, get a raise, or get a better job. Some worry if they'll have enough for retirement. People are worried about credit card debt and bad financial decisions they've made. Most of us really want to be generous. God gave so much to us. We want to put God first. "Seek first his kingdom and righteousness, and all these things shall be added unto you" (Mt 6:33). Let me just mention I am grateful to be living in the most prosperous nation at the most prosperous time in the history of the world. I'm also very sobered at the truth that our Lord gave us: "To whom much is given, much will be required" (Lk 12:48). With that in mind, wouldn't you agree that although maybe you are already a generous person, that you want to grow in generosity. The passage we are looking at this morning teaches us a great truth.

Generosity is an important indication of your spiritual growth in Christ and maturity. What does that mean? It doesn't mean that if you give a lot of money that you are spiritually mature. That's not true. Plenty of bad people give lots of money to philanthropic causes. What I am saying is that if you are growing spiritually you will grow in generosity. Your heart grows bigger and bigger as you grow in Christ. Jesus teaches us this. "Where your treasure is there your heart will be also" (Mt 6:21). If you love self, that's where your treasure is. If you love God and his kingdom and his causes, that's where your treasure will be. What does your bank account say that you love? When we came to know Christ, he gave us a new heart that is totally surrendered to him. That's the heart of faith. His Spirit is united with our spirit and Christ becomes head of our lives. Christ puts off the old life for us and he gives us a new life to live. And one of the results is a heart of generosity.

I prayed for my sister to be saved for ten years. One of the first things she told me after her salvation is: "I can't wait to tithe this Sunday." She had given her all to Christ, and one tangible way she could demonstrate Christ's ownership and lordship over her is giving the firstfruits of her labor. All God's people have this spiritual desire within them.

We have some amazingly generous people in our church, both rich and poor. But it might surprise you that some of the poorest people in our church are the greatest givers. I don't know what people give, but I know that I've been shown such generosity personally by some of the poorest people in our church. I could tell you amazing stories.

I've seen people in our church give cars away. I've seen them give houses away. I've seen poor people in our church give all they have to the kingdom. I'm amazed and blessed at the generosity of our congregation. It shows that there are some very spiritually mature people in our church. I also think that we have a long way to go as far as spiritual maturity in our church. And as we grow deeper and closer in Christ, I believe he will give each of us here a breathtaking ability to give generously, no matter what our financial profile may be.

One awesome example of a very poor church that became breathtakingly generous is the church at Philippi. This is our last message in this book. Remember Paul is writing from what is in essence a prison. He's in a rented house (Acts 28:30) in Rome, chained to a Roman soldier 24/7. There are six shifts, four hours a piece. Pastor Epaphroditus shows up, having risked his life. Epaphroditus faithfully delivered the financial gift from his home church and then went above and beyond the call of duty. In his fervor to serve the Lord by hand-delivering this gift to Paul, Epaphroditus became seriously ill and, in fact, almost died (2:25-30). And now, Paul, as he closes this letter, recognizes their exemplary spiritual maturity and highlights three areas they have glorified God by their generosity: partnership, worship, and stewardship.

Maybe you have really been convicted and burdened that you want to be more generous and a better steward of all that Christ has given you. I know I want to be a better steward! Well let's stand and listen to what Paul says in Philippians 4.

> **Philippians 4:14-23** | Yet it was kind of you to share my trouble. [15] And you Philippians yourselves know that in the beginning of the gospel, when I left Macedonia, no church entered into partnership with me in giving and receiving, except you only. [16] Even in Thessalonica you sent me help for my needs once and again. [17] Not that I seek the gift, but I seek the fruit that increases to your credit. [18] I have received full payment, and more. I am well supplied, having received from Epaphroditus the gifts you sent, a fragrant offering, a sacrifice acceptable and pleasing to God. [19] And my God will supply every need of yours according to his riches in glory in Christ Jesus. [20] To our God and Father be glory forever and ever. Amen. [21] Greet every saint in Christ Jesus. The brothers who are with me greet you. [22] All the saints greet you, especially those of Caesar's household. [23] The grace of the Lord Jesus Christ be with your spirit.

Why is giving so vital to the Christian life? It's a major part of our growth in Christ. It shows us we are partnered with God and not the world. It put's God first in worship. It shows we have kingdom priorities. We grow in partnership (4:15-17). We grow in worship (4:18). We grow in stewardship (4:19-23).

### *People and Money*

I heard about an elderly gentleman who had married a beautiful young girl, but he was worried that perhaps she married him because he had so much money. And so, one day, he said, "Tell me the truth, sweetheart. If I lost all my money, would you still love me?" And she said, reassuringly, "Oh, honey don't be silly. Of course, I would still love you. And I would miss you terribly."

Seriously though, the church of Philippi is the most generous church in all of the New Testament. They are repeatedly extolled for being good stewards, for being generous givers. For example, in 2 Corinthians 8 and 9, they are lifted up as an example to the Corinthian church of what a good, giving, generous, church should look like and how it should conduct itself. The rich Corinthians are not very willing to help Paul as he gathers an offering for the poor Jerusalem saints, but the Philippians, being the poorest of the poor are always giving so much.

### *The Bible and Money*

The Bible talks a great deal about money. About 800 times, in fact, scripture speaks of money, wealth, finances, possessions, and the like, between the Old and the New Testament. Furthermore, Jesus teaches on finances and wealth about 25 percent of the time, which means were I to speak of money as much as Jesus, we'd take one whole Sunday a month and I would just talk about money.

So we come to one of three motives we have for generosity. When you really love someone, it's easy to give to their ministry. That's the motive of partnership. The Philippians loved Paul. Remember he risked his life to bring the gospel to them. He was in the prison, beaten and bloodied with Silas. He was singing. You had Lydia the seller of purple that had been converted. You had the slave girl that had been converted. Now you have a Phillippian jailer and numerous others who are connected in their hearts with Paul. They love him. That brings us to the first motive of giving.

## GIVING GROWS US THROUGH PARTNERSHIP (4:14-17)

The Philippians entered into partnership with Paul's worldwide and world changing ministry. How? They contributed financially in a sacrificial way for Paul.

> **Philippians 4:14-17** | Yet it was kind of you to share my trouble. [15] And you Philippians yourselves know that in the beginning of the gospel, when I left Macedonia, no church entered into partnership with me in giving and receiving, except you only. [16] Even in Thessalonica you sent me help for my needs once and again. [17] Not that I seek the gift, but I seek the fruit that increases to your credit.

Look at their pattern of giving in 2 Corinthians 8 and 9 from the churches of Macedonia.

> We want you to know, brothers, about the grace of God that has been given among the churches of Macedonia, ² for in a severe test of affliction, their abundance of joy and their extreme poverty have overflowed in a wealth of generosity on their part. ³ For they gave according to their means, as I can testify, and beyond their means, of their own accord, ⁴ begging us earnestly for the favor of taking part in the relief of the saints— ⁵ and this, not as we expected, but they gave themselves first to the Lord and then by the will of God to us.
> —*2 Corinthians 8:1-5*

They were the poorest of all the saints, but they gave the most! The churches of Macedonia included congregations at Philippi, Thessalonica, and Berea. There was constant war going on in Macedonia with the Romans. This is like the Afghanistan or Syria of the Roman Empire. Not only that, there was a great persecution against Christians. They were stripped of everything, but they desired above all to give to Paul. The prosperous Corinthians didn't give to Paul. It was the poor Philippians. I find that so interesting and intriguing, don't you?

**Philippians 4:15-16** | And you Philippians yourselves know that in the beginning of the gospel, when I left Macedonia, no church entered into partnership with me in giving and receiving, except you only. [16] Even in Thessalonica you sent me help for my needs once and again.

How is it that the poorest of the poor have such a stellar generosity? The secret? Love. They love Paul. We are to love God's servants. We have 20 missionaries. I believe God would be pleased if everyone of us got connected with each of them. Now it might be impossible to get connected with every one of them, but what if you chose one?

The Philippians gave so much and were such amazing examples of sacrifice even though they were the poorest of the poor because they had a personal connection with Paul, more than the rest of the churches. No other church entered into partnership with him in giving and receiving, except the Philippians only. That's amazing. The Corinthians didn't. Other prosperous churches were too busy with their own prosperity. But the suffering churches. The Macedonian churches. The Philippian church. They entered into partnership with Paul. Why? They loved him. Perhaps Lydia was still there. Perhaps the slave girl that came to Christ was still there. Maybe even the jailer was still there. They were all so thankful for Paul's ministry because they were connected.

## The Power of Partnership

When Paul had to leave Macedonia because of persecution, the only church that helped Paul and his fellow missionaries was the Philippian church. Why? Partnership. Where ever Paul was they found him and gave him financial support and fellowship at times. It had been ten years since Paul had been in Philippi, but that relationship was lasting. The power of partnership is that it is lasting. When you really get to know someone, years can pass, and you feel like not a day has gone by. There were years when they did not see Paul's face, but they kept him supplied. They met his needs. They sent financial support. This has some implications for us.

### How Do I Partner with People for the Gospel?

We are called to partner in the gospel with people. The great commission has at least three implications: evangelism, church planting, and the training of leaders. Paul was evangelizing. Paul was planting churches. Paul was training leaders for gospel ministry. Each of our twenty missionaries is in one of these three primary areas of the great commission work. Not all of us are called to be evangelists, though some of you have that gift. We all evangelize but not all of us hold an office of evangelist. We are not all planting churches or training leaders, but we are called to partner with people who do these things.

Personal contact. You can do that by encouraging our missionaries by email or WhatsApp or Skype. I love that. I'm in contact with some of our missionaries personally every week. We are all called to do that.

Personal prayer support. One of the best things you can do is to pray for our missionaries. Look over their requests. Pray for them.

Personal visit. You should, if you are able plan on every so often taking a trip on the mission field to visit a missionary. The first time you do it, it will change your life. You will never feel disconnected again from that missionary.

Personal support. I think we should all do this. I know of many great churches that support their church's missionary program above and beyond their tithes and offerings. We should all do this. One way you can do this is to choose a missionary and adopt them. Mike Klikas did this for me when I was in Spain. He and his family supported me with special gifts, like Hickory Smoke BBQ sauce. You can't guy that in Spain. He sent me and my family Hickory Smoke BBQ sauce! Now that was a bonus, but he and others supported our family financially. He would write me an email from time to time encouraging me. Who's your missionary? Adopt one. Support the missions program of the church and designate over and above your tithe for a missionary you adopt from our church. When you enter into partnership with a missionary, they become part of your family. Pray for them. Contact them. Go out and see them. Support them. Write and encourage them. Partner with them.

### The Fruit of Partnership
What's the fruit of this partnership?

> **Philippians 4:17** | Not that I seek the gift, but I seek the fruit that increases to your credit.

Paul says, "I'm not seeking a gift" (4:17). "I don't need your financial support." He's just told us: "I have learned in whatever situation I am to be content" (3:11). He knows that it's God who supplies his needs. He's not ever in actual need. God will always supply. But Paul's motive is to credit fruit to their account. This is a banking term. It means compounded interest. It signifies *continuing* multiplication that creates compound spiritual interest credited to their account.[116] I love this spiritual banking equation. It means Paul is reaching people who are reaching people, but your investment is getting compounded interest to your own account. You have a part. You are holding the ropes for our missionaries, our pastors, our local church. You are holding the ropes.

He says no other church has entered into partnership with giving and receiving. This financial support has a profit, a receiving. It means they invested with money but they received souls to their account. They could not physically go with Paul, but they could support his ministry, and that fruit, that receiving was laid up to their account. When we give of ourselves to the work of the gospel around the world, God counts that as fruit to our credit. Isn't that an amazing promise? I can't go to Uganda. But I can encourage and give toward the amazing gospel work

---

[116] Hughes, *Philippians*, 192.

of reaching orphans for the kingdom. And that fruit abounds to my account. There are going to be orphans in Uganda waiting for us at the gates of heaven thanking us for partnering with our missionaries there who shared the gospel with them, opened their homes for them.

I can't live in Spain right now, but God is reaching people through our missionaries there in Spain. There are people flowing through Spain from all of Latin America, Africa and Europe that will be so grateful when we meet them in heaven. I'm not there and you're not there, but God is crediting fruit to our account because of our sacrifice. Listen, pray, give, and go! Pray daily for those preaching. Give generously. And go! Go visit them. If God stirs you up, then go and train to preach the gospel. Go over there and do the work yourself if you can! That would be the most glorious offering you could give: yourself.

So let me ask you: Are you growing spiritually? There are many marks of spiritual maturity. Maybe you have the fruit of Bible knowledge and knowledge of walking with Christ and the fruit of the Spirit. You say: Pastor Matt, my whole character is changing day by day into the image of Christ! Praise the Lord! The Bible says in Psalm 1:1-3 that the blessed may meditates on the law of the Lord day and night, and it says you'll have lasting fruit that doesn't wither.

Do you have fruit that God is crediting to your account because of your generosity towards missions and missionaries? Do you know our missionaries? They are doing all they can to reach out to us, but are you reaching out to them? Here are some ways you can partner with our missionaries. Let me review them. Personal contact: Email, Skype, FB messenger. Now in the day of internet, we can personally contact our missionaries. Get to know them. Pray for them: we are designing a daily missionary prayer book that you can use each day of the month and pray for missions. Adopt a missionary: Give financially to missions. Adopt a missionary to give to. Go! Go visit them! You'll never be the same!

Another way your generosity helps you to grow, Paul says, is worship.

## GIVING GROWS US THROUGH WORSHIP (4:18)

Paul now comes to a second reason why giving is so vital to our spiritual growth: the motive of our giving is worship! David speaks of the benefit of worship in two ways: as a payment and as an offering.

## A Full Payment

**Philippians 4:18a** | I have received full payment, and more.

Paul gave everything to the Lord, and God was over abundant in supplying all his needs. Paul says, "I've received full payment, and more" (4:18). Paul gave his life to the Lord, and the Lord took care of him. He's basically saying, "I'm living an abundant life that is full and overflowing!"

Can you agree that if you give your all to the Lord, he'll take care of you? God's on payment system is not like this world. If you put him first, he'll take care of you. Malachi 3 says that God will rebuke the devourer if you put him first. Often when we sacrifice for God by faith, he'll stretch the paycheck. Can you testify? God's accounting system is so different than our accounting system. But the people that were providing for Paul's needs are here painted as worshippers. The reason we give to God is not mainly because we need to keep the lights on here at Living Hope or in all the churches and evangelists and training centers we are supporting around the world. We give to God. It's our worship. It's our love offering to God. It's our way of putting God first. That's how Paul describes it.

## A Fragrant Offering

**Philippians 4:18b** | ... I am well supplied, having received from Epaphroditus the gifts you sent, a fragrant offering, a sacrifice acceptable and pleasing to God.

The picture suggested by a "fragrant offering" is that of the Old Testament's burnt offering in which the offering was consumed, so that a sumptuous roast-like aroma rose up to God as an acceptable and pleasing sacrifice.[117] If you were to go by the Tabernacle or Temple in the Old Testament times, you would smell the sweetest smell of bar-b-que. It would be the most wonderful aroma of the best grill out you can imagine. God loves the aroma of a generous heart!

Paul's main concern is to express that their financial giving to his work serves a much higher purpose than simply meeting his needs. Their stewardship is an act of worship that is being given to God. Here is the ultimate purpose and the greatest motive for our financial giving

---

[117] Fee, *Philippians*, 451.

to gospel ministry. More than meeting the needs of God's ministers, the highest aim is the pleasure it brings to the Father. Such sacrificial gifts are offered as an act of worship that brings pleasure to God. When you realize that your financial support of God's servants is a fragrant sacrifice that brings great pleasure to God, you will find you are a sacrificial giver who can be classified as what Paul called a "cheerful giver" (2 Cor 9:7).[118]

### David's Generosity

Remember what David said? When he wanted to offer an offering to God, a man named Araunah the Jebusite wanted to give the king the altar on Mount Moriah and the animal offerings for free. David refused and purchased a very important piece of land. It was in the very center of Jerusalem which would later become the Temple Mount. David said, "I will not offer to the Lord that which cost me nothing" (2 Sam 24:24). God desires us to give our all to him.

God loves a cheerful giver. So if you have a grumpy, stingy heart, I beg you, please do not give to this church or any other church. That kind of giving does not please God. God wants us to see what a joy it is to give. Giving is an act of worship. David understood that. God doesn't want our tokens. He wants our heart. And if we give our heart to God, he'll have our treasure too.

### Your Generosity

God loves the aroma of a generous heart! Of course, God's not mainly impressed by the amazing smell of the Old Testament animal sacrifices but of the generous heart behind the sacrifice. That's what God finds well-pleasing and fragrant. Can I ask you a question? What does God smell when he smells your heart? Is your heart filled with the well-pleasing aroma of sacrifice? God says: I love the aroma of a generous heart! A generous heart is a fragrant offering to me! What about you? What's your heart smell like?

I love my daughter Katie. She's here for the summer and then she's taking her sister and heading to South Carolina for college. But when Katie was a little girl, her greatest compliment was to walk right up to you and tell you, "You smell good!" That's a pretty good compliment. That's what God says when he sees the generosity of your heart. He

---

[118] Lawson, *Philippians*, 222.

says, "You smell good!" God knows our heart. Your gifts to him are a sweet-smelling sacrifice to him for his glory and kingdom.

## GIVING GROWS US THROUGH STEWARDSHIP (4:19-23)

Finally, we see that the last motive of sacrificial generosity is one of stewardship. You understand the principle of stewardship right? It means: I own nothing. God owns everything. Let's say that together: I own nothing. God owns everything. Turn to your neighbor and say: God owns everything. Amen.

### God's Care for You

So here's the first principle of stewardship: God will take care of you.

> **Philippians 4:19** | And my God will supply every need of yours according to his riches in glory in Christ Jesus.

I love the words of CH Spurgeon. He says:

> "In all of my years of service to my Lord, I have discovered a truth that has never failed and has never been compromised. That truth is that it is beyond the realm of possibilities that one has the ability to out give God. Even if I give the whole of my worth to Him, He will find a way to give back to me much more than I gave."

Can you testify to that? Amen. You can't out give God. He promises to take care of you. But remember the context. They are giving money out of their poverty. They are sacrificing. They will not give God what cost them nothing. When you give like that, God promises to give more than you. He will provide according to his riches in glory in Christ Jesus. You are united with his Son. He's not going to neglect his Son.

### We Care about God's Glory

God cares for us, and we care for his glory. That's what Paul says. I want God to get the glory for everything. This giving is not about getting our name in print.

> **Philippians 4:20** | To our God and Father be glory forever and ever. Amen.

Our giving is always for the glory of God, amen?! Our motive in giving is to magnify the Lord, to expand his kingdom and glory. Our motive is that all nations everywhere would worship him!

## We Care for God's Family

Paul says, our primary motive is the glory of God, but our secondary motive is the love of the saints. This comes out in his final good bye to the Philippians. He says:

> **Philippians 4:21-23** | Greet every saint in Christ Jesus. The brothers who are with me greet you. [22] All the saints greet you, especially those of Caesar's household. [23] The grace of the Lord Jesus Christ be with your spirit.

This isn't just Paul saying goodbye, but within this goodbye is the family ethic. For Paul, the gospel is not merely a religion, but a family. He calls them brothers (and sisters). This is about connection to the saints. He greets them. He encourages them that the kingdom is expanding even in "Caesar's household". The soldiers were getting converted! That's joyous. Caesar's household is now our household. Caesar's family were really considered the unreachables. Who could ever reach them? Paul's arrest and imprisonment for two years were not in vain. People in Caesar's household: the soldiers, perhaps some in the emperor's own family were now worshipping Christ. Whatever your set back, God's got a purpose for it.

## Conclusion

As we close, I want to make this message personal to us all. We've had the amazing privilege in the last seven years to bring on 3 pastors. We began at Living Hope 7 years ago with 20 missionaries that we still support to this day.

You may obtain this and many other fine resources made available by Proclaim Publishers by contacting us:

**Web**:
proclaimpublishers.com

**Email**:
contact@proclaimpublishers.com

**Postal Mail**:
Proclaim Publishers
PO Box 2082
Wenatchee, WA 98807

Soli Deo Gloria

www.ingramcontent.com/pod-product-compliance
Lightning Source LLC
Chambersburg PA
CBHW031314160426
43196CB00007B/526